AL-JAZEERA

*Dedicated to all those who
lost their lives on September 11, 2001.
To the victims of a disaster that touched all walks of life;
every race, creed and gender. To the hundreds of
children orphaned on this tragic day and
all those who have suffered from similar
heinous acts of terror and war around the world,
we pray for a safer tomorrow where
freedom and democracy thrive.*

CONTENTS

PREFACE

In a time when opportunists in politics point to the writings of a handful of doomsday writers who warn of an inevitable clash of civilizations between the Western world and the Arab Middle East, we see the need for mutual understanding. The attacks of September 11, 2001, and the ensuing wars in Afghanistan and Iraq reflect an absence of meaningful understanding between peoples. We do not subscribe to such prophecies of doom, yet they are increasingly difficult to counter given all the rhetoric about "unbridgeable differences" between West and East, Americans and Arabs.

The true clash of civilizations, however, is not being forged on the battlefields of war but in our very own living rooms and in our mind-sets. Contentious ideas about "the other" are the staple of modern war coverage in the media, each idea promising to tell something more real about the enemy. Although we try to avoid shoehorning people into generalized groups, we promise here to reveal a glimpse of the Middle East in a way that helps readers comprehend the origins of strife and explain the roots of turmoil.

We wholeheartedly believe in intercultural, interreligious, and interracial dialogue for better understanding our common humanity. This book should be read as not only a historical account of how a satellite television network emerged in the Middle East; it is also the story of peoples' quest for freedom of opinion and expression, a quest that if curtailed—as it has been for many years—can lead to catastrophes like those the world witnessed on September 11. The emergence of militant religious fundamentalism is a product of decades of oppressive regimes and the virtual nonexistence of a public sphere where issues are discussed and resolved.

Since the original publication of this book, Al-Jazeera has become a global trendsetter among mass media networks, shaping public opinion and politics from London to Jakarta. The war on Iraq has also served to place Al-Jazeera among the elite of television broadcasters worldwide. Likewise, the remarkable attention this book has received has been extremely encouraging, offering us a glimmer of hope that public opinion in the Arab world matters to the American people and to the future of peace. We are gratified to know that this volume provides the only meticulously concise, fair, and balanced account of this unique and revolutionary phenomenon to date.

The success of the "Al-Jazeera effect" is evident in the way it has transformed the media environment in the Middle East, giving rise to several similar and semi-independent satellite stations, while at the same time maintaining the Al-Jazeera trademark of holding world governments from Washington to Islamabad accountable for their foreign policies.

The realization that there is a definite dearth of information about media in the Middle East, and little data about how the Arab public living there responds to current events, provided the greatest motivation to undertake this project. Although a book of this sort is overdue, the need was accelerated by the recent crisis. It not only catapulted the Al-Jazeera network to international celebrity; it also demanded a deeper understanding of the media's effect on the Arab world's religious, political, and economic communities.

More important, in a world where agendas are determined by channels of interest, readers should understand that the authors of this book remain independent, autonomous of any governmental or personal influence; they are not connected to any vested media interest. If we have any agenda, it is to support and promote free democratic expression in the Arab world even as we illuminate realities about this world to Americans. We have conducted extensive research on Al-Jazeera for years, monitoring virtually every aspect of the station's operation. Here we attempt to bring forth all possible perspectives on Al-Jazeera and its audience, reserving our opinions for the most important issues in the debate. We also take care to present as many other opinions as possible and have labored to present the reader a perspective that is fair, untainted, and insightful.

Sometimes the only way to accomplish these goals was to assure confidentiality to our sources. Therefore, we use pseudonyms when necessary to protect sources' privacy and ensure their anonymity. We see this as the only way to present an unvarnished view of Al-Jazeera, its audience, and recent world events.

While we were putting this book together, countless people have supported us throughout.

Our sincere appreciation goes to both our families. We offer our deepest regards to Rasha El-Gendi (Mohammed el-Nawawy's wife) for her continuous support and encouragement. Thanks to Adel Iskandar's family, Dr. Talaat I. Farag, Essam Farag, and the late Magda El-Badramany for their unceasing support. We are also thankful to the renowned Egyptian cartoonist Ahmed Toughan for his generous contribution to this book. Special thanks go to Dr. Douglas A. Boyd at the University of Kentucky for his continuous support of this project. We are indebted to Holly Hodder, our extraordinary publisher and editor, our publicist, Greg Houle, and all the staff at Westview Press and the Perseus Books Group. We owe much gratitude to Davide Girardelli for his innovative ideas from the very inception of the book. We would also like to thank Khalid Al-Jaber, a Qatari graduate student at the University of West Florida's Communication Arts Department, for his help with facilitating interviews between the authors and Al-Jazeera's management.

Mohammed el-Nawawy   *Adel Iskandar*
Easton, MA   Lexington, KY
April 25, 2003

AL-JAZEERA

1
WE ARE WHAT WE WATCH

————◆————

Sherif Helal, a Muslim Canadian of Middle Eastern descent, barely stirs when his alarm clock goes off at the same time every Wednesday morning. Even though the clock is set at its highest volume, the entire household sometimes wakes before Sherif lifts his head from the pillow. The snooze button is within striking distance, but lately Sherif hasn't been using it. His sleep is intermittent and shallow, interrupted occasionally by nightmares of falling buildings, exploding bombs, and mass graves. On one occasion, he dreamed he was trapped in the basement of one of New York City's World Trade Center towers, in absolute solitude, rubble all around, listening to shouts and rescue calls overhead. With his shirt covering his mouth and nose, he screamed at the top of his voice "Here! I'm here!" The images he's seen on television—of the motionless escalators and ghostly white debris blanketing everything—flash back constantly. Like the millions who watched the events of September 11, 2001, unfold in utter disbelief, Sherif's life had changed.

Now he wakes on the first ring of the alarm and rushes straight to the living room to find out any news he may have missed overnight. His father, Kamal Helal, beats him to the television by a half-hour, giving his twenty-three-year-old son the one-line synopsis. "They're on the doors of Kandahar," Kamal explains.

1

As the family sits at the breakfast table, all eyes are fixed on the television, located close by in the adjacent living room. All chairs are turned toward the screen. A year ago, the Helal family became addicted to the news. "Even if they bomb Afghanistan to the ground, they won't find Osama bin Laden. He's an elusive rascal," remarks Sherif, breaking the attentive silence.

"Do you really think he's in Afghanistan? He knows that if the Americans think he's there, they will come and get him. He must be somewhere else," says Sherif's mother, Naama Helal.

"What about the videotape of bin Laden on Al-Jazeera? Some geologist said that the rocks behind him are from a precise area in the Afghan mountains," suggests Sherif.

"I think he's just playing cat-and-mouse games with the Americans. Sends them to Afghanistan when he could be in Sri Lanka," replies Kamal. "Well at least they're getting rid of the Taliban," he continues.

Sherif interrupts: "But what about all the casualties in Afghanistan? I mean all these photos Al-Jazeera is showing. It's frightening. And you don't see any of them on CNN."

"Well, of course. What do you expect? America has to sell the war to its people, and showing these images won't do that," responds Kamal.

"So it's just like the Intifada (uprising) in Palestine. You only see something on CNN when Israelis are killed but not when Palestinians are killed," Sherif retorts.

"Well, maybe. But in Afghanistan, the Americans are stakeholders. This is *their* retaliation to what happened in New York. So they have a lot more invested than in Palestine," Kamal adds.

This is ordinary conversation among the Helal family every morning as they try to make sense of the information they receive from Al-Jazeera, the Arabic satellite TV news network that broadcasts from the tiny peninsular country of Qatar, located in the Arabian Gulf. For the first time, table talk revolves around politics, instead of what new music CD is selling, what the kids will do that evening, school reports, and phone bills. These days, Al-Jazeera sets the agenda. Although the Helals got Al-Jazeera as part of an Arabic satellite package a number of years ago, they took real notice of Al-Jazeera only the year before, in October 2000. Since the beginning of the second Palestinian Intifada, the network has been the preferred source of news for the family.

The discussion is interrupted only by a glimpse at the clock on the wall. Sherif picks up his coffee in one hand, tosses his knapsack over his other shoulder, waves his good-bye *salams* and walks out the front door. Like many students living in eastern Canada, Sherif sets off for campus.

One year ago, on a morning in October 2000, Sherif sipped a cup of coffee while hastily striding to his electromechanics class. A third-year student, Sherif is living up to the family expectations and carrying on the tradition of becoming an engineer. He is one of hundreds of Palestinians who lived in Kuwait whose families emigrated to the eastern Canadian maritime city of Halifax, Nova Scotia, in the aftermath of the Gulf War. Sherif lives as any Canadian would; he received citizenship at a ceremony one year earlier.

When he arrived at class, he scanned the room and found a vacant seat next to his friend and classmate, Samy Mounir, a Copt (Egyptian Orthodox Christian). A handsome, clean-shaven, and keen-dressing young man, Samy often saves a seat for Sherif. An Egyptian who landed in Halifax the same year as Sherif, his family also moved from Kuwait in the aftermath of the liberation, although under different circumstances.

It doesn't take a visitor long to notice that the number of students of Middle Eastern descent is disproportionately large in the Dalhousie University engineering program. Historically, the eastern Canadian province of Nova Scotia, of which Halifax is the capital, has seen little overall immigration compared to the larger provinces of Ontario, Quebec, and British Columbia. However, Halifax's Middle Eastern community, owing to the large influx of immigrants that started in the early 1990s, is now the city's second largest visible minority group after African Canadians. Many of those who moved from Kuwait, Saudi Arabia, Iraq, and the United Arab Emirates sought more secure lifestyles in Canada. The Gulf War had destabilized many regions in the Middle East, and those who arrived—entrepreneurs, investors, refugees—found safe harbor in Nova Scotia. Home to Canada's second largest port and the largest city in far eastern Canada, Halifax provided ample opportunity for work, education, and comparatively inexpensive travel back to the Middle East during holidays.

For many of the city's inhabitants, the immigration seemed overwhelmingly quick. It was as if floodgates from the Middle East had opened, pouring in peoples from a host of countries and cultures. It seemed that Arabic became a second language almost overnight on the streets of this fishing town. Although the Arab community in Halifax is nowhere near as established as those in the U.S. cities of Dearborn, Michigan, and Toledo, Ohio, the community and cultural landscape have changed swiftly and dramatically in less than a decade. Arab-owned stores have sprung up on every major street, and local community radio station CKDU-FM is home to the largest number of Arabic-language specialty programs.

The first word of Arabic was broadcast here on October 7, 1995, by a group of amateur programmers hosting a show called *Radio Egypt*. Four years later, the program won an award from Canada's National Campus and Community Radio Association in the category of community involvement for its all-day broadcast of the political specialty program *Through Arab Eyes*.

Courses on Islam and Arabic language classes are now regular offerings at each of the city's universities.

Six years since arriving, Sherif and Samy now call Halifax home. Known for hosting the G-7 conference in 1995 and made famous by the *Titanic*'s wreckage off its cost, Halifax leaves its newcomers little to desire. They participate in the city's local restaurants and nightlife—Thursday's wing night at the Oasis or Your Father's Moustache, the occasional beavertail (a hot wheat pastry that resembles a beaver's tail with sweet and savory toppings), or an occasional night out at the Palace disco. However, their apparent adjustment to life in Halifax should not be mistaken for complete assimilation. Sherif and Samy, like many Arab immigrants, remain profoundly connected to their Middle Eastern roots. The satellite package that provides Arabic television reception 5,000 miles away from its source also provides Arab families with a "real" connection to their favorite Arabic programs.

Before their move to Halifax, Sherif's father, Kamal, worked for a civil engineering company in Kuwait for twenty years. Kamal's parents, now deceased, had moved to Kuwait in the 1960s, escaping from dire conditions in the Palestinian town of Ramallah. Kamal's three children, Sherif being the youngest, were all born in the same maternity ward in Kuwait. The Helals still speak fondly about the years they spent in Kuwait, the country that Kamal's children knew as their only home. It wasn't until the Iraqi invasion of Kuwait in the early hours of August 2, 1990, that everything changed. The machine-gun fire in the streets, artillery fire, curfews, rising inflation, lack of running water, and food rations made for difficult living conditions that lasted the seven months between the Iraqi invasion and the U.S.-led liberation. Naama, Kamal's wife, recalls how Sherif would hide, shivering under his blanket from the sounds of explosions. He would become nauseated and sick when the building shook from the shelling. Sherif would calm down only when the bombing ceased.

Following the liberation of Kuwait in February 1991 by the Coalition forces led by the United States, the country's reinstated government under the Al-Sabah family implemented policies that prevented many Palestinians who resided there from renewing their permits and employment contracts. This was an act of protest and retaliation by Kuwait's rulers against the Palestinian Liberation Organization's support of Saddam Hussein. On numerous occasions, Palestinians were charged with cooperating with Iraqi occupying forces during the short-lived occupation. The conclusion was simple: The Palestinians, who once comprised the largest percentage of expatriate workers in Kuwait, were branded as traitors and had to leave. A few who were fortunate enough to have travel documents issued by other Arab states after the 1948 Arab-Israeli war were admitted into these countries. Many others were not.

The Helals were among the lucky. They endured considerable discomfort at the airports and customs desks, but their Egyptian travel documents allowed them to leave Kuwait and live temporarily in Cairo, where they had distant relatives and many friends. Life was not much easier in Cairo. Kamal was jobless, and Naama had never worked. There was much talk and gossip about emigrating to Western countries. Kamal heard that immigrating to Canada was relatively inexpensive and that the procedures were less difficult than those in the United States. It was an option that surely appealed to many of those formerly employed in Kuwait. Kamal opted quickly to stand in line at the Canadian embassy in Cairo for days in those scorching sun to speak to an official and start the emigration process. It undoubtedly tried his patience, and anxiety racked his family.

Although a child at that time, Sherif remembers the day when his father came home from the embassy smiling broadly—his father hadn't laughed or joked for months. Sherif, oblivious to the details at the time, knew something good was imminent. Kamal clicked open his leather Samsonite suitcase, pulled out a large yellow envelope, waved it around, and let out a cry of relief that echoed in the little apartment they were all crammed in: "We're going to Canada!"

A little more than eight years after that monumental day, Sherif and family are full-fledged Canadians, possessing the full rights and responsibilities of citizenship to go with their navy-blue passports to document it.

While the instructor recited and reviewed one formula and problem after another, Sherif was too restless and distracted to focus. Twenty minutes into class, Sherif turned to Samy, signaling to him. He reached over Samy's right ear and asked, "Did you see Al-Jazeera yesterday?" Samy shook his head, but his curiosity was aroused. Sherif rarely watched Arabic television and commented that he despised its "backward" programming style. He added that he preferred American networks, choosing *The Simpsons* on Fox and Jay Leno on NBC's *Tonight Show* over any Arabic film or soap opera. He argued frequently with his parents about Arabic music and how it lacked creativity.

"The Arabic music videos are all the same, and all the singers sound alike," he would say. Sherif added that he would much rather watch the music charts on Much Music, the Canadian version of MTV. For this reason, the question from Sherif— "Did you see Al-Jazeera yesterday?"—was unexpected.

But his question was also rhetorical, for Samy's family, unlike Sherif's, has no satellite dish. In fact, two days earlier, Samy's family, the Mounirs, visited Kamal and Naama specifically to watch Al-Jazeera. "No. What was on?" replied Samy.

Sherif uttered a few sighs and resorted to paper to explain. He tore a sheet from his notebook, scribbled a few words, and passed it to Samy. As he read Sherif's note, Samy's face turned to one of shock and disbelief. The note read, "18 in Israel. The most since 1956."

The news since late September, 2000, reported little more than numbers, statistics, body counts. Sherif had been providing Samy with daily Palestinian death tolls from the ongoing conflict in Israel, the West Bank, and Gaza. This day's numbers were shocking because all the dead were Palestinians in Israel, not the Gaza Strip, West Bank, or other occupied territories. It was indeed the biggest single-day death toll for Palestinians living inside Israel since 1956.

Many Arabs attribute the beginning of the so-called New Intifada, or second Palestinian uprising, to Israeli Prime Minister Ariel Sharon's visit to the Temple Mount on September 28, 2000. From that moment forth Arabs worldwide have avidly watched their televisions. The Intifada has resulted in a tally of deaths on both sides. The few days after September 28 were especially gruesome. Just two days later, Samy's family visited the Helals and watched as Al-Jazeera rebroadcast the footage of twelve-year-old Mohammed Al-Durra's death. He was shot by Israeli fire in his father's arms; the short clip was unforgettable. Eight men, women, and children sat, tears filling their eyes, in that Canadian home, silently watching the clip and the interviews that followed, a reaction that is known to have been shared by many Arabs around the world.

Only days after the broadcast of the death of Al-Durra, a song called "Jerusalem Will Return to Us," featuring some of the top Arab recording artists reciting the young boy's name, was broadcast on some of the major Arabic networks. From that point forth, Al-Durra had become an icon of the Intifada.

Sherif's family was one of the first to subscribe to Arabic satellite television. As subscription prices fell, most Arab homes in Halifax installed the service, and those who didn't subscribe before the September 11 attacks on New York City and the Pentagon are now buying and installing satellite dishes. When the Helals initially decided to install their satellite package, their reasons were different. Shortly after the family moved into their home in Halifax, Kamal and Naama often quarreled with their children over their behavior, religious traditions, and customary rituals. Sherif, who at one time hardly missed a single prayer (Muslims pray five times a day), now habitually procrastinated. His parents also noticed his growing preference for speaking English instead of Arabic at home, something that prompted them to take action.

Unlike most Arab families, the Helals have not returned to the Middle East since their departure six years earlier. This lack of contact with the Arab world surely prompted Kamal and Naama's decision to bring Arabic television into their home. In some ways, they hoped it would help preserve their children's sense of culture and religion. In all likelihood, Kamal and Naama also had personal reasons. As recent immigrants, they would have missed their homeland, yearning to watch anything Arabic on television. They taped their favorite Arabic *masrahiyaat* (comedy plays) and watched them so frequently that they could recite the scripts by heart. The satellite dish, once installed, would change all this.

On the many evenings following September 28, 2000 and the Intifada, the Helals would huddle around the television to watch Al-Jazeera's latest news and onsite reporting from Jerusalem and the Palestinian cities of Ramallah, Beit Jala, and Bethlehem. "We used to watch CNN to hear the news from the Arab world, but now we have Al-Jazeera," Kamal explained in a conversation we shared. Although he is a fluent English-speaker, his command and comprehension of Arabic is far superior. But language, he said, wasn't the problem he had with some of the American and Canadian networks. It's what they chose to cover.

Samy would join the Helals to watch the latest developments of the Intifada on Al-Jazeera. With a fresh approach to news and talk shows, it immediately became the favored station for the Arabic community living in Halifax. In circumstances that must have been replicated throughout the world, Haligonian Arabs would talk incessantly about the Al-Jazeera coverage. Never before had firsthand, day-to-day events inside Israeli and Palestinian controlled areas been so widely broadcast—and in Arabic, no less. During the early days of the Intifada typical chit-chat between, say, shop owners, taxicab drivers, and their customers would eventually lead to a discussion about the uprising and Al-Jazeera. The two had become inseparable.

During breaks from computer games and snacks, Sherif and Samy would return to the living room to catch up on Al-Jazeera's latest broadcast. A small discussion would ensue, after which they would return to their games.

In the beginning, the Helals' satellite hookup was something of a novelty, and the family received many visits from neighbors and friends; together they would watch entertainment shows, Lebanese concerts, Syrian soap operas, and Egyptian classic films. In those earlier days Al-Jazeera was just another news channel, but the recent outbreak of violence in Israel and the Palestinian territories transformed it into must-see TV in a painfully personal sense.

In November 2000, Samy Mounir's family connected the satellite service to their own home and watched Al-Jazeera just as avidly as the Helals. "It's contagious," says Samy. "I mean, it's exactly what I want to see from a news station. It focuses on the area of the world I'm interested in and it's very critical, unlike all the other stations."

Having spent his life in the Arab world and then in Canada, Samy, like most Arab immigrants, has a basic awareness of their differences. He has much to say about government corruption in the Middle East. Today, he speaks less Arabic compared to when he first emigrated to Halifax, yet there is something intrinsically Arab about this young man. From outward appearance, Samy's ethnicity could fool the keenest eye. Like most students his age in Canada, Samy dresses in clothing purchased from popular retail chains; his goatee extends up to his sideburns, reflecting the style of North American hip-hop culture.

Over the years Samy has grown more opinionated and critical of his world. His parents and friends often complain that nothing pleases him, claiming that if finding fault in everything was a sport, then Samy would be its Wayne Gretzky. He argues over religion, politics, daily lifestyle, and most anything else. It appears that many of his opinions have emerged from his dual cultural experiences. "There are so many things that I disagree with in the Arab world and so many other things that I value," explains Samy. "The same goes for living here in the West. There are things that I like and others that I don't."

Samy states that Al-Jazeera is an undeniable influence. Its talk shows, although sometimes too argumentative even by Samy's high standards, reflect a whole spectrum of ideas and values. "I must say that when I first watched some of the talk shows, I was completely shocked," he explains. "They are battling it out on Arabic TV. I had never seen anything like it."

Traditionally, most discussion programs on Arabic TV stations are noncontroversial and do little else but serve as a public relations outlet for governments. Al-Jazeera provided the first exposure to opposing voices, using the power and persuasion of television. Samy admitted that at first he could not even fathom live broadcasts of what were once behind-closed-doors conversations.

"Some of the opinions on these shows you can get arrested for in most Arab countries," Samy said. "I can't believe most of the people they've criticized on Al-Jazeera haven't been able to close the channel down." More important, Samy said he feels that Al-Jazeera has asked all the questions he's ever sought about his identity as an Arab Canadian. Thus, as Samy and Sherif struggle to define their identities, so too does the Arab world.

Al-Jazeera is playing a big part in this changing cultural definition. By questioning everything, Al-Jazeera has opened a window to issues long avoided and restricted by the Middle East. Samy acknowledges this as Al-Jazeera's greatest accomplishment: "More Arabs and even non-Arabs need to watch Al-Jazeera. It'll make us reflect more on how we think."

Even when it comes to coverage of recent events, Al-Jazeera is Samy's preferred source because it provides him with the news he wants, when he wants it. "I want minute-by-minute news from the Middle East, and that's what Al-Jazeera gives me," he explains. He adds that Al-Jazeera is sometimes like having an Arabic equivalent to *CNN Headline News*.

The Mounir family is similar to most Arab Canadians. Samy speaks for his family—if not his whole community—when he describes the primary reason for opening the satellite feed into his home. There is precious little reporting from the Middle East on the major American and Canadian networks.

Before their subscription, they would use the Internet and read the online versions of Arabic newspapers or BBC's World Service on the Arabic website. These were the primary news sources on the Middle East. When asked why he needed such sources for news on the Middle East, Samy said he believed Western TV networks assume that Americans and Canadians are simply not interested; as a result, events in that region are not covered in detail.

"They just don't have enough information about what is happening there," Samy complained. "The news is almost always recorded, never covered live. I wonder what they edit out?" he questioned. Samy continued, "They always seem to favor non-Arabs in their reports. I don't want to hear Wolf Blitzer tell me what his impressions are of how the Arabs feel! I want to hear what the people in the street think." He also complains that political statements by Arab leaders are reduced to soundbites.

"When I watch the local networks, if I even find what I want, it's usually processed and then shown in little pieces. They spend more time covering an L.A. Lakers game than the death of twenty people in the West Bank," he explains, then backtracks: "Don't get me wrong, I'm a big Lakers fan! You know what I mean. . . . that's why I watch Al-Jazeera. The station and I agree on what is important."

The Helals claim something very different. Kamal believes very strongly that the true reason why U.S. TV networks do not show enough about the crisis in Israel and Palestinian territories is due to a Jewish media conspiracy. "Jews and Zionists control the media in the United States, so they don't show any images that are sympathetic to the Palestinians," he states adamantly.

He adds that he refuses to buy into the notion that commercial media networks are independent of political groups. When provoked, Kamal will spout dozens of statistics he retrieved online about the number of Jews involved in the media industry. "It's a complete monopoly," he argues. "It doesn't take a genius to figure it out. Just count the number of Israeli officials they speak to instead of Palestinian civilians," he responds when challenged.

When alternative possibilities are suggested, Kamal asserts that "there is no other explanation. . . . If there is a suicide attack in Israel, they have full coverage. But if twenty-five Palestinians are killed in one day in the Occupied Territories, then it gets two minutes on the news or it scrolls in a little headline across the bottom of the screen."

He argues furthermore that this conspiracy goes beyond TV programs. "Even Hollywood is run by Zionists," he states bluntly. "When they show Arabs in Disney movies, they're always evil and ugly, but when they show a movie about Jews, like that cartoon *Prince of Egypt*, then they are sad and noble and deserve sympathy."

When told that the movie is a biblical story, Kamal immediately interjects by saying, "Okay, okay. . . . And then after the movie, they should show the audience what these same Jews are doing to Palestinians today. Right?"

When the Helals see on Al-Jazeera that the violence is intensifying in their hometown of Ramallah, they attempt to reach family members by phone to make sure they're safe and unharmed. Phone connections are difficult at best, often taking an hour before a connection can be established. It always has been an effort to call Ramallah, and once the call gets through the family would gather around, listening to glean any hint from the caller's voice about events happening thousands of miles away. This time, once the phone picked up, Kamal spoke into the handset loudly to ensure that he was heard on the other end.

"Allo . . . allo," he repeated. "Allo, *Al Sallamo Aleikom*" (an Arabic greeting, meaning "peace be upon you"). Hearing this, Naama and Sherif run down to the living room. Bringing their ears as close as possible to the handset, Naama and Sherif try to hear both sides of the conversation, to no avail. Kamal remained unfazed and continued conversing.

Kamal's aunt Fatma was on the other line. By far the most talkative member of the family, she could summarize several months of events in a ten-minute conversation. Since the beginning of the Intifada two weeks earlier, they had spoken to her twice. During each call, Fatma would describe horrifying stories of the Israeli soldiers, bombings, arbitrary arrests, and mass funerals. It wasn't very different from what the Arab Canadian families had seen on Al-Jazeera.

Today, Fatma was unusually quiet. Often volunteering unnecessary information, this time Fatma had little to say. Naama and Sherif heard the alarm growing in Kamal's voice as he pressed Fatma for information. "What's wrong? You're not yourself? Did something happen? Is everything all right? How is Aisha? What about Mohammed? Ibrahim?" With every name Kamal uttered, Naama and Sherif sat, waiting, apprehension no doubt rising.

"Who was it? Those bastards!" shouted Kamal.

"What's wrong? Tell me!" asked Naama, as Sherif embraced her.

"It's Fakhry, the neighbor's son," said Kamal with his hand muting the telephone receiver.

This was the first time that the effects of the Intifada struck close to the Helal family. After the phone call, the three sat silently for what seemed like hours. Fakhry was born the same month as Sherif. Kamal recalled stories about the young man, whom he had carried on his shoulders as a child. This time it was different. It was too close.

Unlike his parents, Sherif had never been to Ramallah. He had never met any of these people: Fatma, Mohammed, Aisha, Ibrahim, or even Fakhry. The only bond he had with them was through his parents, several casual phone conversations, and Al-Jazeera. Still, his heart must have ached as he imagined himself in Fakhry's shoes.

From that point on, Sherif made it a personal job to educate and inform everyone around him about the conflict in the Middle East. Through his involvement with local peace groups, Arabic societies, and Muslim associations, he organized public lectures, panel discussions, workshops, and the occasional demonstration.

Kamal's reaction to the violence and bloodshed could be seen in the family's household and in the way he controlled how the family watched Al-Jazeera. Kamal would sometimes act as self-titled censor: Anything that questioned the tenets of Islamic faith, according to Kamal, a relatively conservative Muslim, would be unacceptable. He would switch off the station.

"Although the station is good in how it covers the news, it sometimes argues about all these things that we think are holy. I think that's very bad," he explained.

Naama agreed, but her view comes from a different place. A fifty-two-year-old housewife, she's received limited schooling. She wears a *hijab* (veil) to cover her hair, but not because anyone has asked her to. Often quite colorful in her selections of the *hijab*, and always matched to her day's attire, she believes it is a sign of modesty and humbleness. Naama's quick wit has always compensated for her lack of formal education. Very selective about her household arrangements, clothes, and culinary specialties, Naama behaves similarly in her choices of TV programs. She knows precisely what she likes and dislikes.

Although the men in her family are fond of Al-Jazeera's news coverage, she maintains that some of what airs is demeaning to her Islamic faith and can be construed sometimes to be outwardly blasphemous. "On some of the shows, they question the words of the Quran [the Muslim holy book] and the hadith [the Prophet Mohammed's sayings]," she says. "Sometimes I can't imagine what they are saying! What are they doing to our religion? I can't believe it." She knows precisely where she draws the line, something she thinks Al-Jazeera does not do. "I also think all these talk shows where people argue should be limited to politics, economic issues, and social stuff, but not religion. They should stay away from the sacred matters."

But she does support other programs aired on Al-Jazeera. "Other shows are okay, especially the political ones." Usually nonopinionated on political issues, Naama has, since Al-Jazeera, grown more vocal. Kamal and Sherif say she now has an opinion on everything.

Kamal has said he is disheartened about his son's involvement with the Arab activist groups. He had hoped his son would be apolitical. Kamal's own experiences living in the Middle East taught him that questioning government authority could be extremely dangerous. Understandably, he would have concerns about his son criticizing Canadian foreign policy toward the Middle East. He had occasional nightmares about his son getting arrested. Opinionated in private, but reserved in public situations, Kamal was soft-spoken everywhere except within his inner circle of friends and family. He would share his opinions only behind closed doors. During his many years in Kuwait as a foreigner, the prospect of deportation was real and ever present. Having watched Kuwaiti and Iraqi television since their beginnings, he grew accustomed to the fact that opposition and dissent were punished. He can recall incidents when local newspapers would be shut down and journalists detained for expressing anything contrary to the government line.

It would seem natural that his son's unchecked political protests would engender consternation in this stoic father.

When Al-Jazeera began its worldwide broadcasts, it took Kamal by more than surprise. Before then, Kamal, like most natives of the Middle East, was accustomed to the kind of brainwashing TV programming that Arabic television stations initially broadcast. All stations followed the same government position. It was only during times of conflict, as in the Lebanese civil war, or the Iraq-Iran War, that he sought news elsewhere, mainly through the radio. The BBC World Service Arabic radio, Voice of America (VOA), and the Middle Eastern Radio

Broadcast out of Cairo, and Radio Monte Carlo–Middle East were among the most reputable.

For Kamal, Al-Jazeera provided a dramatic contrast to his previous media exposure. He recalls the days of the Iraqi invasion of Kuwait (August 1990–February 1991), during which the local residents of Kuwait, who were reduced to a quarter of the country's original population, were exposed to Iraqi propaganda that was unparalleled in its fabrication of reality. Iraqi President Saddam Hussein's daily *bayanaat* (announcements) on Iraqi TV would tell a story about the crisis that completely contradicted what the world heard from BBC, Voice of America, Middle Eastern Radio Broadcasting, and other Arab radio stations.

Iraq orchestrated an elaborate scenario and used its media to disseminate war propaganda. Once the Iraqi forces took control of Kuwait's telecommunications building, they replaced the existing service with their own. On the first day of the invasion, August 2, 1990, Kuwaiti residents watched a new broadcast, shabby and unconvincing.

Kamal recalls seeing a blank screen with handwritten lettering on a cardboard sign that read, "The Television of the Provisional Government of Free Kuwait." Even though the implication was that the broadcast was part of an interim independent Kuwaiti government, it didn't take the local audience long to realize that what was interim was the state of Kuwait itself. The illusion of a military coup led by Kuwaitis that toppled the existing monarchy was perpetuated on both Iraqi and Kuwaiti television. In an attempt to make the illusion believable, Iraqis aired coverage of Ala Hussein Ali, the supposed Kuwaiti army official who led the alleged coup. The makeshift news programming showed Saddam Hussein greeting and congratulating Ali.

Ali, who was also named prime minister, defense minister, and interior minister in the so-called provisional government of free Kuwait, announced a week later that Kuwait would be incorporated into Iraq and that he would become the deputy prime minister of the new expanded Iraq. As Kamal recalls, "I remember they had celebrations on television to commemorate the union between Iraq and Kuwait. They were unbelievable."

He also remembers some of the rhetoric the Iraqi government crafted to deceive its people and those living in Kuwait. "The union is like the 'return of the branch to the tree,'" explained Kamal. "Once the incorporation was complete, they started referring to Kuwait as the 'nineteenth province' of Iraq."

Part of the Iraqi rhetoric, according to Kamal, harkened to the superiority of the ancient Iraqi empire that once stretched from the area of Zakho in northernmost Kurdistan to the sea on the coasts of Kuwait. Thus, the "incorporation" of Kuwait, the only outlet to the sea, was considered a restoration of the age-old empire. Having been exposed to such deliberately blinding programming, it is no surprise that Kamal saw the advent of Al-Jazeera as a breath of fresh air.

The experiences of the Helal and Mounir families with Arabic television through the Arab eyes of Al-Jazeera are emblematic of a larger dynamic. Their experiences tell us something valuable about Arab audiences, wherever they may be, the histories behind their lives, the social and religious dimensions that inform them, and the relationships they have with their governments.

How does Al-Jazeera cater to the Arab audience and the issues that matter to it most? How has it changed the political landscape in the Middle East? How does Al-Jazeera maintain journalistic integrity in a region where covering the news objectively is nearly impossible?

The tensions experienced by Sherif, Arab audiences, Al-Jazeera's advocates, and critics are part of the Arab peoples' experience of globalization, migration, and emigration. Al-Jazeera is a major stakeholder in such processes.

Why is it that Arabs in Halifax, Cairo, Sydney, Toledo, and Amman cry together at the sight of a dead Palestinian boy? And, conversely, why are there so many enclaves of hostility among Arabs themselves? Al-Jazeera has successfully identified characteristics of the Arab audience that show similarities, as well as differences. By detecting and highlighting the links that connect Arabs worldwide, Al-Jazeera has become part and parcel of the Arab world. It speaks to and for it.

The connections that bind the 300 million Arabs in twenty-two countries are often abstract. It's not a military alliance, a political truce, an economic cooperative, or a simple linguistic tie. It may not even be reduced to a common religion. Instead, what brings Arabs together is a notion of joint destiny. As with the human nervous system, a single pinprick can be felt throughout the rest of the body. And somewhat like a body of water, where ripples spread and rebound across the surface, the Arab world can occasionally seem like a single entity. And although divisions of nationhood, religion, and economics are often pervasive, certain characteristics unify the Arab public mentality. Whether or not similarities represent a pan-Arab phenomenon is unimportant. Rather, the way in which we come to understand the Arab world from an insider's point of view can make a profound difference in international relations. More than any other time in recent history, there is a need for greater understanding between the West and the Arab world: What can be accomplished through collaborative political engagement among the regions of the world?

If there's any truth to the popular saying "we are what we watch," then to understand the Arab public we must venture into the Al-Jazeera TV news network. Such a unique look at the world through Arab eyes can open windows.

2

A MAJOR LEAGUE CHANNEL IN
A MINOR LEAGUE COUNTRY

On Sunday, October 7, 2001, Americans were glued to their seats as they watched an unfamiliar and sobering dose of real-life adversity unfold on their TV screens. Cable News Network (CNN) broke its regular coverage of the first day of the U.S. strikes on Afghanistan to broadcast a live feed from Al-Jazeera showing America's iconoclastic arch-nemesis, Al-Qaeda leader Osama bin Laden. The man who has been accused by the U.S. administration of being the prime suspect behind the September 11, 2001, attacks on New York and Washington had his six and a half minutes of fame as he made his case to a world-wide audience—Western and Eastern, Muslim and Christian. His words, translated crudely by a stuttering interpreter, chilled Americans and other Westerners. For the first time in recent memory, the U.S. adversary was speaking directly to the U.S. public.

From that point on, the once-anonymous Al-Jazeera, the Arabic satellite TV news network, became a household name. With its exclusive broadcast of the first video footage of Osama bin Laden, Al-Jazeera had scooped the world. As the world's eyes fixed on Afghanistan, Al-Jazeera scored again with exclusive footage of U.S. strikes against Afghanistan. Its monopoly on reporting from within Taliban-controlled Afghanistan must have been a source of envy for most Western TV stations. Virtually every U.S. network has since dedicated some show, panel, forum, feature, or program to this remarkable phenomenon in Arab-based TV news. In the initial stage of the Afghanistan crisis, American audiences received a daily dose of Al-Jazeera. In covering this crisis, CNN and other news stations that normally might have broken the news themselves used Al-Jazeera footage. In fact, many U.S. broadcasters simply showed Al-Jazeera broadcasts live during their own programming, together with translations. The controversies that surround the network, its operations, audience appeal, journalistic integrity, and coverage of the war have catapulted it into the harsh media spotlight, with articles appearing in the *New York Times* and other major newspapers that give the network credit for championing free speech; others accuse it of galvanizing Arab radicalism.

Controversy is not new to Al-Jazeera. Since its inception in 1996, the network, based out of the tiny Middle Eastern peninsula of Qatar, has been raising eyebrows in the Middle East and elsewhere for its provocative approach to news analysis. In fact, in June 1999 it showed the first televised broadcast of a ninety-minute discussion with bin Laden to a mass Arab audience. Since then, Western states and moderate Arab governments have periodically condemned Al-Jazeera for being a supporter of and mouthpiece for the Taliban and Al-Qaeda. How Arabs perceive Al-Jazeera has also been a topic of concern. Arab views toward Al-Jazeera vary tremendously, with some Arab regimes accusing it of being an avenue for dissident voices and a conspirator in antigovernment movements, others acknowledging the network as the sole voice of journalistic objectivity in a conflict-ridden region. The network's habit of presenting provocative and nontraditional views sets it aside from other TV stations throughout the Arab region. Whereas most Arab stations reflect an univocal attitude toward the Palestinian-Israeli conflict, Al-Jazeera airs full interviews with Israeli officials, an absolute taboo by most Arab media standards.

Al-Jazeera's seemingly evenhanded reporting and uninhibited critique of authoritarian regimes have rattled the Arab world. Rumor has it that Egyptian President Hosni Mubarak, during a trip to Qatar in January 2000, paid an uninvited visit to the Al-Jazeera studios sometime after midnight. Surveying the facility and chatting with the onsite staff, Mubarak turned to his minister of information, Safwat Al-Sharif, and exclaimed: "All this trouble from a matchbox like this!"

While it seems Mubarak was remarking sarcastically about the size of the network and the country that hosts it, his metaphor could not be more accurate. Regional governments as far west from Qatar as Morocco have considered the network's coverage and choice of programming nothing short of heresy. More recently, accusations against Al-Jazeera are laden with claims that the satellite network's framing of Middle Eastern and world events is igniting Muslim and Arab anger and fury against the United States, its military campaigns, and its foreign policies. Over the last five years, the network's executives have been asked to censor their reporting by everyone from Palestinian Authority leader Yasser Arafat to U.S. Secretary of State Colin Powell. In each of these circumstances, Al-Jazeera management and staff, backed by the Qatari government, have consistently countered these requests by stating their journalistic commitment to presenting news and issues reflecting "the opinion, and the other opinion," a clause that has since become the network's motto and slogan.

What makes the Al-Jazeera news network so provocative and enraging to world governments, yet so engaging and riveting to its viewers? How did Al-Jazeera become such an important player in the U.S. war on terrorism? Most political and media analysts might agree that Al-Jazeera is nothing short of a second Desert Storm, a war fought on airwaves instead of battlefields.

Since the network's inception, Al-Jazeera officials have fended off critics. The network and its founders are keen not to be categorized as partisan on any political issue. In an attempt to avoid being viewed as beholden to any single party or bias, Al-Jazeera is swift in maintaining balanced coverage. Following the broadcast of bin Laden's video on October 7, Western officials, in an attempt to counter the Al-Qaeda leader's message, spoke to Arabs worldwide using Al-Jazeera. Attempting to win over public opinion in the Middle East for strikes on Afghanistan and to help explain the U.S. initiative, National Security Advisor Condoleezza Rice and British Prime Minister Tony Blair both sought interviews by Al-Jazeera. In each case, they were given the opportunity to make a case through an impartial medium to a receptive Arab public.

As the so-called war on terrorism makes headlines worldwide, the hot story in political and media circles is not only the war on the ground; it is also Al-Jazeera, the first twenty-four-hour all-news network in the Arab world. An upstart satellite TV news network, in just a few years of existence Al-Jazeera has grabbed the world's attention, placing the tiny Gulf state of Qatar on the international map. Whether they be critic or advocate, most people consider it to be the Arab world's CNN.

Although Al-Jazeera has taken heat from the West in general, the United States has taken special umbrage with the network, citing its willingness to provide airtime to the Taliban and Al-Qaeda, for spreading "inflammatory rhetoric" against the U.S. mission in Afghanistan. Questions and accusations were directed toward Al-Jazeera after the Taliban prevented all foreign media—except Al-Jazeera—from reporting out of Taliban-controlled regions of Afghanistan. Initially, Al-Jazeera was the only network with correspondents reporting live from the besieged

Afghan capital, Kabul, and the city of Kandahar, the Taliban's religious center and a top target in the U.S.-led war. However, ever since Taliban troops pulled out of Kabul in early November 2001, several U.S. and other Western news agencies have entered Afghanistan to broadcast live from Afghanistan's heartland. On November 13, 2001, the Kabul office of Al-Jazeera was destroyed by a U.S. missile. No one was in the office when the missile hit. However, with its two star reporters out of action after their building was destroyed, Al-Jazeera was temporarily reduced to airing footage from other networks before it was able to regroup its correspondents in Afghanistan.

Al-Jazeera has been the only news media outlet to receive exclusive footage and messages from bin Laden and members of his organization. Since the U.S. attacks started in Afghanistan, Al-Jazeera has channeled reports from bin Laden several times and is likely to remain an exclusive conduit through which bin Laden will choose to speak to the world. Al-Jazeera's exclusive access has prompted U.S. and European networks to court it— and Western governments to try to tame it.

The complaints and criticism were met with Qatari steadfastness. Al-Jazeera staff wore them as badges of honor; the whole world had been forced to take it seriously. And while most Arab governments continue to maintain some control over local news coverage—censoring unfavorable news and punishing reporters who adopt the journalistic freedoms practiced by CNN and other Western media—Al-Jazeera operates under very little government restriction.

Today, Al-Jazeera's influence extends beyond the Arab Middle East. This is doubly extraordinary given that Al-Jazeera is an exclusively Arabic-language network. Not only has it become the news station of choice for many Arab communities in the United States and elsewhere; it is also playing a vital role in strengthening the Arab cause in the West through credible and effective journalism. More important, Al-Jazeera has opened a new front: information war. From propaganda to media broadcasts to covert intelligence, information is more vital to this war than any other in recent history. Describing what will be an extended conflict, the U.S. government faces some opposition at home and more abroad, and its administration is forced to shape public opinion. Al-Jazeera, with its distinctively Arab style, beaming from the center of the Arab world and scooping the U.S. networks, can affect U.S. public opinion by providing the first glimpse of the daily grind of Arab life—warts and all. Al-Jazeera could potentially affect U.S. foreign policy and have a direct impact on the course of the current crisis. Who would have imagined that a network like Al-Jazeera could win the first round in this information battle, where large and established media outlets compete for supremacy?

But Al-Jazeera's success is not unfounded. Arab audiences see Al-Jazeera as a television and information system that not only uncovers the scandals and corrupt policies in their respective countries but also sympathizes with the issues they hold dearest. Often enough, Arabs complain about the U.S. inability to conceptualize the Arab narrative, story, and position. They bemoan the fact that the American public fails to comprehend the Arab position on most issues. This discrepancy became painfully obvious during a CNN *Larry King Live* program, aired in late October 2001. The guests were Dana Suyyagh, the soft-spoken senior producer for Al-Jazeera, and Judith Miller, a *New York Times* columnist. As Suyyagh tried to explain what she described to be misconceptions about Al-Jazeera, she was cornered by Miller about the veracity of Al-Jazeera's objective news reporting. It could be assumed that the network, even as it insists on interviewing Israeli as well as Arab officials, is known to reflect Arab empathy toward the Palestinians and their plight. This is exactly what Miller targeted when she accused Suyyagh's station of faking objectivity.

"So there is a difference between terrorists who kill people—civilians in Israel—and terrorists who kill Americans," Miller claimed. In response, Suyyagh appeared to be content by affirming simply that "it's all in the cause" and that the attacks on September 11, as opposed to attacks on Israel, were "causeless."

This goes to the heart of the fundamental conflict that commenced with the establishment of the Israeli state and the dispossession of Palestinians some five decades ago. Israeli control of the Occupied Territories and the violent acts committed between the Israeli and Palestinian soldiers have resonated in Arab minds. For most Arabs, some forms of resistance against Israeli occupation is legitimate. This may be the reason why, in accordance with many Arab empathizers, Suyyagh stated that one attack reflected one "cause" more so than another. How can there be two differing definitions of "the cause"? The journalistic standard applied here required some form of *contextual objectivity*, because the medium should reflect all sides of any story while retaining the values, beliefs, and sentiments of the target audience. In this case, one could argue that Al-Jazeera determined what was important for the public to know even as Al-Jazeera was itself influenced by its audience. One could further argue similarly that U.S. TV coverage, operating as a free press, has reflected the views of mainstream America in the aftermath of the September 11 attacks while at the same time helping to create public opinion on the streets. This dual relationship underscores the conundrum of modern media. How then can the news media be truly objective?

Larry King posed it well when he asked if we "should be listening to the other side." This is precisely what Al-Jazeera strives to attain. Its philosophy is built on demonstrating how objectivity can be attained only if all subjective views and opinions on any issue are presented and aired. The coverage must exhaust all possible ideas and perspectives. Suyyagh reinforced this when she added that Al-Jazeera labors to cover every conceivable side of every story. "It's a balancing act," she said; "we try our best to listen to everyone."

This formula grew out of a group of individuals who themselves were a conglomeration of various opinions, perspectives, and views. Yosri Fouda, Al-Jazeera's London bureau chief, described in early 2001 the atmosphere in the network as a unique system that is unrealistic and rare compared to most other organizations. "It is a mixture of the tribal and the urban, the Eastern and the Western, the leftist and the rightist, and the religious and the secular." This multiplicity of diverse voices is what some view as either an act of heroism or of heresy. The one thing that is certain is that this eclectic presentation has angered everyone across the political spectrum.

This approach is what network officials consider best for public discussion and political activity in the Middle East. Any viewer of Al-Jazeera immediately notices the degree of sophistication and intellect reflected in many of the network's talk shows and programs. A comprehensive discussion from all possible angles on many issues—including Islamic law, Arab nationalism, and freedom of expression—is bound to nourish democracy and free speech in an Arab world that has seldom enjoyed such privileges. Qatari media scholar Ali Al-Hail argued that Al-Jazeera and its type of programming are the best way to reinvigorate a sense of freedom, democratization, and liberty throughout the Arab world, in addition to fostering a vibrant civil society.

WHAT IS AL-JAZEERA?

Al-Jazeera, which means "the island" or "the peninsula" in Arabic, broadcasts out of a region with little tradition of a free press. It seeks to be provocative in a region where news reporting is often limited to directives from government information ministries; it is a region where dissent has been tightly controlled so that the political regimes can remain in power. Al-Jazeera has, indeed, revolutionized the media environment in the Arab world by broadcasting what no other Arab news organization dared to: the hard, often harsh truth of Arab life, culture, and politics. Before Al-Jazeera, most Arab regimes' broadcasting dictated a steady diet of mind-numbing entertainment and bland, often harmless news and talk shows.

Today, many shudder when Al-Jazeera tackles unusual views and controversial political debates and broadcasts them to millions of viewers in the Arab world and beyond. And many wonder, too, how they ever watched television before Al-Jazeera. The network's daring approach touches on issues considered by Arab standards to be forbidden, like sex, polygamy, corruption of governmental regimes, women's civil rights, and Islamic fundamentalism. Moreover, it was the first Arab network to feature interviews with top Israeli leaders, including former Israeli Prime Minister Ehud Barak. This has angered many Arab leaders who were accustomed to tight control over the state media.

More than anything, Al-Jazeera gained fame for its graphic and frequent depictions of the Palestinian uprising (the New Intifada), the streak of violence between Palestinians and Israelis that started in September 2000 and galvanized the world's 1.2 billion Muslims. Complete feature films and hour-by-hour coverage of the demonstrations, coupled with an unvarnished presentation of death, casualties, and destruction, have had a monumental impact on Arab audiences.

In November 2000, we spoke with Tawfik Mahroos, a twenty-two-year-old pharmacy student at Cairo University in Egypt. Like many Arab youths his age, he was enraged at the sight of what he calls "unpunished atrocities" that have been airing on

Al-Jazeera's nightly news. Before the student's family subscribed to the satellite service, all they had access to was Egyptian television, which covered the Intifada more subtly. Since then, the student has demonstrated alongside thousands of fellow students to urge the Egyptian government to take action. "I never knew the situation was as bad as it is," he said. This student's experience reflects a fundamental aspect of civil action: mass mobilization. Many U.S. and Israeli officials have accused Al-Jazeera of inciting public demonstrations as a consequence of its coverage. Once again, Al-Jazeera staff remained steadfast, stating that they cover what they see and that public reaction is simply the logical consequence.

Even during times of peace, Arab audiences find that government programming is divergent with long-held popular interests. This persisting tension provides yet another reason for why Al-Jazeera is so successful. The gap between the Arab viewers' environment and the pictures they see is enormous, whether audiences are watching a state-run national network or satellite networks. International media professor and Middle East specialist Douglas Boyd described this phenomenon in a seminar held in Cairo in February 1999 organized by the London-based International Center Against Censorship:

> The hardware of getting the signal out in a professional way becomes the goal, instead of the means, while the software is left to the existing diet of government news, cheap Arabic soap operas and the worst Hollywood programming. Once the signal is out, and the picture of the king or the ruler is seen against a background of classical music, the operation is declared a success.

Al-Jazeera grew out of the termination of a contract in April 1996 between Rome-based, Saudi-owned Orbit Radio and

Television Service and the Arabic TV division of BBC News Service. A disagreement between the Saudi Arabian kingdom and the BBC News Service concerning editorial independence led to the Saudi investors' abrupt withdrawal of financial support only twenty months after the deal was signed. It was reported that the Saudis pulled the plug following an argument over the broadcast of a special documentary about executions in Saudi Arabia.

The premise of the Arabic TV division of the BBC News Service for television was conceived and built initially on the assumption that the success of BBC's Arabic radio network (BBC World Service Arabic Radio), which attracted an estimated 14 million listeners in 1994, was replicable on TV screens. With the financial backing and subsidy of the large Saudi corporation Mawarid, it was understood that this new TV service would be the largest and most influential media force in the Arab world. Soon enough, with the rush of success, the aspirations of both groups clashed over the issue of editorial independence. One side held firm that the BBC violated cultural sensitivities; the other claimed nothing more than a series of journalistic scoops. Many of the details of this confrontation, which left both parties sour and at odds, are indistinct, but a winner soon emerged. And so it was that Al-Jazeera was unexpectedly conceived during this period. It became a reality when the founders of Al-Jazeera decided to recruit the majority of the BBC's disheartened Arabic TV service editorial staff. In fact, Al-Jazeera inherited not only most of the staff of the former BBC network but also its editorial spirit, freedom, and style.

The BBC's Arabic TV network collapsed, leaving the remaining twenty Arabic-language media professionals jobless. Al-Jazeera executives, still in the process of structuring the new network, were swift in their recognition and acquisition of the BBC staff. Much of the programming talent and employees stationed in London were moved to the Qatari city of Doha. (The Al-Jazeera executives had solicited and recruited a subsidy from the Qatari government in an effort to reinstate the service in Qatar, where they would run the network's operations.) This move proved to be decisive for both the network and its newly recruited staff. The staff of editors, reporters, and producers—of various Arab nationalities—were grafted into what seemed like an experimental station in an obscure location. Since then, this core group has gone on to formulate the vision and direction of Al-Jazeera. The staff was trained in the Western journalistic tradition; wielding the expert knowledge and understanding of Arab politics and audiences, they were the final ingredient in the recipe for Al-Jazeera's eventual success.

Growing out of a country whose population is little more than an average-size U.S. city (744,500, according to 2000 estimates), Al-Jazeera is a textbook example of what media scholars Joseph Straubhaar and Marwan Kraidy call "asymmetrical interdependence." As millions of Arab satellite subscribers throughout the Middle East, North America, and Europe tune in to watch Al-Jazeera, it could be convincingly argued that the network's influence and impact on international affairs and public opinion is disproportionate to the miniscule amount of power that the Qatari state exerts politically.

The power that Al-Jazeera holds as a media force in the Middle East is asymmetrical to Qatar's actual leverage in the international arena. This in itself shifts patterns of dependence in the region. In the 1960s, larger Arab nations like Egypt and Saudi Arabia exercised a great deal of influence throughout the Middle East through centralized media like Egypt's Sout Al-Arab (Voice of the Arabs) radio. Today, Qatari- and Lebanese-based news media are some of the most widely viewed foreign networks throughout the Middle East. Al-

Jazeera's London bureau chief, Yosri Fouda, expressed the anguish and frustration of Al-Jazeera's satellite competitors when he stated that some people "just could not accept the fact that the 'country of goats,' Qatar, could actually produce such a professional success."

Ali Al-Hail, a Qatari scholar and consultant to the network, recently reported that approximately 70 percent of Arabs who own a satellite dish rely primarily on Al-Jazeera for news, documentaries, and political information. The September 11 attacks and the ensuing war are surely having an immeasurable impact on that audience today. In fact, an official from Al-Jazeera estimated that subscriptions to Arabic satellite services have increased by more than 300 percent in the month following September 11. It is no longer accurate to claim that Arab audiences are impacted mostly by the long-standing satellite networks out of Egypt and Saudi Arabia. Instead, those countries' officials, in an attempt to court Al-Jazeera, and despite reservations about programming and content, have started to collaborate with Al-Jazeera. For example, the Egyptian government has since allowed Al-Jazeera to use its studios and facilities for its programming.

Al-Jazeera received its funding in November 1996 from Qatar's progressive emir (the Arabic equivalent to prince), Sheikh Hamad bin Khalifa Al-Thani, as part of his move to introduce democratization to his tiny state. The British-educated emir, who overthrew his father after a nonviolent coup in 1995, planned for Al-Jazeera to be an independent and nonpartisan satellite TV network free from government scrutiny, control, and manipulation. Sheikh Hamad offered an initial pledge of $140 million to help launch and subsidize Al-Jazeera over a five-year period through November 2001, after which the network was to become financially self-sufficient from advertising revenues. Al-Jazeera has not made that transition yet. In fact, the Qatari government has been spending roughly $100 million each year to sustain the network, which has not attracted enough advertisers to date. Although the market for satellite TV advertising in the Arab world is estimated to exceed $500 million annually, most of it is spent by multinational corporations that are reluctant to risk alienating Arab governments by advertising on Al-Jazeera. However, this trend may change with Al-Jazeera's newfound success and growing popularity.

Today, five years since its launch, Al-Jazeera houses a staff of some 350 journalists and fifty foreign correspondents working in thirty-one countries, including the United States. One of those correspondents, Hafez Al-Mirazi, the chief of the Al-Jazeera bureau in Washington, D.C., said: "Al-Jazeera has a margin of freedom that no other Arab channel enjoys. Our motto is 'the view and the other point of view.'"

More important, the operators and directors of Al-Jazeera have identified a market demand for serious and independent journalism, thereby narrowing and specializing their content exclusively to political matters. This serves as a contrast to most other Arabic-language satellite services, which dedicate much of their airtime to entertainment. Although there are no reliable statistics to document the exact number of satellite-package subscriptions made specifically for Al-Jazeera, and no documentation of actual viewing time, estimates put the number of Al-Jazeera viewers at approximately 35 million.

WHO IS HAMAD BIN KHALIFA AL-THANI?

What would make an Arab monarch like Sheikh Hamad introduce democracy and allow freedom of information within his tiny emirate? One can speculate that Hamad's policies stem from his education in Great Britain, where he graduated from the Royal Military Academy in Sandhurst in 1971.

With this military background, much of Hamad's political attention has been military- and security-oriented. Under his authority, an old border dispute between Saudi Arabia and Qatar
has been revived. Before appointing himself emir, Hamad was
active in modernizing both the military as well as the country's
physical and economic infrastructures. In 1977, Hamad was appointed crown prince, whereupon he was also appointed minister of defense. Under his direction, Qatari military forces partic-
ipated in the Coalition attack on Iraq following the invasion of
Kuwait in 1990. In June 1995, while his father, Sheikh Khalifa,
was in Geneva, Hamad took control of the Qatari government
in a peaceful coup. Hamad has been on good terms with his father since December 1996, when they met in Rome for the first
time since Hamad took power. The personal meeting marked
the formal end of the dispute, which had tied up the finances of
Qatar for eighteen months. Under an agreement reached between their representatives, the father's foreign bank accounts
have been unfrozen, and some of those monies were transferred
to the Qatari government under the control of his son.

AL-JAZEERA AND QATAR

Like all Arab countries, the emirate's citizens and inhabitants
follow the official religion, Islam, and speak the official language, Arabic. A minority (25 percent) of the population are
Qataris (Arabs of the Wahhabi sect of Islam), while the rest are
expatriate workers who reside in the emirate with state-approved
employment visas. These workers are largely Pakistanis, Indians,
other Arabs, and Iranians.

Qatar is a traditional monarchy, where a provisional constitution enacted in 1972 called for elections to the thirty-five-seat
advisory council, although none have been held to date. Instead,
council members continue to be appointed by the ruling family.
Like its neighbors in the Gulf, Qatar's economy is dominated by

oil, which accounts for more than 90 percent of exports and government income. Qatar has the world's third largest gas reserves after Russia and Iran. Its huge offshore northern field contains reserves of more than 350 trillion cubic yards (10 trillion cubic meters), an asset that will guarantee economic prosperity for years. Qatar is a member of the Arab League, the United Nations, and the Organization of Petroleum Exporting Countries (OPEC).

As was the case with other Gulf nations, during the 1991 Gulf War international Coalition forces were deployed on Qatari soil; as in postwar Kuwait, Palestinians were expelled from Qatar in retaliation for the pro-Iraq position of the Palestine Liberation Organization. Since the war, relations with the Palestinians have normalized. After the Gulf War, Iraq was still regarded as a threat to Qatar's oil interests. Qatar signed a defense pact with the United States but also restored relations with Iraq. The emirate has long called for a regional initiative to end the economic sanctions imposed on Iraq after its invasion of Kuwait. Upon the launching of Al-Jazeera, senior producers and directors have made this a vital issue on the network's agenda, with various documentaries aired to demonstrate the plight of the Iraqi people under the sanctions.

Qatar has been marked by policies independent from other Arabian Gulf monarchies. Adopting a moderate course of action in the late 1990s, Sheikh Hamad eased press censorship. Moreover, he sought improved relations with Iran and Israel. He also moved steadily to democratize the nation's government and institute the delayed elections. Israel opened a trade office in Doha in 1996 despite criticism from other Gulf Arab states. But Qatar froze ties with Israel in response to criticism from Muslim countries.

Although Qatar has one of the smallest populations among the Gulf states, its emir's democratic goals may be among the grandest. Sheikh Hamad's vision points toward a more liberal political system, starting with an elected consultative council. Of the other Gulf states, only Kuwait has an elected parliament. All the others have appointed councils that advise the ruler, carry out investigations of government services, and conduct interrogations of cabinet members. Sheikh Hamad further distinguished the Qatari government when he announced that in addition to an elected council Qatar will have elected municipal officers. During a recent visit in 2001 to the United States, he promised that he will hold parliamentary elections in two years.

Sheikh Hamad went one step farther when he announced an end to media censorship. He abolished the Ministry of Information, responsible for censorship; it ran radio and television, set quality standards for local newspapers, and assisted foreign journalists and scholars seeking information about Qatar. There is no other Arab government that functions without such a ministry or its equivalent. Even in the United States, many of these kinds of media controls are scattered among various federal departments (for example, the Federal Communications Commission), agencies, and commissions. In place of the Information Ministry, Sheikh Hamad established an association named the General Association for Qatari Radio and Television.

Furthermore, Sheikh Hamad is emphasizing women's education in a country where both female and male attendance in primary and secondary school is mandatory, and where women already outnumber men in the national university. He is calling for removing all remaining barriers so that women can realize their full potential in cultural, economic, and professional life. And in a radical departure from the practices of traditional governments in the Gulf, Sheikh Hamad allowed all citizens over age eighteen, including women, to vote in municipal elections.

At the end of 1996, one of Sheikh Hamad's three wives led a delegation of specialists in the educational and medical fields served by Sheikh Hamad's personal charitable and educational foundation to visit leading U.S. institutions. In doing so, she apparently became the first wife of an Arabian Gulf ruler to lead a delegation abroad unaccompanied by her husband.

The developments within the Qatari government have elicited favorable comments in the Western press; however, they have drawn mixed reactions in more conservative Middle Eastern circles. In fact, listening to conflicting accounts of what is happening in Qatar is like viewing a painting or a mosaic floor designed to fool the eye. Looked at one way, it presents a smooth and inviting path. Looked at another way, it seems an impassable surface.

AL-JAZEERA AND ARAB SATELLITE TELEVISION

Al-Jazeera is one of several Arab satellite networks that have been launched by Arab governments and entrepreneurs over the last few years. Several Arab states, witnessing CNN's impact on an international scale during and after the 1991 Gulf War, realized the strategic importance of satellite television during times of conflict. These states launched their own national satellite TV networks.

Several networks that serve Middle Eastern audiences are based outside the Arab world. A quick glance at the six leading Arab satellite networks reveals that where free speech is concerned ownership matters more than location. The London-based Middle East Broadcasting Center (MBC) belongs to Sheikh Walid Al-Ibrahim, a brother-in-law of Saudi Arabia's King Fahd. King Fahd is believed to have underwritten a large portion of MBC's costs. The Egyptian Satellite Channel (ESC), broadcasting out of Cairo, is part of an enormous state-run monopoly, the Egyptian Radio and Television Union (ERTU).

Emirates Dubai Television (EDTV), broadcasting out of the United Arab Emirates, is state-owned. Of the two private Lebanese networks that expanded into satellite television, one, Future TV, is partly owned by Lebanese Prime Minister Rafiq Hariri. The other, the Lebanese Broadcasting Corporation (LBC), is controlled by a board dominated by ministers and officials close to the Syrian government. Both networks are located in Beirut.

Many of these Arab satellite networks are offshoots of state-run TV networks. Many were set up purposely so that Arab governments could extend and exert influence beyond their national borders. They broadcast mostly official propaganda, and they spend more money on the technical side of broadcasting than on the quality of the programming. This is reflected in the content. The news programs in many of these networks broadcast "protocol" news, that is, items in government news bulletins about officials' activities, visits, and announcements. Viewers of the nightly news in Kuwait watch the step-by-step daily agenda of the emir, Sheikh Jaber Al-Sabbah, and his cabinet as they open new schools, meet foreign delegates, and celebrate national occasions. The dearth in issues-oriented coverage on Arab government TV screens can be generalized to most Arab countries.

Even privately owned satellite networks like the Lebanese Broadcasting Corporation, Middle Eastern Broadcasting Company, and Arab Radio and Television provide primarily entertainment-oriented programming that only mildly tackles issues of social and political sensitivity.

It used to be the case before Al-Jazeera that Middle Easterners would listen to foreign-based Arab-language short-wave radio broadcasts, such as the Voice of America, Radio Monte Carlo–Middle East (RMC-ME), and BBC World Service Arabic Radio to get reliable and authoritative sources of news that were accurate, objective, and comprehensive. However, these foreign

services have given way to Al-Jazeera, now that it presents the
policies of the Arab world more clearly and effectively, as well as
uncensored discussions and opinions. In fact, we believe that Al-
Jazeera's mission is similar in some ways to that of VOA and
Radio Free Europe, which is to provide news, analysis, and discussion of domestic and regional issues crucial to successful
democratic and free-market transformations, and to help
strengthen civil societies by projecting democratic values.

It is interesting to note in this regard that U.S. officials, like
Secretary of Defense Donald Rumsfeld, who claimed that Al-
Jazeera was serving as a "mouthpiece" for the terrorists by
broadcasting their messages to the world, have also tried to stop
VOA from airing an exclusive interview with Taliban leader
Mullah Mohammed Omar. Though the interview was eventually aired, the attempts to persuade VOA from running the program angered the network's new director, Robert Reilly, who
was quoted in the *New York Times* on October 12, 2001 as saying, "During the past few days, there has been a systematic attack on the Voice of America." VOA's interview with the
Taliban leader came at a time of controversy over its role and
degree of independence. Some members of the U.S. Congress
say the government-funded radio network, which broadcasts in
fifty-three languages, should be more of an advocate for U.S.
interests. But VOA's professional staff has long maintained that
it will lose credibility and listeners unless it reports news that is
balanced and objective.

For this reason, in times of distress, most Arabs have sought
national and international news from sources like BBC World
Service Arabic Radio, Voice of America, and the French-based
Radio Monte Carlo–Middle East. Those living in Kuwait for the
few months of Iraqi occupation in 1990 huddled around radios
to listen to BBC and VOA news reports when the Iraqi media
disguised the Iraqi invasion as a supposed Kuwaiti military coup

that overthrew a corrupt Kuwaiti monarchy. For Arabs outside of Kuwait, it wasn't until the Gulf War commenced that they were introduced to the form of TV news coverage provided by CNN. In fact, since Al-Jazeera's inception, many of its officials have repeatedly announced that they hoped to tailor their style after CNN. And in more ways than one, then, it is becoming evident that these two networks have a great deal in common. The current war in Afghanistan, according to Ibrahim Hilal, Al-Jazeera's chief editor, in an interview with CNN's Christiane Amanpour on the program *International Correspondents*, explained that the way the Gulf War gave CNN its worldwide fame is happening again—but this time the news agency to gain media celebrity is Al-Jazeera. Al-Jazeera is in a way the CNN of the war in Afghanistan.

Yet the BBC still serves as the primary model for Al-Jazeera. Much of the network's objectives mirror its British forebear. As explained by Al-Mirazi, from Al-Jazeera's Washington D.C. bureau, "We [Al-Jazeera] follow the BBC model in that we are a public corporation that enjoys editorial independence. It used to be the case that Arab people used to prefer Western media over Arab media, thinking that you cannot have an independent media body in the Arab world that is free from government control. Al-Jazeera broke that rule."

In an interview conducted by S. Abdallah Schleifer, senior editor of the electronic *Transnational Broadcasting Studies Journal*, the managing director of Al-Jazeera, Mohammed Jasim Al-Ali, explained what TV news was in the Arab world prior to CNN, and how the war coverage changed the future Arab media and audiences thereafter:

> *You often get here someone reading an item about leaders arriving in the country, sitting together—it's not news, they only do it to give them TV time. The view is of leaders sit-*

ting together, talking together, and everything is fine, there's no news. But behind the scenes, everything is not fine. They never put that on the screen. People saw something dramatically different in CNN's coverage of the Gulf War. At that time everyone was watching CNN; no one was watching any entertainment then, just the news. There were so many stories in the war, human interest and war stories even took the place of entertainment.

Today, there is one exception to the rule of Arab state ownership of satellite news networks, and it is Al-Jazeera. The other Arab TV news stations are now having to find either another niche market or compete with Al-Jazeera, a challenge for which few are prepared.

Officially, Al-Jazeera is an independent network, its only connection to the Qatari government being its funding. This freedom has allowed Al-Jazeera's considerable scope. Political talk shows are now a regular feature of Al-Jazeera's program listings, and viewers are now openly encouraged to call in and voice their opinions. Only Al-Jazeera has dared to challenge Arabic traditions and political restraints by airing programs open to all opinions. Al-Jazeera's staff prioritize stories according to their newsworthiness, not their acceptability to local politics, and much of Al-Jazeera's material is broadcast live.

Al-Jazeera was criticized by Arab governments that did not welcome the airtime given to political opponents. Generally, Arab leaders are mindful of two risks as far as the media are concerned. First, they feel that foreign, and especially Western, values could undermine their traditions and roots. Second, they need to maintain citizens' respect for their leaders, who govern predominantly by tribal and religious guidelines. Support for freedom of the media is circumscribed by local tenets, the traditional and often cited "national interest" being one example.

For the Arab satellite networks that have sprung up in the past decade and attempt to compete with Al-Jazeera, many spice up political coverage by adding a lineup of political debates, talk shows, and social comment—this after mind-numbing years of drab propaganda, endless soap operas, and outdated cabaret acts. "It's a new phenomenon and the idea behind it is that in the new world of television, censorship basically does not exist," said Hussein Amin, a communications professor at American University in Cairo and a senior official in the Egyptian Radio and Television Union, in an interview with Reuters News Agency in June 2001.

However, Arab governments still exercise some control over satellite networks, and they continue to push their policies through them. For example, Egyptian civil rights activist Saad Eddin Ibrahim (who also holds a U.S. passport) said that he gave a lengthy interview to the Egyptian Satellite Channel explaining his recent trial and defending himself against charges of defaming Egypt, forgery, and illegally accepting foreign funds; it was cut to two minutes and spliced into a program about Egyptian spies. "I am not charged with espionage, so I considered that defamation," the sociology professor said during an interview with Reuters in the summer of 2001. The new freedom on the airwaves is "contrived at best," said Ibrahim. "It's one step forward and two steps back." Amr Al-Leithy, host of one of the Egyptian Satellite Channel's talk shows, was quoted by Reuters in June 2001: "We can't say the red lines have gone, but there are fewer of them. . . . Political programs are being approved by the [Egyptian] minister of information personally."

It appears that Al-Jazeera has been able to eliminate all the red lines (i.e., substantive editing) from its political talk shows. However, four questions need to be addressed in this context. First, with all that Al-Jazeera has done to the political landscape in the Middle East and worldwide, what role will the network play in world politics in the years to come? Second, if Al-Jazeera existed wholly in the private sector, would its relatively independent and free approach be curtailed by possible government-driven commercial boycotts? Third, do Qatari officials genuinely believe in freedom of information, or are they using Al-Jazeera as a public relations tool to enhance their country's image overseas? And fourth, how can Al-Jazeera and similar media networks help foster better understanding between the United States and the Arab world?

Although there are no definitive answers to these questions, Al-Jazeera has set new standards for freedom for all the other Arab satellite networks. Credibility, audience size, and financial resources will serve as the essential criteria for the survivability of Al-Jazeera as well as other Arab satellite networks in the immediate future.

No Arab satellite TV network other than Al-Jazeera has ever attempted to present Arab views, opinions, and beliefs to the West with such vigor and legitimacy. Al-Jazeera officials seem to understand the power of public opinion, the role it can play in the vital formulation of policies in the West, and its influence in decisionmaking worldwide. Still a fledgling in the world of international media, Al-Jazeera is providing the Arab world with its own version of CNN, as a transnational—not just regional—network broadcasting real news and conducting free dialogues. It can be effectively argued that given the rise of Al-Jazeera, Arab views and concerns are directly presented to the world without censorship. It can be also argued that the West in general, and the United States especially, have seldom noticed the Arab world unless there was a crisis that threatened Western oil interests. One of Al-Jazeera's major accomplishments in this crisis was to force the West to look at the Arab world, as the Arabs would say, "with a new eye."

3

THE BATTLE FOR
THE ARAB MIND

It is 9:00 P.M. on a Tuesday night. At their home in an upper-class neighborhood in Cairo, Egypt, the Ragab family sits transfixed, watching their TV set. They are not watching a soap opera or a movie. It's a talk show broadcast on the Al-Jazeera network named *Al Ittijah Al Mo'akis* (The Opposite Direction). Similar to CNN's *Crossfire*, this is the most popular and controversial talk show in the Middle East.

The Ragab family has always been skeptical of Arab media news in general, the Egyptian media in particular, because, according to family members, they did not get any "reliable" news from either. Like many Arab natives, if they watched local or satellite channels, entertainment programs were all that was available. Accordingly, they described news about their own country received from Western networks, like CNN or BBC, as "more credible and comprehensive." Now all they watch is Al-Jazeera. In fact, Al-Jazeera programming makes more sense to the Arab communities than any Western network.

What interests Arab viewers—beyond the national obsession of soccer—is domestic, regional, and world news. Today, Al-Jazeera satisfies this demand and more. Perhaps the Arab public was primed for better television, including programs that offered comprehensive news, news analysis, and talk show programs—even those that fostered flat-out confrontation. Although Al-Jazeera is not a Western media network, its managers and producers have taken a page from the Western media's playbook. Its talk-show hosts are younger and bolder, trained in journalism and imagemaking. Gone are the stiff and stonefaced pedants who dominate Arab TV news. Gone are the bland, traditional, and boring styles and formats of traditional news programs. For example, the first third of the fifty-minute prime-time news bulletin aired on the local Egyptian state-run network is devoted to little more than a review of the president's meetings and telephone calls, cabinet members' inaugurations of new projects, and senior officials' daily activities (it should be noted that virtually all Arab leaders are male). Al-Jazeera's news bulletins, however, provide in-depth investigative analysis of the day's events as they unfold, eschewing government officials' comings and goings.

Al-Jazeera, almost single-handedly, motivated millions of viewers in the Arab world, and in many Western countries, to buy satellite dishes to watch its programming. It could be argued convincingly that some Arabs have saved money specifically to buy satellite dishes at the expense of purchasing basic necessities. For example, in Egypt, where the satellite ownership level is still far below the 20–60 percent recorded elsewhere in the Middle East, the cost of a satellite dish is approximately L.E.1,400 (U.S. $280). During an interview Abdullah Al-Hajj, Al-Jazeera's deputy manager, explained that in several Arab countries women have gone as far as selling their jewelry to purchase a satellite dish to watch Al-Jazeera. In the streets of any Arab capital today, satellite dishes cluster everywhere along the rooftops. Even in Saudi Arabia, where satellite dishes are banned officially, locals purchase and install them, ostensibly to watch Al-Jazeera.

In the Palestinian territories, where economics prevent many from purchasing satellite dishes, the Palestinian Central Bureau of Statistics recently calculated that 78.2 percent of Palestinian households in the West Bank and Gaza Strip have some kind of access to Al-Jazeera.

Mohammed Jasim Al-Ali, Al Jazeera's managing director, described his network's goal, even as it competes with the local BBC or CNN news stations. "The challenge now is how to bring the audience back into watching their own channels. We treat them as intelligent, we give them the true story. For the first year, people watched us, but were very cautious. They wondered how long we could carry on, who's behind us, what our aim was. After that, our audience has grown, and we've grown," he says.

Al-Ali does not have access to sophisticated ratings systems to measure the numbers of viewers who watch Al-Jazeera (there is no Arab equivalent to the Nielson or Arbitron ratings systems used in the States). Satellite subscriptions provide incomplete data—it is complicated to calculate exact numbers of Arab viewers because satellite subscriptions come in multiple packages. The few surveys and polls conducted are questionable because their sampling methods are not statistically reliable. Too often, these surveys do not access random population samples or the samples are too small, so they do not provide accurate figures.

Although flawed, some studies and surveys may provide an initial indicator of the market penetration that Al-Jazeera has achieved. The Qatari newspaper *Al-Sharq* (The East) published an article on November 20, 2000, that reported the results of a survey it conducted among Arabic Al-Jazeera viewers in Washington, D.C., Jordan, and Sudan. In Washington, 79 percent of those surveyed, when asked for their opinion of Al-Jazeera, stated that they "strongly support it." As for their preferences, 64 percent said they prefer Al-Jazeera's talk shows; 29 percent said they like the news; and 7 percent said they like the correspondents' reports. Respondents were also queried about

why they watched Al-Jazeera: 43 percent cited reporters' freedom to pose any question to their sources; 22 percent cited programs that tackle sensitive issues; and 14 percent pointed to the
apparent lack of outside government pressure.

The respondents in Jordan had somewhat different responses:
60 percent said they support Al-Jazeera; 16 percent said they opposed it; and 24 percent said they had "reservations" about its
programs. Some 79 percent of respondents in the Sudan said the
main reason behind Al-Jazeera's success was due more to the
"weakness" of other Arab networks to take on different issues.

Al-Jazeera is popular partly because satellite ownership
throughout the Middle East has become more than fashion-
able—it almost seems indispensable. In the more affluent Gulf
countries, some 70 percent of the population has regular access
to satellite television. One source reported that Al-Jazeera is
broadcast into 60 percent of all Middle East households.
Although interesting, this assertion is questionable because
many households in the more populated Arab countries cannot
afford to pay the service fees for Al-Jazeera. Nonetheless, many
households that lack Al-Jazeera are never far from viewing its
broadcasts. The network is available in many public cafés, and in
more restrictive states, like Iraq, local bazaars sell videotapes of
previously recorded Al-Jazeera programming.

Another Qatari newspaper, *Al-Watan* (The Nation), in an article published May 5, 2000, presented the results of an online
survey that was conducted by the Al-Balagh Cultural Group for
Serving Islam Online. The survey, comparatively large, included
1,026 participants and was conducted through the Islam Online
website. In regard to the nature of "free" (i.e., balanced) news
coverage, *Al-Watan* reported that 625 respondents said Al-
Jazeera contained the most; 204 respondents cited the Saudi-
owned Middle East Broadcasting Center, and 150 cited the Arab
News Network (ANN).

Three years earlier, the same newspaper conducted a similar survey not long after Al-Jazeera started broadcasting. Results of the survey were published on May 17, 1997. That survey, which included a random sample of 500 Qataris in the capital city of Doha, showed that 79 percent thought that Al-Jazeera did not represent the Qatari identity. Much has changed in only a few years.

Al-Jazeera, although headquartered in Qatar, has managed to project an identity that transcends its physical location, reflecting an amalgam of Arab states. A diverse staff from different Arab countries helped establish this pan-Arab identity, which also reflects a broader editorial commitment. In an exploratory study recently published in the *Transnational Broadcasting Studies Journal*, media researcher Mohammed Ayish showed that 73.3 percent of Al-Jazeera's coverage is pan-Arab and that virtually no coverage is local to Qatar. Instead, Al-Jazeera's management attempts to locate issues that will resonate across many Arab audiences.

Given that the majority of the Arab audience appears to desire objective news coverage, Al-Jazeera is racing to stay ahead of the curve to fill that demand. The 1997 *Al-Watan* survey also reported that 61 percent of respondents said the channel was objective; 30 percent said it was not objective. Another 55 percent said they would prefer that Al-Jazeera be supported by the private sector, not by the Qatari government. And another 85 percent said Al-Jazeera needs still more independence.

In the five-plus years of its existence, Al-Jazeera has not only become the most-watched satellite-TV network in the Arab world but also infuriated every Arab government from Libya to Kuwait—both of which once threatened to pull their ambassadors from Qatar in protest.

Initially Al-Jazeera drew attention for airing sensitive issues and controversial debates. During the Algerian civil war, Al-Jazeera had the temerity to cover Algerian opposition party views and the Islamic fundamentalists' role in the internal struggle. Al-Jazeera even dared to produce and broadcast a program that debated a most sensitive ongoing issue: Who is a Jordanian? (The majority of residents are of Palestinian descent.)

Such programming is not especially radical, and Al-Jazeera should not have caused such consternation among neighboring governments and citizens. On the one hand, much of Al-Jazeera's news would be considered perfectly normal on English-language television. On the other hand, its political debates reflect the everyday arguments that Arabs privately carry on among family and friends. The fact is that by broadcasting such issues in public—and in Arabic, no less—Al-Jazeera violated long-established customs. "It makes a hell of a difference when you say it in Arabic," says Yosri Fouda, Al-Jazeera's deputy executive director, in an interview with the *Guardian* newspaper in October 2001. Many Middle Eastern states control the supply and media distribution of information, so it is understandable that these same states protested when audiences turned away from official programming.

Another Al-Jazeera mainstay is studio debate, during which viewers can phone in to ask questions and argue with talk-show guests and hosts. Sometimes arguments between hosts and their guests go on for hours, the antagonists wagging fingers and screaming at one another. According to Jian Al-Jacuby, an Iraqi reporter working in the Al-Jazeera newsroom, "For Arabs, Al-Jazeera is revolutionary. Arab people, for a long time, just wanted somebody to listen to them. That is the importance of Al-Jazeera: to let people talk." Where public expression is often suppressed, Al-Jazeera has become an instrument for both marginal and silenced voices, whether radical or liberal, Muslim or Christian. Its programs often contain fiery debates and arguments that appear to be on the verge of fistfights, but Al-Jazeera's producers strive to maintain more than a semblance of intellectual rigor as well.

Al-Jazeera presents an array of views: secularists debate fundamentalists, Israelis debate Palestinians, Iraqis debate Kuwaitis. There is no bias. When Al-Jazeera hosted former Israeli Prime Minister Ehud Barak on one of its talk shows in 1998, and when it interviewed the Israeli Foreign Minister Shimon Peres more recently, Israeli officials praised the network for its credibility and professionalism.

In an interview with the *Jerusalem Post* on September 2, 2001, Gideon Ezra, former deputy head of the General Security Service (GSS) there and who has become a regular guest on Al-Jazeera's talk show lineup, claimed, "I wish all Arab media were like Al-Jazeera." Ezra acknowledged further: "There I was in Jerusalem, with Marwan Barghouti [West Bank Fatah chief] in Ramallah, and the moderator was sitting in Al-Jazeera's London studio, and they were hearing me out, even though little of what I said could have been agreeable to them." Ezra adds, "All of a sudden, an Israeli called in claiming to be a former GSS man who quit because he could no longer stand coercing Palestinians into becoming collaborators. Now that's what I call a free discussion."

Another aspect of Al-Jazeera—one that is considered unique among Arab networks—is that it broadcasts major events live from the scene. When the hijacked airliners crashed into the World Trade Center in New York on September 11, 2001, Al-Jazeera reporters were there, and they transmitted to Arab viewers live scenes of the twin towers crashing to the ground.

Moreover, when the United States and Britain commenced the bombing campaign against the Taliban and Al-Qaeda forces in Afghanistan on October 7, 2001, Al-Jazeera's correspondents were very close by. In fact, they were the nearest among all the broadcast stations in Afghanistan. Before the anti-Taliban forces' takeover of Kabul, in fact, Al-Jazeera was the only network to have a twenty-four-hour satellite link to the Afghan capital. (Other stations started to report from Kabul around mid-

November 2001, after the fall of the Taliban regime.) Al-
Jazeera's Afghan outpost was little more than a small, ramshackle
building where guests had to be filmed outside or, more likely,
on the roof. The rudimentary set occasionally produced its own
breaking news, as on the first night of U.S. strikes when
Mohammed Halimi, a member of the Taliban foreign ministry
staff, was being interviewed live on the roof. "While Halimi was
speaking, we heard a big noise, like a bomb," says Mohammed
Kicham, the Qatar-based anchorman of Al-Jazeera. "Suddenly
we had no picture and no sound at all. After about five minutes,
the sound came back and Tayseer Allouni [Al-Jazeera's Kabul re-
porter] reported that a bomb had fallen nearby. 'I'm sorry,' he
told the studio in Doha, 'but the cameraman has disappeared
and I've no idea where he is.'" The cameraman, it turned out,
had fallen off the roof. "Fortunately, it's not a high building,"
Kicham adds. "So he climbed back and finished the interview."

   In Cairo, the largest city in the Arab world and a longtime focal point of Islamic and Arab activism, the usual hustle and bus-
tle of the crowded streets did not exist on that first day of U.S.
strikes on Afghanistan. Most Egyptians gathered around TV sets
in their homes and coffee shops, watching the news. They were
not watching CNN; they were watching Al-Jazeera. "America,
Afghanistan, boom! boom!" one Egyptian viewer said to a reporter. When he learned that the reporter was American, he
shrugged and smiled, then went back to watching the set.

IS AL-JAZEERA BIASED?
Many Westerners have accused Al-Jazeera of being biased toward the Palestinian cause. Al-Jazeera has a practice of describing Palestinian suicide-bombers who strike in Israel as "martyrs," which many consider a violation of objective news
reporting. Walid Al-Omary, Al-Jazeera's correspondent in the
West Bank town of Ramallah, described the complexity of his

position: "To be objective in this area is not easy because we live here. We are part of the people here. And this situation belongs to us also, and we have our opinions."

Perhaps this is one reason why Arab viewers relate more to Al-Jazeera than to Western networks. Many Arab viewers who watch CNN believe that American television is biased against Arabs. They have argued, for example, that the word "assassination" is seldom used in the U.S. media when describing the Israeli policy of assassinating anti-Israeli political activists who belong to various Palestinian factions. Such events are instead referred to as "targeted killings." This often feeds into a belief in much of the Arab world that the Western media skew coverage in ways that Israel would prefer, preventing Palestinians and Arabs from airing their positions as often as the Israelis.

Today, Al-Jazeera presents Arab views using a manner and language to which Arab audiences can relate. It is intrinsic within many Arab cultures to consider Palestinians who are killed by Israeli soldiers in the Palestinian territories as shuhada ("martyrs") because, to Arabs, they sacrificed their lives to defend their right to live in Palestinian territories. This runs contrary to much of the tone that is broadcast by Western TV media, yet it reflects more accurately the nature of the Arab view of Middle East events. However, following the September 11 attacks on New York and Washington, there is some debate among the Arab press, media, and public as to whether attacks on Israeli civilians constitute martyrdom. A war of words has been waged on Al-Jazeera between clerics in the region that have varying interpretations of resistance to what they see as Israeli occupation.

Al-Jazeera's managing director, Al-Ali, explained,

We came with our own ideas and our own perspective. . . . Al-Jazeera, from the idea up to the launch, was built by a staff coming from Arab countries. Maybe they had experi-

*ence working with Western media—they are ex-BBC, ex-
U.S. media—but all are Arabs. So they take the professional experience from the BBC, but their background as
Arabs means we can adapt this experience and apply it to
the Arab world. We know the mentality of the Arabs—but
we also want the expatriate Arab audience, who are used to
Western media.*

To a certain degree, what Al-Ali expressed is true. There is a fine
line between a real reporting bias and presenting the news from
an Arab point of view to Arab viewers throughout the world.
Arabs educated in the West, and Arab immigrants in North
America, go to CNN as the preferred source for any news about
their respective home countries.

Sharon Waxman, a staff writer for the *Washington Post*, said it
well in her article about Al-Jazeera on December 2, 2001. She
stated correctly that every news organization is a product of the
native culture in which it was conceived. "American-based news
networks, for example, make the unspoken assumption that the
state of Israel has the right to exist and that Osama bin Laden is
evil," she explained. "In the Arab world, that looks like bias."

One well-known Saudi journalist, Jamal Khashoggi, stated that
Al-Jazeera has a major problem with objectivity. "They are being
led by the masses," he asserted, "they don't lead the masses."
Should the media be led by the people? Is it the duty of the media to lead the masses? It would seem that the theory of contextual objectivity—the necessity of television and media to present
stories in a fashion that is both somewhat impartial yet sensitive
to local sensibilities—is at work.

Another pointed criticism is that Al-Jazeera blindly pursues
audiences and relies on sensationalism to gain those audiences.
The talk shows have been dismissed consistently by Arab officials as nothing more than Jerry Springer–style shock TV. Nabil

Osman, head of Egypt's State Information Services, told Waxman that Al-Jazeera is "no more than a tabloid." There is an old Arabic saying, *khalif to' raf,* which in English means "oppose and be known." It could be argued that in the spirit of this saying Al-Jazeera has established a name for itself by creating and then driving controversy. Perhaps Arab audiences are now ready for such controversy.

AL-JAZEERA AND POLITICAL MOBILIZATION

Many wonder if Al-Jazeera plays a real role in developing Arab audiences' political awareness and in mobilizing public opinion to take political action. Is Al-Jazeera ushering in a new era of political change and accountability?

Some observers have claimed that it would be overly optimistic to conclude that Al-Jazeera can affect the nature of political systems in the Arab world. These observers add that Arab viewers may well change their minds because of something they see on television but that this might not effectively translate into political action. According to these observers, the political decisionmaking systems in most Arab countries are preconfigured to maintain a progovernment, centrist majority that allows increasing debate and discussion but that keeps real decisionmaking in the hands of small elite groups who have managed public affairs and matters of state for decades.

The argument that Al-Jazeera cannot promote a move toward greater Arab democratization and political mobilization seems one-dimensional. It is true that Al-Jazeera's talk shows have neither initiated coups nor motivated the Arab people to revolt violently in the streets. However, Al-Jazeera has been credited with playing a major role in mobilizing support for the Palestinians and sustaining their current uprising, which started with the second Palestinian Intifada in September 2000. Millions of Arabs from the Persian Gulf to North Africa to the United States have been watching footage of Palestinians clashing with Israeli forces. Many of those Arab viewers watched the Intifada live—a first. Al-Jazeera aired graphic scenes of Palestinian casualties and Palestinian stone-throwers fighting Israeli tanks and heavy artillery in Palestinian territories. These scenes, many of which were not broadcast by U.S. media, have increased Arab sympathy for Palestinians and augmented Arab hatred for Israeli leaders and their policies.

In this sense, it can be argued that Al-Jazeera has united Arabs behind a single issue for the first time since the early 1970s, when Um Kalthoum, the legendary Egyptian diva to whom a magnificent shrine was recently built in Cairo, rallied the Arab world with her stirring monthly radio concerts. Fans from all corners of the Arab world would gather around their radios and TV sets on the first Thursday of every month to listen to her sing. Not since her death in the mid-1970s have Arab audiences been united in watching or listening to any single mass medium. Today, Al-Jazeera's programs and talk shows have the same effect. No matter what they are doing, or where they happen to be, during the time a certain Al-Jazeera program is aired, Arab viewers drop everything and rush to watch. On the day Um Kalthoum's $1.2 million museum was opened, a fifty-nine-year-old fan, Mohammed Abdel Ghani, was quoted in a December 28, 2001, BBC interview as saying that "she united us as Arabs, she united our souls." In more ways than one, it can be said that Al-Jazeera has done the same with its news coverage.

Al-Jazeera's coverage of the Palestinian uprising ignited pro-Palestinian demonstrations throughout the Middle East. But when the network broadcast opinions from Arabs calling on their leaders to do more for Palestinians, Arab governments reacted swiftly, accusing the network of inciting violence. Several Arab governments, including Egypt and Jordan, stated that Al-Jazeera's coverage of the uprising threatened the stability of their regimes and exposed them to criticism by their own people. In fact, Egypt and Jordan have been more critical of Al-Jazeera than has Israel. The Israeli government could have cause for concern if Al-Jazeera's coverage helps incite Palestinians to riot, yet it continues to allow Al-Jazeera correspondents to operate freely within its borders.

Al-Omary, the network's correspondent in the West Bank, says his portable phone rings around the clock with news tips, many of them from Palestinians in far-flung villages. "The credibility of Al-Jazeera is very high among the Palestinian people because they hear the facts that they didn't hear from any other media— including their own. They trust us," says Al-Omari.

Will this trust truly foster political action? It could happen. The evidence more than suggests that Al-Jazeera's coverage of the Palestinian uprising inspired the Arab populace to pressure their governments to assist war-torn Palestinians. It could have happened with the coverage of the U.S. bombing of Afghanistan. Al-Jazeera at first was the only news network in the world whose correspondents reported right from the heart of the action, from the Afghan cities of Kabul and Kandahar. Al-Jazeera was the first to cover the Afghani refugee camps, and the pictures it transmitted—showing Afghani refugees suffering in camps near the borders with Pakistan—elicited Arab anger against the U.S. military.

And even though the Western news media have devoted enormous amounts of airtime to cover the plight of the Afghanis, their suffering through decades of war, and the harsh strictures imposed by the Taliban regime, it is difficult to tell whether their coverage of the U.S. humanitarian aid campaign has had any impact in the Arab world. If the war for public opinion in the Gulf states is any indication, prospects are dim for a rush of converts to the U.S. point of view. On the contrary, experts say the United States has been unable to explain and highlight the goals of its humanitarian campaign to a widely hostile and suspicious audience focused on casualties rather than the humanitarian aspect. According to Michael Hudson, an expert in Arab issues at Georgetown University, the United States needs to run "a more believable" humanitarian campaign. "It has to do a lot more than dropping a few pallets from an airplane," said Hudson during a recent interview with the *Christian Science Monitor*.

Al-Jazeera first realized it had the ability to consolidate Arab audiences when it covered the DESERT FOX U.S. military operation against Iraq in 1998. As with the conflict in Afghanistan, Al-Jazeera was the only network on the ground in Iraq at the onset of the bombing. From that point forth, footage from the raids and extensive discussions of the sanctions on Iraq fed Arab fury. The UN-sanctioned economic embargo seemed, in a word, unjustified. Al-Jazeera strengthened its position as the news network of choice two years later when it provided on-the-ground coverage of the Intifada.

AL-JAZEERA AND CIVIL LIBERTIES

In the United States and Europe, where political and social policies are openly debated, the powerful media conglomerates and their programming can advance civil rights. In the United States, enormously popular TV programs and talk shows like *Politically Incorrect*, *The Tonight Show with Jay Leno*, and the *Late Night Show with David Letterman* regularly address ills and issues in American society, albeit under the guise of comedy, wit, and humor.

It is vastly different throughout the Middle East. There, a population of 300 million, the majority of them young and living in very strict societies, dreams of liberation, of basic freedoms. Half that population is illiterate, ruled by governments whose top priority is to stay in power, to keep control at any cost. Somehow, given the different Arab societies—some more open, others tightly closed—Al-Jazeera was launched, and it appears that a previously untapped audience was discovered as well.

Al-Jazeera has provided the new Arab audience with so-called interstate representation of civil rights and liberties. One of the civil liberties promoted by Al-Jazeera has been the empowerment of Arab women to exercise their right to seek and receive information and ideas. For example, one of Al-Jazeera's programs, *Akhbar Riyadiyya* (Sports News), has devoted several episodes to the role of Arab women in sports and highlighting the championships that have been won by various female sports figures. Moreover, Al-Jazeera programs have made it possible for Arab women from Morocco, Tunisia, Egypt, and Yemen to witness the developments and impact of women's movements in other parts of the world, including the Arab world.

Al-Jazeera has immense potential for Arab viewers, as a forum for the exchange of thoughts and ideas, as a means to gain a public platform for development and empowerment, and as a medium for education that overcomes barriers of distance and time. Al-Jazeera is an ideal venue for enhancing civil liberties among the Arab community scattered across the globe.

AL-JAZEERA AND THE CONSPIRACY THEORY

Our story of Kamal Helal, living in Halifax, Nova Scotia is emblematic of a generation of Arab citizens whose distrust of the state of Israel is so great that all ill that befalls the Arab world is related to an Israeli state-sponsored conspiracy to dissolve Arab unity and wreck havoc in the Middle East. Kamal's suspicion that the U.S. media are an instrument of Zionist propaganda is part of that distrust. Whether it is the introduction of HIV into Arab countries neighboring Israel, or the abundance of illicit drugs on Arab streets, Israel is always thought to be a mastermind of such ailments.

The same social problems exist tenfold on the streets of New York City; in fact they exist everywhere to some degree. But this Zionist conspiracy theory has become such an obsession that almost every tribulation is blamed on Israel. Some of the press in Egypt, for instance, has reported that HIV-positive tourists cross the border from Israel to Egypt and intentionally infect Egyptians with AIDS in an attempt to infiltrate and disrupt the state. Others have reported that drugs are intentionally distributed by Israeli drug lords to destroy Arab youth. As wild as these ideas sound, many Arabs find them believable and convincing.

Thus conspiracy theories prevail among Arab societies. Unlike in the West, where such theories today are the preserve of alienated fringe elements, they enjoy widespread mainstream popularity in the Middle East. They flourish on the street, in the palace, and everywhere between. In order to understand the Middle East, Western and other societies will need to recognize the distorting lens of conspiracy theories, make allowances for them, and perhaps even plan around them.

Within the context of this theory, many Arabs believe that all suffering in the Arab world has been a result of a grand plan hatched by Britain and France after World War II, with the United States as an ally and perpetuated by Israel—the pampered U.S. protégé—for more than five decades. Thus there is a general thinking among the average Middle Easterner that the West is conspiring against the Arab and Islamic world and that there is a Zionist plot planned by the United States and Israel to stop any kind of development in Arab and Islamic countries.

Conspiracy provides a key to understanding the political culture of the Middle East. It pervades life, from the most private family conversations to the highest and most public levels of politics. It helps explain much of what would otherwise seem illogical or implausible, including the region's record of political extremism and volatility, its culture of violence, and its poor record of modernization. The conspiracy mentality also extends beyond the region, skewing the way outsiders see the Middle East and fostering conspiracy thought in other parts of the world.

Since the beginning of the U.S. war on terrorism in Afghanistan, much talk among the U.S. media has focused on how the United States plans to win it, not on any Arab or Muslim angle. Yet the images of demonstrators around the Muslim world burning effigies of U.S. President George W. Bush and Israeli Prime Minister Ariel Sharon that filled newscasts told a different story. Many of the Muslims and Arabs demonstrating against the U.S. campaign believed there was little evidence to incriminate Osama bin Laden for the September 11 attacks and that this new U.S. action was an attack against Islam. Despite the U.S. government's release of the videotape of bin Laden on December 13, 2001—in which he discussed his plan for taking down the World Trade Center and which seemed to provide definitive self-incriminating evidence—some Arabs remain unconvinced of his culpability. In addition to the culture of conspiracy theories, it is difficult for many Arab moderates to accept that the perpetrators of such heinous crimes sprang from their religious, national, or ethnic ranks.

Thus for many who demonstrate against the U.S. military action in Afghanistan, virtually any other explanation seems more plausible than the one provided by the U.S. administration. The Zionist conspiracy theory is perhaps the most popular and pervasive.

Just a few minutes' chat with an average Middle Easterner makes it clear how public issues are filtered through the prism of conspiracy. The conspiracy thinking promotes distorted explanations for myriad events and crises that have occurred in recent history. It would appear to them that the Western powers built up Iraqi President Saddam Hussein, colluded with him to design OPERATION DESERT STORM, and even provided him with the weapons to stay in power after his "defeat"—all for the purpose of gaining control over oil resources in the Gulf. By extension, some believe that the late Iranian religious leader, Ayatollah

Ruhollah Khomeini, who appeared anti-Western, actually served the British and U.S. governments right up to his death.

Before the United States undertook the war on terrorism and the strikes on Afghanistan, a popular belief in the Arab world was that the September 11 attacks were not the work of Osama bin Laden and Islamic extremists. Instead, it was a plot by Israel and Mossad, the Israeli intelligence agency, to discredit Arab and Islamic countries. In the days following the attacks, the Arab press reported that 4,000 Jews employed in the World Trade Center had been tipped off not to go to work that day. Entire websites have been dedicated to explaining how the pieces of the conspiracy puzzle come together. One website that propagated such twisted explanations and was widely circulated on Arab list-servers ("Exposing the 11th September Lies," located at http://11september.20m.com/), provides a substantial collection of incoherent, disjointed, and unsubstantiated news pieces, some fabricated, in an attempt to connect the September 11 attacks to Israel and Mossad.

In fact, some allegations have gone so far as to accuse Israeli Prime Minister Ariel Sharon of being the mastermind of the attacks on New York and Washington. Given that Sharon is perceived as a war criminal in the Middle East, it is not far-fetched for the Arab public to believe such nonsense. With his heavy-handed approach toward Israeli security and frequent incursions into Palestinian-controlled territories, along with a past that Arabs see as horrific, Sharon has become the arch-nemesis. He has been the target of satirical TV programming (one called *Tales of Terror*, broadcast on Kuwaiti and Abu Dhabi TV networks during the Muslim holy month of Ramadan, depicted Sharon as a pale-faced, blood-drinking killer). Such programs, and the daily political cartoons that fill the Arab press, are consistent in representing Sharon as a terrorist. One joke that circulated among Arab online discussion boards reflected the Israeli conspiracy, suggesting that Sharon had prior knowledge of the September 11 attacks:

Sharon calls up George W. Bush.
Sharon: Oh, President Bush, I send my condolences. The Israeli people share your pain. This is a terrible, terrible tragedy that has happened, and we sympathize with your grief. Words cannot begin to describe the horror of this act.
Bush: Excuse me, but, what are you talking about?
Sharon: Oh, damn, I forgot about the seven-hour time-zone difference.

Such allegations of a vast Jewish conspiracy, silly and ridiculous as they are, continue to circulate in the Arab world, although they are less popular now following the broadcast of the incriminating bin Laden videotapes. Many forget that Jews and Israelis died in the twin towers, along with Muslims, Christians, and others of many different heritages.

For some time, some Arabs and Muslims were in denial that members of their faith, ethnicity, or nationality could have committed such heinous acts. This may be one reason why some were quick to blame Israel instead of acknowledging the perpetrators were possibly members of their own constituencies. With bin Laden's culpability now established by his own words, some have come to recognize how much the September 11 attacks—not to mention the unreasonable denials of Arab involvement—have hurt the global image of Arabs and Muslims.

Yet incredible as it may seem, when Al-Jazeera televised the videotape of bin Laden saying the World Trade Center and the Pentagon had been "hit by God in one of its softest spots . . . thank God for that," it changed only a few minds in the Arab world still clinging to the conspiracy theory. "No Arab has the necessary technology to make such a broadcast," an Egyptian lawyer says about the bin Laden tape. "Mubarak, King Abdullah, all of them know that Mossad did it, so that America could be goaded to destroy the Palestinians, and so that the world's eyes would be closed to the Palestinians' fate." Several of Al-Jazeera's talk-show hosts have been trying to counter such absurd assumptions by ridiculing the conspiracy theories spreading among Arab peoples since the September 11 attacks. For example, during the November 20, 2001, episode of the Al-Jazeera's talk show *The Opposite Direction*, one of the guests, an Arab intellectual, accused the United States of planning to close down the Al-Jazeera bureau in Qatar because, according to him, the U.S. administration is afraid of the network. The program's host, Faisal Al-Kasim, discredited his guest's claim and asked, "Why make these allegations against America, when you don't have concrete evidence?"

Al-Jazeera was accused of inciting violence in the Middle East by showing footage of Palestinian casualties in the ongoing Intifada. The same Arab audiences that accused Al-Jazeera of inciting violence also accused it of being pro-Israeli and of betraying the Arab cause by hosting senior Israeli officials on talk shows. Some people went so far as to accuse the network of collaborating with Mossad and the U.S. Central Intelligence Agency. "I am very suspicious of Al-Jazeera's intentions. It is not really a free channel. It is allying with Israel and the United States to portray the Arabs in a negative way," says an Arab American in Baltimore.

According to Judith Kipper, director of the Middle East program at the Center for Strategic and International Studies in Washington, "It is always the Arab answer to say that it [Al-Jazeera] is conspiring against the Arabs. It is easy to say, but it is a different story to really evaluate the effect of Al-Jazeera, which *is* a free channel operating in one of the most limited regions in terms of freedom of expression."

On the other side, U.S. officials have accused Al-Jazeera of collaborating with the Taliban leadership because it was initially the only network allowed in Kabul. Moreover, Al-Jazeera has been called the mouthpiece for Osama bin Laden, especially after the network aired bin Laden's tape on October 7, 2001. Ironically, this recalls the role CNN played in the 1991 Gulf War, when CNN correspondent Peter Arnett was, initially, the only Western correspondent in the Iraqi capital of Baghdad. Alone, Arnett had the opportunity to cover the damage that the Coalition bombing caused within the city. Given some of the more farcical aspects of his coverage (the infamous "Baby Milk Factory" episode among them), Arnett, who indeed was in a unique position, was criticized by U.S. officials, other media, and viewers alike.

AL-JAZEERA AND ITS FANS IN NORTH AMERICA

Al-Jazeera's rise to prominence following its scoops in Afghanistan and its broadcasts of the bin Laden tapes may help it expand far beyond the Arab-speaking world. The network's list of nearly 200,000 subscribers in the United States and Canada is growing by 2,500 weekly, according to managing director Jasim Al-Ali. The network already has an Arabic-language website (www.aljazeera.net) that reaches even more users than viewers. Most of the 300,000 daily hits on the Al-Jazeera website originate from North America, according to Al-Ali.

For many Arabs living in the United States, Al-Jazeera is their main source of news about home countries. "I watch it almost daily," says Fuad Ateyeh, a businessman living in San Francisco. "I watch Al-Jazeera and CNN—but I get more coverage from Al-Jazeera." Ateyeh is one of 150,000 U.S. subscribers who pay $22.99 per month to receive Al-Jazeera on Echostar's DISH Network, the Colorado-based distributor of Al-Jazeera programming in the United States.

Another Al-Jazeera viewer, Nadia Semia, says she watches Al-Jazeera programs and talk shows religiously. "I watch Al-Jazeera at my friends' house, and I like its programs because they reflect an honest and straightforward picture of what is going on in the Arab world. I plan to buy the dish, just to watch Al-Jazeera," says Semia, a Moroccan living in Baltimore. Yasser Ahmed, an Egyptian American also residing in Baltimore, says he watches Al-Jazeera on a regular basis. "Al-Jazeera is the only Arab channel that provides me with true news about the Middle East in general and my home country, Egypt, in particular; I wish all the other Arab channels were that brave," he says. And Ghassan Dib, a Palestinian American who lives in Montgomery, Alabama, says the twenty-five Arab families living there depend on Al-Jazeera for news about the Intifada. "I don't know what we would do without it," says Dib, a used-car salesman.

Several Arab coffee shops around the United States have installed satellite dishes so customers can watch Al-Jazeera. The owner of an Arab café in Southern California says that many patrons subscribe to Al-Jazeera at home but come to his café to sip tea or Turkish coffee, watch the news, and discuss the day's events with friends.

The main reason for Al-Jazeera's growing popularity among Arab viewers in North America undoubtedly relates to the cultural connection that the community has re-created on Western soil. The perception of serious uncensored coverage of Arab and world events, presented by Arab anchors and announcers and packaged in a familiar style, helps nurture this sense of Arab community. Part of the Arab tradition is to argue and discuss issues passionately. In the Middle East, where political debate is often limited to the private spheres of the home and places of prayer, Al-Jazeera has projected closed-door discussions via satellite worldwide, an act seen by many as one of courage and defiance. Showing an Iraqi dissident denouncing Saddam Hussein, or a Palestinian and Kuwaiti debating the effects of the Gulf War, are interpreted as extremely radical acts. Al-Jazeera has expanded the Arab tradition of debate and discourse. It has debunked many Middle East sacred cows and is unflinching in its evenhanded coverage of Arab world news. For expatriate Arab viewers, Al-Jazeera, with its in-depth analysis of Middle East issues and integration of Middle East histories, is superior to any U.S. news network.

The Arab-language companion website to Al-Jazeera was launched in 1998. Like many popular Internet sites that accompany new TV programs, aljazeera.net allows users to view live programming through streaming video at no charge. The largest number of visitors to aljazeera.net comes from Arabic speakers residing in the United States. The website has recently recorded up to 1.2 million daily hits since September 11, increasing to 3 million hits daily by the second week of strikes on Afghanistan, 40 percent of which came from Arab Americans. Furthermore, the website provides complete, uncondensed coverage, supplemented with complete transcripts of all talk shows that can be read and obtained at no charge. The huge numbers of satellite viewers and website users suggest that mainstream Middle Easterners have grown more accepting of progressive ideas and genuine debate.

Al-Jazeera correspondent Jamal Demiloj told reporter Ned Parker in a *Christian Science Monitor* article that "Al-Jazeera provides a space of freedom to the Arab viewer. Before, Arabs didn't have any idea of media freedom." One of the reasons Al Jazeera appeals to the Arab masses throughout North America boils down to economics. "We are beamed freely on air," says Ahmed Sheikh, a program editor. You just have to own a $300 satellite dish. The power is simple, according to Sheikh: "When you talk about things considered taboo in the past, it encourages people to be more open-minded and courageous about issues. When we talk about human rights violations, we are instructing them that they have basic human rights that they need to stand up for." According to Farouk Al-Kassem, a journalist at Al Jazeera, "The people are hungry and thirsty to express themselves."

In an interview conducted by Stephen Wu, published in the fall 1999 issue of *Harvard International Review*, Mohammed Jasim Al-Ali adds, "We have only one of two choices, to win the government or to win the audience."

PUBLIC DISCOURSE

In some of the most totalitarian states—Syria, Iraq, Sudan, and Libya—there is virtually no freedom of the press. In others, state censorship of the news is loosening. In Jordan and Egypt, an opposition press of sorts has emerged with official consent, but even they hew to the official line on the major issues and often make for very dull reading. Lebanon was the only state where Arabs experienced a free press until Syria imposed its control in the last year of the 1975–1990 civil war.

A decade ago, all typewriters in Iraq had to be registered with the authorities. Today, the authorities are easily outmaneuvered by an international phoneline or satellite antenna. Many Arabs still lack such luxuries. Politics has always been the exclusive province of the middle and higher class. Faisal Al-Kasim adds, "The media can be a catalyst in the process of democratization. The dirt in our society has been swept under the carpet for too long."

The press in the Arab world is getting bolder and affecting the political culture of the region, which brings to mind the role that journalists have played in democratizing other areas of the world. Al-Kasim and colleagues have set in motion an insistence on international standards of press freedom in their own countries. They are learning from recent history. Middle East states can learn from those journalists pushing for democracy and freedom of speech.

The formula that Al-Jazeera's editorial and managerial boards adopt is built on recognizing what Arabs find important. Saddam Hussein played the Palestine card in his attempt to win Arab public support in the early 1990s. Osama bin Laden attempted the same in the fall of 2001. The Palestinian Intifada—the single-most pervasive and persistent issue in the Arab world—has been Al-Jazeera's most frequently covered news topic. Whether Al-Jazeera frames the Intifada as a consequence of Israeli or Palestinian aggression is unimportant. Instead, Arab audiences remain passionate about the Intifada, and that passion drives Al-Jazeera's coverage: Supply meets demand.

Al-Jazeera's role in this context is built on its ability to air contending ideas and issues. When the Palestinian Intifada is openly discussed in the public sphere, as with any democratic issue, it is less likely that any radical position will prevail. The lunatic militants in the Middle East today are a product of decades of suppressed expression and forced silence. Moderate voices that employ rational thought and discourse can do more than displace psychotic beliefs and extreme actions. They can help create a vibrant civil society.

4

BIG VOICE, TINY COUNTRY:
AL-JAZEERA IN QATAR

———————————

This is Al-Jazeera television from Qatar. . .

—Words uttered by Al-Jazeera
announcers everyday and heard by
millions of Arab viewers worldwide.

To understand Al-Jazeera, one must understand its host country,
Qatar. Qatar's leader—a maverick by any definition—and his
small peninsular emirate in the Arabian Gulf sit atop huge natu-
ral-gas reserves. And ever since Qatar became host to the headquarters for Al-Jazeera, its political weight on the world stage
has increased. Al-Jazeera has made tiny Qatar a major player
among the world's news media.

THE QATARI TRADITION

Before the U.S. strikes on Afghanistan on October 7, 2001,
hardly any American had heard about Qatar, the self-pro-
claimed "pearl of the gulf." But U.S. charges of "inflammatory
rhetoric" in Al-Jazeera's coverage of the Afghan war turned the
spotlight on Qatar, which has projected itself as a champion of
the free press in a region where news blackouts predominate. Is
that really the case? Has Al-Jazeera fostered freedom of speech

in Qatar, as it seems to have in the rest of the Arab world? Have civil liberties in Qatar been enhanced thanks to the presence and actions of Al-Jazeera?

Qatar is a monarchy without democratically elected institutions or political parties. It is governed by the ruling Al-Thani family headed by its emir. Qatar burnished its international profile when, starting in 1997, it hosted a number of sizeable international gatherings, including the Middle East and North Africa economic summit, as well as leaders of the Organization of the Islamic Conference (OIC) in 2000 and the ministerial meeting of the World Trade Organization in 2001.

Yet Qatar is a place where 95 percent of women are veiled, where Bedouin tribesmen, chattering to one another on their portable phones, herd their sheep on foot, where falconry and camel races are the preferred royal sports. It came as a surprise, therefore, when on the morning of June 27, 1995, Sheikh Hamad bin Khalifa Al-Thani, the forty-five-year-old son and heir of the ruling emir, undertook a peaceful coup and seized the government from his father, who was vacationing in Switzerland. The takeover was supported by the leading branches of the Al-Thani family, together with other leading Qatari families. Several factors may have led up to the event, the most likely being the weakness of Sheikh Hamad's father, Sheikh Khalifa, who had delegated most of his ruling responsibilities to his sons following the 1991 Gulf War. Moreover, corruption prevailed in various governmental sectors, and the revenues from the country's oil and natural gas were not used to improve the country's infrastructure.

This transition of authority did not represent a change in Qatar's basic governing order. The emir still holds absolute power, the exercise of which is influenced by religious law, consultation with leading citizens, and rule by consensus of the nation's elite. The emir generally legislates public policy after meeting with his appointed advisory council (the Majlis Al-

Shoura). In 1999, the emir convened a legislative committee to draft a permanent constitution that would provide for parliamentary elections. The committee has met regularly and is projected to complete its recommendations by the end of 2002.

For its part the judiciary branch is nominally independent, but judges are appointed by the emir's government. Qatar has efficient police and security services, and interior ministry has a special state security investigative unit that performs internal security investigations and gathers intelligence. There have been allegations that members of the security forces have tortured civilians in detention.

Sheikh Hamad bin Khalifa is making good on his promise of greater democracy, a promise he made when he came to power. The patron of Al-Jazeera has called for greater political openness, with some small steps having been taken. In the past five years, Sheikh Hamad bin Khalifa has resisted pressures from Arab leaders to intervene in Al-Jazeera policy and nudge it back into the region's conformist traditions. Sheikh Hamad bin Khalifa's refusal to bow to such pressure typifies his single-minded determination, which has edged his tiny nation toward democracy, an open forum for debate at home, and a foreign policy that promotes independence abroad.

The Qatari process of political change, led by the emir, has enhanced the credibility of what was formerly one of the most conservative countries in Arabia, one of the least inclined to explore social and political reforms. In fact, Sheikh Hamad bin Khalifa's actions in the conservative, autocratically governed Qatar amount to a one-man revolution. In a speech at Georgetown University four years ago, the emir echoed John F. Kennedy's words that those who fail to make peaceful revolutions possible make violent revolutions inevitable. He said, "We have simply got to reform ourselves. We're living in a modern age. People log on to the Internet. They watch cable TV. You cannot isolate yourself in to-

day's world. And our reforms are progressing well. In a tribal
country like Qatar, however, it could take time for everyone to accept what we've done. But change, more change, is coming."

It might have been his own personal characteristics that convinced the emir to launch Qatar's most effective revolutionary
enterprise, Al-Jazeera, Qatar's loudest voice. The emir had already lifted press censorship in Qatar in 1995, when he also announced plans to increase citizens' participation in government.
Since his government launched Al-Jazeera in 1996, the station
has grown to become the hallmark for freedom of the media
across the Middle East. It appears that Al-Jazeera's growth is directly reflective of the emir's governmental plans.

However, it is not until a permanent constitution is drafted that
Qataris can make their democratic voice heard. Despite bin
Khalifa's reforms, political parties are illegal and parliamentary
elections have yet to be held. Yet bin Khalifa in July 1998 enacted a
crucial piece of legislation that allowed for a democratically elected
Central Municipal Council with representatives from the entire
country. And on March 8, 1999, he presided over the first elections
in Qatar's history—for twenty-nine seats on that same municipal
council; he has worked closely with its members ever since.

Bin Khalifa also gave Qatari women the right to vote and to
run for election to the municipal council. Seven women decided
to run, campaigned throughout the Qatari capital, Doha, and
debated on television and radio. None of the women won, but
the fact that they stood for election and ran political campaigns
is remarkable. One of the women, Moza Al-Malki, forty-three,
was educated in the United States and is Qatar's first practicing
psychotherapist. When recently asked by a reporter from *The
New Yorker* about the election experience, Moza said,

> *It was a dazzling development, and it was so sudden. None
> of us expected it. I sent a questionnaire to my constituents,*

and I asked them, "Have you ever heard of democracy?"
Fifty percent responded no. My mother's awareness of what
this was all about centered on the word "municipal." She
was furious when I decided to stand, and she asked me what
I would do—collect the garbage?

Moza went on to explain why all the female candidates had lost:

Simply because women didn't vote for any of us. Eighty per-
cent of our votes came from men. Was it tradition? Custom?
Jealousy? Or was it a combination of the three? We have a
long way to go. For a number of years, I was the only
woman in this country who went on TV. But during the
campaign I persuaded one of the other candidates to appear.
She went totally shrouded in her veil. No one could see her!
But what's important is that she went. (New Yorker,
November 20, 2000)

Since public pressure to reform is virtually nonexistent in Qatar,
there is plenty of speculation about the emir's motives for promoting political openness. One suggestion is that he sees the
gradual evolution toward democracy as conducive to long-term
economic growth. Another is that by boosting the legitimacy of
his government, Qatar might prevent the type of violent unrest
occurring in other Arab states, as in neighboring Bahrain. Some
critics have accused the emir of paying lip service to democracy
with only subtle reforms that accomplish little more than conservative applause from Western governments.

Freedom of the Press

In reality, by Western standards, freedom of speech and a free
press are severely restricted in Qatar. Public criticism of the ruling family or of Islam is forbidden. Even after formal censorship

was lifted, newspapers have been shut down twice for publishing articles that ran contrary to Qatar's interests. The Ministry of Endowments and Islamic Affairs censors cable television and imported print material.

The nature of censorship in Qatar is a walking contradiction. In 2000, some Qatari journalists were reportedly pressured by the government after publishing articles that criticized some officials. At least one Arabic-language newspaper has polled its readers to determine the most popular and least popular ministers, and a popular radio talk show regularly criticizes Qatari government ministries. Yet one Ministry of Education official who wrote a letter in 1999 critical of the emir's decision to allow women to vote and run for municipal council elections remains in custody.

Television and radio in Qatar are state-owned and controlled, but the privately owned Al-Jazeera operates freely. Recently, radio and television call-in programs and talk shows criticized the emir for meeting with the Israeli prime minister at the United Nations Millennium Summit in September 2000. And the Qatari government was criticized by several Qatari journalists for allowing the Israeli Trade Office to remain open prior to the Islamic Conference hosted by Qatar in November 2000. Apparently, in such circumstances the emir and his government are willing to accept such criticism.

The Qatari government is less understanding on other issues, however. Freedom of association is limited to private, social, sports, trade, professional, and cultural societies, all of which must register with the government. Participation in organizations that are critical of the government is prohibited. Political demonstrations are also prohibited.

Although the Qatari government reduced restrictions on freedom of speech and the press, many Qatari journalists continue to practice self-censorship due to real or perceived social and political pressures. For example, no explicit criticism of any citizen—whether in public or private life—has been noted in local newspapers. A Qatari journalist told Reuters in March 2000 that "as a reporter, you still assume that certain things are taboo. Seventy percent of the problem is actually the journalists' own inhibition," the journalist said on condition of anonymity. But occasionally stories break through. Recently, Al-Jazeera and local Qatari newspapers were allowed to publicize citizens' views on the ruling family's financial disbursements, unprecedented even in some of the more liberal Gulf countries.

Still, local journalists remain cautious. If powerful individuals take umbrage with critical news reports, there is no assurance that journalists can rely on their editors to defend them. One Qatari reporter said that the "independence enjoyed by the press is genuine . . . it is a function of how much you want to exercise it." Yet there are reports indicating that some ranking officials insist on reviewing articles affecting them before they go to print. Some officials are reluctant to provide interviews without assurances that the articles can be vetted before they are published. Such actions, albeit more subtle, impose prior restraint on reporters.

In addition, limitations on the availability of information are a challenge for Qatari journalists. Interior officials in the past often did not volunteer information regarding criminal investigations and the treatment of political detainees. For example, according to the 1999 Amnesty International Report on Qatar, up to a dozen political opponents of the Qatari government were detained during that year, and most of them stated in criminal court that their confessions had been obtained as a result of torture. Reported methods of torture included beating with truncheons, particularly on the genitals; hanging the detainees upside-down until they were compelled to urinate while so suspended; dragging detainees on the floor; and electric shocks.

Such allegations of torture were hidden from the Qatari media by officials.

The Censorship Office within the Ministry of Information was abolished (together with the entire ministry) in 1996, yet officials still censor broadcast media under the supervision of the Ministry of Religious Endowments. The restrictions on dissemination of information include items that may offend religious sensibilities, reveal military information or compromise national security, and damage Qatar's relations with friendly states.

Pornography and expressions deemed hostile to Islam are also subject to censorship. Customs officials screen imported print media, videocassettes, and other items for pornography but have stopped blocking the import of non-Muslim religious items. A newspaper editor was fired in 1998 on instructions from the government after he published a fashion picture showing a woman's breast, an act that violated the press law and was alleged to be religiously unacceptable. Strict regulation also applies to direct defamation of the head of state. In June 1998, the emir ordered the arrest of an official who wrote a letter criticizing several of the emir's decisions as anti-Islamic. Yet today Qatari newspapers publish material critical about, for example, the provision of services and the maltreatment of workers in Qatar, two items that would have been thrown into a waste bin by the censors four years ago, according to one Qatari editor.

A growing number of Qatari citizens and residents have access to the Internet, which is provided through the state-owned telecommunications monopoly. Internet service is censored for pornographic content through a proxy server, which blocks websites that contain certain keywords and phrases linking to censored sites. However, a user who believes that a site is censored mistakenly may submit the address to the Internet service provider to have the site reviewed for suitability. The government is responsive to such submissions. According to a research unit of the *Internet Arab World Magazine*, there are currently sixty-one Internet users for every 1,000 Qataris; subscription numbers grew by almost 64 percent in 2000.

Thus for a Gulf state, at least, Qatari citizens enjoy a comparatively broad freedom of speech, yet they tend to restrict themselves by the social and family restraints of their long-held traditions. There is no apparent fear that their government monitors private speech. There is also no legal provision for academic freedom. Most instructors at the University of Qatar, like their fellow citizens, exercise self-censorship.

Religious Practice

Qatar's state religion is Islam as interpreted by the puritanical Wahhabi branch of the Sunni tradition. The government officially prohibits public worship by non-Muslims, but it tolerates and protects private services conducted behind closed doors—as long as prior notification has been given to local authorities. The police provide traffic control for authorized Catholic services, which are sometimes attended by up to 1,000 or more persons. The government recently began to issue visas to the Christian clergy under foreign embassy sponsorships. There are no restrictions on non-Muslims who provide religious instruction to their children. However, non-Muslims may not proselytize, and conversion from Islam is theoretically a capital offense (although there is no recent record of an execution for such a violation).

Militant Islam has virtually no politically significant presence in Qatar, unlike many countries in the Gulf. However, there are several radical Islamists, known as "traditionalists," who oppose the new reforms that Sheikh Hamad bin Khalifa introduced. In a recent interview with *New Yorker* magazine, Yusif Al-Karadawi, an Egyptian expatriate in Doha who appears frequently on Al-Jazeera and one of the most respected religious clerics in the region, said that most of the traditionalists' opposition to the emir's reforms are misplaced:

> *There is nothing in the Quran which says that a woman can't stand for election, drive a car, or get a Ph.D. These people who want to stay frozen in time, who see everything as haraam—forbidden—are mixing up tradition and custom with Islam. The danger lies . . . in the growing presence of the United States military, not just in Qatar but across the Gulf. . . . Everywhere [the U.S.] military goes it has insisted on alcohol, night clubs, discos, and bars. And, in Islam, these things are all very definitely haraam. (New Yorker, November 20, 2000)*

No one, it seems, is immune from official surveillance. The traditional Islamists' activities are closely monitored by bin Khalifa's intelligence service and police. The ranks of the intelligence include many civil servants as well as members of the ruling family, among them the emir's own second son, Fahd.

The Qatari government does not permit the existence of local human rights organizations, and no such organization has asked to investigate conditions in the country. However, Amnesty International and foreign embassies were invited to send observers to sessions of the public trial of those accused in the 1996 coup attempt against bin Khalifa, who had taken control of the government less than a year earlier (a cousin and thirty-two conspirators attempted to wrest control from the new emir in February 1996). Agence France Presse reported on February 29, 2000, that bin Khalifa's father, the ousted emir, was alleged to have instigated the failed coup from abroad to regain his throne (father and son have since reconciled). Qatar could have fallen irreparably into the instability that prevails in many other Middle Eastern countries. Instead, bin Khalifa struck back quickly and decisively. He arrested the conspirators and sent them to court, regaining control and further solidifying his government.

Foreign observers attended parts of the trials during 2000. In February, a high criminal court sentenced the coup-plotters to life in prison. Although not a direct result of the trials, it has been reported that there are plans to establish two nongovernmental human rights groups. One will be an international committee dealing mainly with freedom of expression; the other will monitor the protection of other human rights.

This overview demonstrates that the emir has endeavored to introduce democratic reforms at all levels of society. Some conservative Qataris worry that bin Khalifa's reforms are happening too quickly, in part due to fears that a democratic Qatar may upset a delicate balance with Qatar's powerful neighbor, Saudi Arabia. Political figures in Saudi Arabia have misgivings about some of bin Khalifa's policies, which they see as destabilizing the entire area by moving too fast for nearby conservative regimes.

Although there has been a visible effort at the highest levels in Qatar and Saudi Arabia to mute such criticism, Saudis also have interpreted bin Khalifa's overtures toward Israel as an attempt to win support from the U.S. administration should any dispute with Saudi Arabia arise. Such overtures to Israel will not likely give Qatar more leverage in Washington because oil-rich Saudi Arabia is one of the most important U.S. allies in the Arab world and a big consumer of U.S. products. Political observers find it inconceivable that the United States would be willing to sacrifice its close ties with Saudi Arabia for a tiny emirate with little political clout. Accordingly, the emir has taken care not to stray too far from Saudi Arabia's conservative political path, which calls for keeping a distance in its relations with Israel. This was illustrated during preparations to host the 2000 OIC summit, when the Qatari government shut down the Israeli trade office in Doha in response to Saudi threats to boycott the summit.

Hamad bin Khalifa thus seems to value the importance of democratic reform in Qatar even as he treads the fine line between tradition and progress. According to a report published on the website of the Qatari newspaper *Al Watan* in February 2000, the emir said he believes that Qatar's future lies "in establishing the building blocks for a democratic state, especially a free, balanced and fair media." He said that the Qatari government respects freedom of the press, does not attempt to control the media, and has its own "methods of dealing with the issue of banning books or newspapers. We only ban on moral aspects and substandard methods in dealing with press issues." He added, "I know that my time will not be that long, but I want to feel happy in the knowledge that I have put Qatar on the right path, and that those who come after me will continue, and correct the mistakes I have made. My hope is to see Qatar as a democracy before I leave."

Hamad bin Khalifa, the first Arab leader to visit the United States after the September 11 attacks, announced during his visit that "within two years [Qatar] will have a parliamentary life with a democracy that dictates that freedom of the press should be granted and the press should enjoy credibility."

But what is Al-Jazeera's role in all this? Has Al-Jazeera enhanced civil liberties in Qatar? Do the domestic Qatari media enjoy the same level of freedom and editorial independence that Al-Jazeera enjoys? Have the domestic Qatari media experienced greater press freedoms since the formal lifting of press censorship in Qatar in 1996? Answers to these questions do not come easily. Yet Al-Jazeera does test the limits of what is acceptable in the Arab world; it also has some effect—whether tangible or not—on the government of Qatar.

AL-JAZEERA: TRADITION VERSUS PROGRESS

In pursuing pluralistic coverage, Al-Jazeera's staff has occasionally fallen short. Nowhere is this more obvious than in its own backyard. Although the station lacks inhibition in critiquing Arab regimes from Mauritania to Oman, it has only rarely gone after the government of Qatar with the same vigor. Many issues—the lack of a viable parliamentary structure, the legitimacy of the monarchy, progress toward democracy—are ripe for an Al-Jazeera special, yet the network doesn't pursue them with any zeal. Real questions, then, remain: How much influence does the Qatari government exert on Al-Jazeera? To what extent does this influence affect editorial decisionmaking? At what point will the station wean itself, as do all private media outlets, from the control of the state?

Media Schizophrenia

Al-Jazeera has been critical of most Arab regimes but barely covers domestic politics in Qatar. The big exception was the 1997 Middle East economic summit held in Doha; Israel was to be included. Several Arab countries, including Egypt, boycotted that conference because of Israel's participation. One of Al-Jazeera's talk shows, aired that same year, conducted an interview with a Kuwaiti professor who strongly objected to Qatar's invitation to Israel to participate, accusing the Qatari government of "playing into the hands of the Zionists."

However, Al-Jazeera has been known to show some deference to the Qatari government's concerns and agendas. Indeed, domestic issues such as the power struggle between Hamad bin Khalifa and his deposed father, as well as foreign policy issues, have not found an outlet on Al-Jazeera. Moreover, bin Khalifa's decision in late 2001 to postpone parliamentary elections in Qatar for two years without any justifiable reason seems to have passed unnoticed by Al-Jazeera.

In response, some Al-Jazeera officials have argued that their host is a small nation with little news and that in any event local news takes a backseat to world news and issues that concern the greater Middle East. In a December 2, 2001, phone interview, Faisal Al-Kasim, host of *The Opposite Direction*, expressed the same argument: "Nothing that happens in Qatar is worth covering." There is also the argument that Al-Jazeera, unlike many government-run broadcasts in the Middle East, is not a governmental entity but a transnational and pan-Arab network that focuses on news and politics from the Arab world and for the Arab world. Another explanation is that events in Qatar are not as important as those in larger, more influential Arab countries. Supposedly, events in Qatar have little impact on the region itself as well as the television audience.

None of these arguments holds much water. The fact is that events in Qatar *are* important, if for no other reason than that it is a member of the network's target audience—the Arab world. Moreover, Al-Jazeera covers events even on the tiny island of Bahrain, located just off the coast of Saudi Arabia. Among the smallest of all the countries in the region, even Bahrain gets its share of political coverage and critique on Al-Jazeera.* Are events in Bahrain of greater importance? Do Bahraini domestic politics affect the region more than Qatar's? The reality is that Al-Jazeera has hosted an opposition figure or dissenting voice

---

*Bahrain has had a long-standing territorial dispute with Qatar over the Hawar Islands. Bahrain has protested Qatar's decision to hold municipal elections in a long-disputed region of these islands, an act seen as an infringement on Bahraini sovereignty. This issue is still before the International Court of Justice in The Hague. This and several other territorial claims have strained the relationship between the two states, something that Bahrain attributes, in part, to Al-Jazeera's targeting of Bahrain in some of its programs. On one occasion, Al-Jazeera hosted a Bahraini opposition figure who launched a fierce on-air attack against his government, which enraged the ruling family.

from every Arab country *except* Qatar. And though Al-Jazeera will claim its interest is serving its Arab audience, it has mastered the art of setting a political agenda.

Unlike in neighboring Arab states, then, Qataris have no televised forum in which to discuss and debate local politics. "The foreign vision is far more powerful than the local vision in Qatar," explained a Qatari student attending university in the United States. "My information about what's going on outside Qatar is much stronger than all the information of what's happening inside."

However, Arab regimes aren't the only ones confused about the relationship between Al-Jazeera and Qatar. Even local Qataris find it difficult to grasp the true relationship. Qataris are told to take pride in their country's freedom of speech and expression. They are also proud to host Al-Jazeera, the Arab world's most-watched network newscast (the fact about which most Qataris are proudest). However, because so little Al-Jazeera content is dedicated to local politics, citizens are confused about whether it is actually a Qatari-based network.

"Does it really belong to us?" asked the Qatari student, who envies other countries for the coverage they receive on Al-Jazeera. He explains how, in his opinion, Al-Jazeera as an institution has far surpassed Qatar when it comes to freedom of speech and expression. To watch TV in Qatar is to live in parallel worlds. The conflicting policies between Al-Jazeera and domestic Qatari stations have left Qataris in a state of media schizophrenia. Thanks to Al-Jazeera they have a real taste of freedom of expression, but when it comes to local issues they see nothing but tiresome government public relations.

When asked about this discrepancy, Abdullah Al-Hajj, deputy managing director of Al-Jazeera, masterfully evades the question. He explains that such questions should be addressed to Qatari television instead: "Each media organization has its own political agenda and its own broadcasting approach that is decided by its board."

Sometimes it would seem as though Al-Jazeera simply emerged out of the blue and was planted into Qatari soil, whereas other times it appears to be an intrinsic element of Qatari society. Which is it? If it is indeed intertwined with the cultural fabric of Qatar, then why do local issues receive so little attention? According to Faisal Al-Kasim in his recent interview, "I am working in a free environment without any pressures, and nobody tells me not to cover something." Adding that there has been internal discussion at Al-Jazeera about Qatari policies, he claimed that he made the final decisions for his program. When asked about specific topics like Qatar's municipal elections, or the absence of a viable parliament, he answered that there is an intention to cover these, but that it will be done "at the right time."

There are some, however, who are less optimistic about Al-Jazeera's future relationship with the Qatari government. "They use [Al-Jazeera] as a PR tool for the outside world," said Mohammed Arafa, a communications expert and former chairman of Qatar University's communications department, during a phone interview on November 22, 2001. This, he added, would explain the neglected coverage of domestic Qatari politics. Put simply, Al-Jazeera has avoided airing Qatar's dirty laundry at all costs.

The hard truth, then, is that if Al-Jazeera is ever to become a major network and earn credibility, it will need to address the critical issues in Qatar on the air. Yet what little coverage of Qatar is aired tends to paint a spotless image. Thus for critics both inside and outside of Qatar, the real reason why Al-Jazeera has turned a blind eye toward Qatari policy is that doing so would sully the country's emerging reputation as a progressive state.

And there is no doubt that there are issues of relevance to report in Qatar; the Qatari student we interviewed rattled off sev-

eral. The first is despotism in government. The political structure in Qatar means there is a virtual absence of any boundary
between government branches. One government position can
unduly attain more influence than the job mandates. As in many
Arab countries, government officials use political stature to exercise influence over branches of government hardly related to
their duties.

The second issue is the lack of an elected parliament. There is
only the Majlis Al-Shoura, an advisory council that has limited
legislative power. "The advisory councils in the Gulf region are
not effective at all," stated Al-Jazeera host Faisal Al-Kasim. Most
such councils in the area are limited by mandate to little more
than discussing budget issues and making recommendations to
executive decisionmakers in government. The outcome of these
recommendations ultimately rests with the executive. Hamad
bin Khalifa has been pressured by the United States and other
Western governments to create a representative and freely
elected parliament that can exercise real authority. If this ever
does occur, it will not be for several years at least. Even then,
critics point out, the monarchical systems in the Gulf countries
will always impede real democratic representation.

Third, there is no press law that explicitly governs the
relationship between media and the government. The current
law (the Law of Print and Publication) dates to 1979 and has
been on hold for several years in the draft phase awaiting action
from the Majlis Al-Shoura. The old law, which was created by
the now-dissolved Ministry of Information, still stipulates three
fundamental restrictions: (1) The media cannot and should not
undermine or criticize the emir in any way; (2) the media are
prohibited from publishing anything that could undermine the
"established order" or endanger the current political regime;
and (3) the state has the right to impose censorship on the
media to ensure restrictions (1) and (2) above. Although these

two restrictions may not be completely applicable to the local
Qatari media today, many Qatari journalists claim that a new
law needs to be written and passed to protect free speech. The
existence of a decades-old law still manages to cast a pall on
many editorial boards in Qatar. Change is overdue, and it is
ironic that the press is being restricted in a country that prides
itself on hosting a free news network. Arafa, the former
chairman of the Department of Communications at Qatar
University, explained that the absence of a protective law
cripples press freedom: "Legally, the press has not a leg to stand
on in Qatar, which is very unusual for a country launching a
free twenty-four-hour news channel."

When Al-Jazeera is subject to criticism, complaints directed to
the Qatari government are dodged by officials who claim the
station is its own governor. However, the lines between government and Al-Jazeera are sometimes difficult to draw. Sheikh
Hamad bin Thamer Al-Thani, a senior member of the Qatari
ruling family and a distant relative to the emir, is chairman of the
Al-Jazeera board. Also, the abolished Ministry of Information
was replaced by another institution, the General Association for
Qatari Radio and Television. Although it is less visible than the
ministry, it oversees Qatari media and is headed by Hamad bin
Thamer—the same member of the ruling family who chairs Al-
Jazeera! Can this be construed as an obvious conflict of interest?
We think there is little doubt that it can be so construed.

We addressed such questions to Abdullah Al-Hajj, deputy
managing director of Al-Jazeera, in November 2001. He responded politely that "they need to be addressed to Sheikh
Hamad bin Thamer personally." Not surprisingly, bin Thamer
was not available for comment.

Al-Jazeera began with a $140 million loan underwritten by the
Qatari government, supplemented by a similar contribution that
would cover operations until November 2001 (when the loans

came due). Abdullah Al-Hajj insists that the network's financial independence is imminent. During the five-year loan period "the channel has been studying other means of financing." He added that large amounts of money are currently generated through advertising, licensing and distribution rights, renting technical equipment, subscriptions, joint productions, and buying and selling programs. However, there has been no formal statement yet that Al-Jazeera is officially free from government subsidy.

Civil Society in Qatar

Qatar appears to be moving toward a healthier civil society owing more to Al-Jazeera than the Qatari domestic media. Although Al-Jazeera does not cover domestic Qatari issues very well, it has succeeded in making the Qatari citizens aware of civil rights through its programming. Many of its programs address sensitive political and social issues without discernible governmental interference or other official pressures.

Ali Al-Hail, a consultant for Qatar television, mentioned in an article published in the spring 2000 online *Transnational Broadcasting Studies Journal* that Al-Jazeera "has influenced certain sectors of the [Qatari] society—through its revolutionary challenge to some taboo subjects—into founding aspects of civic activity, that in turn may lead to civil society in Qatar." According to Al-Hail, this was exemplified by the turnout of Qatari women at the 1999 municipal election and the decision by some leading Qatari women to run for office. This single event is an emblem of rising feminist consciousness. More will follow.

Thus throughout the Middle East there is rising criticism and a call for change. The absence of serious coverage of Qatari politics in Al-Jazeera broadcasts has prompted Arab governments to see the station and its host country as hypocrites. They argue that a country lacking an active civil society is in no position to criticize others. One prominent Egyptian journalist sent a clear message to Al-Jazeera and Qatar in one of his recent pieces: "Those in glass homes should not cast stones."

Local and regional Arab audiences are lobbing similar criticisms at Al-Jazeera. Most media that are criticized for neglecting any topic are swift to defend themselves yet will change their programming to avoid losing audience share. Al-Jazeera's staff needs only look outside their windows or pick up a local paper to understand the importance of covering local news. It seems absurd that Al-Jazeera's news editors put forth little about Qatar when they meet to pitch ideas about the day's broadcast. With all the effort that goes into retrieving information from foreign bureaus thousands of miles away, the activities next door are routinely ignored. Is Al-Jazeera turning a blind eye? Or is there an unspoken official barrier beyond which Al-Jazeera staff cannot trespass?

The station's ability to divorce itself from the government of Qatar—in terms of finances as well as editorial decisionmaking—will determine the network's long-term viability.

Northern Africa and the Middle East

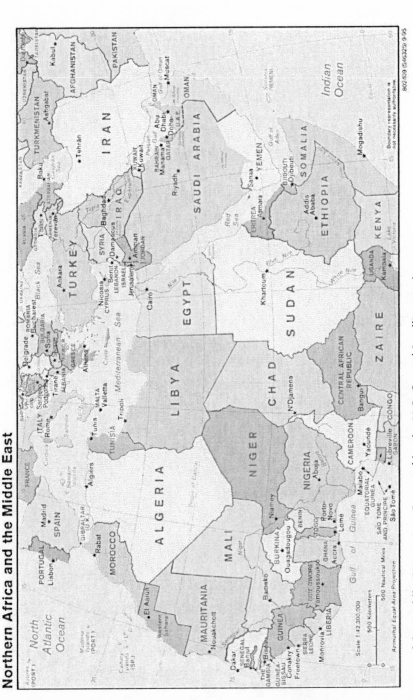

Map of the Middle East region. Prepared by the U.S. Central Intelligence Agency.

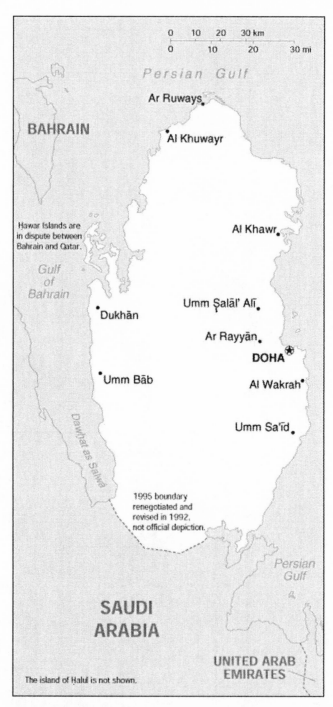

Map of Qatar. From *The World Factbook 2001*, U.S.
Central Intelligence Agency.

Big Voice, Tiny Country. Cartoon reproduced courtesy of Ahmed S. Toughan. Toughan is one of the most recognized political cartoonists in the Arab world.

Al-Jazeera's headquarters in Doha. Photograph courtesy of Al-Jazeera
Satellite Channel, Doha, Qatar.

Inside Al-Jazeera's studio, Doha. Photograph courtesy of Al-Jazeera
Satellite Channel, Doha, Qatar.

Osama bin Laden, and Ayman Al-Zawahri, one of his senior
Al-Qaeda aides, as they appeared on the videotape released by
Al-Jazeera on October 7, 2001. Photograph courtesy of Al-Jazeera
Satellite Channel, Doha, Qatar.

Osama bin Laden, as he appeared on the videotape released by Al-Jazeera,
October 7, 2001. Photograph courtesy of Al-Jazeera Satellite Channel,
Doha, Qatar.

Qatar's emir, Sheikh Hamad bin Khalifa Al-Thani. Photograph courtesy of Al-Jazeera Satellite Channel, Doha, Qatar.

Al-Jazeera's chairman, Sheikh Hamad bin Thamer Al-Thani. Photograph courtesy of Al-Jazeera Satellite Channel, Doha, Qatar.

Al-Jazeera's managing director, Mohammed Jasim Al-Ali. Photograph courtesy of Al-Jazeera Satellite Channel, Doha, Qatar.

The Opposite Direction. Talk show host Faisal Al-Kasim and guests. Photograph courtesy of Al-Jazeera Satellite Channel, Doha Qatar.

Kaduja bin Guna, one of Al-Jazeera's Doha-based news anchors.
Photograph courtesy of Al-Jazeera Satellite Channel, Doha, Qatar.

Al-Jazeera's deputy managing director, Abdullah Al-Hajj. Photograph
courtesy of Al-Jazeera Satellite Channel, Doha, Qatar.

5
BOXING RINGS:
AL-JAZEERA'S TALK SHOWS

"Has the American media slogan become: 'No voice is louder than the voice of war?'"

"Have the Western mass media become mouthpieces for Western governments?"

"Why have the Western news media lost their abilities to listen to any opposing opinions?"

"Why was the Al-Jazeera bureau in Afghanistan bombed?"

"Are the Western media really free?"

But on the other hand. . .

"Isn't the media war an essential part of the military war, which makes it any country's right to use any means to win the war?"

"Isn't it the Western media's right to fashion their coverage to adapt to the exceptional circumstances that the United States is going through?"

"Isn't the American public opinion supportive of its government's policies?"

"Isn't it unfair to accuse the American media of becoming a mouthpiece for the government or a public relations machinery?"

"Aren't the Western mass media still the best example of free speech?"

—Questions posed to guests of the talk show
Al Ittijah Al Mo'akis (The Opposite Direction) on
November 20, 2001, following the bombing of
Al-Jazeera's bureau in Afghanistan on November 13.

During each weekly episode of the program, Al-Jazeera's top talk-show host, Faisal Al-Kasim, spends the first two minutes of the flagship show, *Al Ittijah Al Mo'akis* (The Opposite Direction), posing questions that reflect opposite positions on a chosen topic. This talk show is just one of many through which Al-Jazeera opens the floor to unbridled and often noisy debates on some of the most sensitive issues in Arab society. Other Arab TV networks would never screen such discussions, which result in floods of telephone calls to the studios and reams of protests throughout the Arab press.

CROSSFIRE IN THE MIDDLE EAST

The Opposite Direction—the most controversial show on Al-Jazeera—is modeled on the format of CNN's *Crossfire*, but this show is more fierce and uproarious than any of its Western counterparts. In a live, two-hour weekly broadcast, two guests from diametrically opposed sides on a variety of issues come face-to-face in debate and take calls and respond to faxes from viewers. Emotions run high between the program's guests, especially after Al-Kasim sets the stage for hot debate and ignites discussion with provocative questions like those listed just above.

Al-Kasim's guests during this episode were Christopher Ross, former U.S. ambassador to Syria and U.S. State Department counterterrorism coordinator, and the current U.S. State Department special coordinator for public diplomacy, and Ibrahim Alloush, a mass-communications scholar and editor-in-chief of an Arab think-tank's website, titled *The Free Arab Voice on the Internet*.

From the early moments, it was clear that the discussion would be contentious to say the least. Al-Kasim's first question, directed to Ross, was: "Why was Al-Jazeera's bureau in Afghanistan bombed?" Before Ross had a chance to answer, Alloush interrupted abruptly, saying: "I think the question we should start with is: Was the bombing of Al-Jazeera's bureau in

Afghanistan a prelude for bombing Al-Jazeera's bureau in Qatar?" Alloush's question alluded to the dominant Arab thought that the United States has been against Al-Jazeera since the September 11 attacks. Although even Al-Jazeera officials noted that U.S. forces were aware of the bureau's location, few were prepared to make such unsubstantiated accusations. This is evidence that Alloush's interpretation is part of the conspiracy theories propagated by fringe thinkers and that his website is but one among the media that foster such a theory in the Arab world.

Throughout the discussion, Ross, who was being interviewed from Al-Jazeera's studio in Washington, D.C., met Alloush's aggressive tone with a smile on his face and poise in his answers. Ross elegantly rebutted Alloush's arguments with rapid-fire and eloquent responses. Ross's answers were not in English; they were in fluent Arabic. A November 6, 2001, article in *Time* described Ross's fluency in Arabic as a "secret weapon to the propaganda war" and "a tremendous asset in making the case to middle-class Muslims countering [Osama] bin Laden's adept exploitation of anti-American grievances in the Muslim world." The article mentioned that "it may take a spokesman with [Ross's] deep appreciation of the nuances of Arab politics—and language—to help reverse the tide of Arab sentiment against the U.S. five weeks into the Afghan bombing campaign."

Ross, who has played a leading role in formulating Middle East policy in various U.S. administrations over some thirty years of diplomatic service, responded calmly to Alloush's allegations. Ross argued that "the United States is not targeting Al-Jazeera's bureaus in Kabul [the Afghani capital], Qatar, or America. And my participation in this program tonight is evidence that there is a kind of media cooperation between the [United States] and Al-Jazeera. As for [Al-Jazeera's] Kabul bureau, the U.S. troops in Afghanistan are after the military sites only, not the civil or the media sites, and despite our efforts in that regard, there is bound to be some faults in using the weapons. Up to this point, we don't know how the Al-Jazeera bureau was bombed, but we know that it wasn't among our targets."

During this early segment in the program, Al-Kasim, in an attempt to question Alloush's perceptions of U.S. policies, challenged him: "Why these allegations against America and against the American troops in Afghanistan?"

Alloush told Al-Kasim that there are several media sources that prove that Al-Jazeera was targeted. Alloush asked Ross to refer to the October 14, 2001, issue of the *New York Daily News*, which he claimed contained an article that encouraged U.S. troops to close down the Al-Jazeera bureau as a response to the network's coverage of the damages to civilian sites in Afghanistan. Alloush also encouraged Ross to check the November 18, 2001, issue of the *New York Times*, which he said included an article written by noted Johns Hopkins University Middle Eastern scholar Fouad Ajami that described Al-Jazeera as "anti-American." According to Alloush, "Al-Jazeera is targeted by the American media, which are monopolized by four or five conglomerates, such as Sony, Time Warner, Viacom, and Walt Disney. Al-Jazeera has broken such media monopoly through its competition in the news market, and the bombing of the Al-Jazeera bureau had a competitive market-driven dimension."

Al-Kasim, who appeared to be unconvinced by Alloush's arguments, responded, "Doctor Alloush, you cited an American newspaper that incites feelings against Al-Jazeera, but can that serve as a sufficient evidence to show that the U.S. administration bombed Al-Jazeera intentionally? Do you have other evidence? Is it just talk? Are you just guessing?"

Alloush seemed at a loss to provide a direct answer. Instead, he claimed that the *New York Daily News* is the sixth largest newspa-

per in the United States and is part of an American media con-
glomerate. He added that CNN lost its preeminence as the
dominant world news medium because of the role Al-Jazeera
played in Kabul. "It was necessary to stop Al-Jazeera's role for
the benefit of the American news media," Alloush argued.

At this point, Ross interjected (in his flawless Arabic, laced
with a Lebanese accent), "First, the New York Daily News does
not by any means represent the opinion of the United States administration. We have hundreds of newspapers, and we have
press freedom guaranteed by the U.S. Constitution. I don't deny
that the American news media are market-driven institutions
that follow the money, and there is nothing wrong with that.
However, our media policies are set by the news editors based on
their readings of the public's concerns, and we don't have a government institution that supervises the media as is the case in
many other countries."

Ross continued his argument in an attempt to explain the U.S.
stand on Al-Jazeera. "You at Al-Jazeera know that since Al-
Jazeera's inception, the U.S. administration has been a great ad-
mirer of the channel. It is true, however, that during a specific
time, some American officials expressed their concerns that Al-
Jazeera was broadcasting announcements made by Al-Qaeda organization officials on a regular basis. The U.S. government considered that to be a message inciting violence." Ross added that
Al-Jazeera's small total revenue from advertising doesn't merit
much worry from huge international media conglomerates.

In the course of the debate, Alloush made the comment that
big media conglomerates with major U.S. holdings are controlled by "some Jews who have Zionist trends." Alloush insisted
that the three largest American newspapers—the New York
Times, Washington Post, and Wall Street Journal—and the three
national U.S. networks—ABC, CBS, and NBC—are owned by
Jews. "Is that a coincidence?" Alloush pressed.

Although U.S. administrations have demonstrated time and again undivided support for the state of Israel based on strategic interests, Alloush's remark remains part of a pervasive, though tragically misinformed, conspiracy theory in the Arab world. This misguided theory purports that there is a Jewish and Zionist plot planned by the United States and Israel to weaken Arab states. In fact, the Al-Jazeera channel itself has been accused by many Arabs of being a Zionist forum because of its interviews with several Israeli leaders, former Israeli Prime Minister Ehud Barak among them. Other Arabs have gone so far as to accuse Al-Jazeera of being financed by the CIA.

Ross responded to Alloush, saying that the American news organizations he cited are publicly traded companies, whose shares are available on the world's stock markets, and that anyone can buy them, including Arab investors.

At that point, Al-Kasim read a fax sent from Paris by an Arab viewer saying that he did not believe there was any correlation between the bombing of the Al-Jazeera bureau in Kabul and the network's role in covering the war. "If this were the case, we would have seen the rubbles of that bureau a long time ago," the viewer faxed.

The episode continued with Al-Kasim asking Alloush for concrete evidence for his allegations and Ross emphasizing his point that U.S. news media provide a forum for all voices and that there was no hidden intention behind the bombing of the Al-Jazeera bureau. At one point toward the end of the show, Al-Kasim reminded Alloush of Thomas Jefferson's saying: "If I were to choose between a government without a press or a press without a government, I would have chosen the latter."

This episode of the talk show was a hit with audiences all over the Arab world. It hosted a renowned U.S. diplomat and gave him the opportunity, in the local language, to respond to an Arab scholar who has deep-seated anti-American positions, strengthened at the time by the U.S. strikes on Afghanistan. And though having Ross address Arab concerns in Arabic was a breakthrough, Al-Jazeera's pan-Arab audiences need exposure to more views from U.S. officials who, like Ross, understand the Arabic language and can address viewers effectively and persuasively. Translations are never as powerful as hearing person-to-person discourse in the native tongue.

Al-Kasim, the outspoken and often domineering host of *The Opposite Direction*, is a Syrian of Arab and Islamic origins. His controversial program has made him a media superstar, a household name in the Arab world. He is a skilled moderator who knows how to elicit responses from guests, instigating them with provocative questions. He runs the show professionally and objectively and makes sure that all possible opinions are presented—often exhaustively. This is no doubt tedious, especially in the Arab world, where people are not accustomed to routine public disagreement and discourse. But Al-Kasim's poise and experience always lead to coherent and persuasive responses from guests. Al-Kasim may have attained early expertise from his study of Drama and Theater at Hull University in England, followed by his ten-year experience as an anchor at BBC's Arabic radio network.

Al-Kasim explained in a recent article that "Al-Jazeera's editorial policy is so lax that I am hardly ever given orders regarding program content. My program is the most controversial show on the network, but no one interferes. I choose the subjects, and I choose the guests. No one has ever influenced my decisions. The network has an even wider scope of freedom than the BBC Arabic radio. I tackle issues that I never even dreamed of covering during my service at the BBC."

Al-Kasim said he started *The Opposite Direction* because he felt it was time that the opposing point of view, virtually silent in the Arab world for more than a half-century, be heard. "I am quite convinced that what hinders progress in the Arab world is the absence of a free press," said Al-Kasim in the same article. "The dirt in our society has been swept under the carpet for too long. But I am certain that this won't be the case for much longer. Arabs are beginning to engage in lively debate over their political and social predicament. And Al-Jazeera offers a ray of hope."

Al-Kasim always makes sure that his guests get equal time on his program, and unlike many other Arab anchormen who sometimes appear unable to stop guests from deviating from the topic or monopolizing the discussion, he manages and controls the discussion like the seasoned veteran that he is. Before he steps in, though, he often allows discussions to get especially volatile.

But sometimes even Al-Kasim loses control of the show. For example, one of his shows discussed polygamy, a topic that arouses strong reaction throughout the Middle East because it is accepted under Islamic law yet roundly criticized by the public. The show, which aired in early 1999, hosted two prominent Arab women who debated the practice of polygamy among Muslim men. One of the guests, Egyptian writer Safinaz Kazem, a Marxist-turned-Islamist, stormed off the set in the middle of the show; then her counterpart, former Jordanian member of parliament Tojan Faisal, rejected polygamy as an antiquated practice. From Kazem's point of view, Faisal's view contradicted the Quran, and for that reason it could have cost Faisal her life. This show was the talk of the Arab world for months, and it infuriated the Islamic religious establishment. It was also the first time on Arab TV that anyone had ever walked off the set in the middle of an on-air broadcast.

BLASPHEMY ON THE AIRWAVES

The Opposite Direction is not a program where guests simply indulge in rhetoric for its own sake. It is a forum for serious, brave discussion on off-limits issues, issues that have otherwise been unavailable to Arab viewers. Contrary to accusations of being a network that promotes radical Islamic views, in many instances the discussions on *The Opposite Direction* amount to outright blasphemy, even to moderate Muslims. One episode aired in 1997 hosted the Egyptian scholar Nasser Hamid Abu Zeid, who was convicted of apostasy (renunciation of a religious faith—a capital offense in Islam) and ordered to divorce his Muslim wife for having questioned the timelessness and divinity of the Quran's teachings. Abu Zeid, who had to flee Egypt to the Netherlands, is regarded by many as the Arab world's equivalent of Salman Rushdie, author of *The Satanic Verses*. For the first time, ordinary Arabs had the chance to see Abu Zeid—so vilified and so controversial that no other Arab TV producer would touch him—and then draw their own conclusions. Al-Kasim was fiercely attacked for that show.

In another episode that aired in late 1998, *The Opposite Direction* featured Jordan's then–deputy prime minister, who debated one of Jordan's prominent Islamist opposition leaders, himself imprisoned many times for rhetoric that bordered on incitement to violence. The opposition leader angrily attacked the Jordanian government throughout the show, and the minister responded in kind. After the Al-Jazeera broadcast, the opposition leader challenged the Jordanian government to rebroadcast the debate so all Jordanians could see it. The government did, but rather than build support for the opposition leader, the result was pure entertainment. To the audiences who tuned in to watch the show using satellite dishes, and later with roof antennas, and later still on videotapes that passed from hand to hand,

Arabic audiences watched, and rewatched, as if viewing a Hollywood blockbuster.

Despite the many rounds of public criticism, Arab and Islamic leaders sometimes give exclusive interviews to Al-Kasim on *The Opposite Direction*. Muammar Qaddafi, Libya's leader, was interviewed by Al-Kasim on October 24, 2001, the first live interview of an Arab leader since the September 11 attacks. Qaddafi, once declared by the United States to be its sworn enemy, told Al-Kasim during the ninety-minute interview that the United States had a right to retaliate for the September 11 attacks, but he also would not brand Osama bin Laden as a terrorist until an international conference agreed on a definition of "terrorism." "We must sit down at any level without emotions . . . and after we define terrorism we agree on fighting terrorism. It is not logical that a country that is a member of the United Nations would shy from fighting terrorism," Qaddafi said. He called the September 11 attacks "horrifying, destructive" and added that they had caused enormous loss of life and economic damage that would affect all countries. Qaddafi reiterated that Washington had the right to seek revenge for the attacks without asking for anyone's permission, but he pointedly evaded answering direct questions on U.S. military strikes on Afghanistan.

Many Arab viewers were surprised to hear these remarks from Qaddafi, the erstwhile U.S. antagonist, who has often assailed the United States for its policies in the Middle East and elsewhere.

The Opposite Direction is not the only controversial talk show featured on Al-Jazeera. Another blockbuster is *Akthar Men Ra'y* (More Than One Opinion). This popular weekly show, which airs on Fridays, offers a platform for opinions and views on political, economic, social, scientific, and cultural issues. The program's host, Samy Haddad—as provocative as Al-Kasim—invites personalities and experts on Arab and international issues to conduct no-holds-barred discussions.

A recent episode of that program, which aired in November 2001, discussed the status of political Islam in Great Britain. The guests were Sir Terence Clerk, the former British ambassador to the Middle East, and Omar Bakry, the head of Al-Mohajeroon (The Immigrants), an activist Islamic group based in Britain. The episode focused on a British law that punishes British Muslims who left for Afghanistan to fight against U.S. and British troops.

Haddad, a finely dressed man in suit and tie, with silvery white hair and thin-framed glasses, claimed that among the British Muslim community there are many who believe that this British law discriminates against them because they are nonwhites. He said, "When the Irish fought in Ulster [Northern Ireland], they were British citizens, and they killed individuals from the British police. But Britain did not accuse them of treason. Why the double standards? Is it because those are Muslims and the others were Christians?" The host's question was blatantly incorrect, because Northern Irish have been killed, imprisoned, and tried for treason by the British government. Yet his underlying objective was to provoke the British guest to defend his case against the logic of his discussant in the show, albeit by twisting the truth.

Clerk, surprised by Haddad's strong but misguided question, said, "The circumstances are different. Those youths, who have chosen to go and participate in what they described as a religious war in Afghanistan, have cut their relationship with the country in which they were born and raised. Those people might be charged with murder if they kill British soldiers." Clerk's answers throughout the program were in English, and the Arabic subtitles were not an exact translation.

Bakry, a plump man with a long beard and a large white turban on his head, responded angrily to Clerk, nearly shouting, "We consider your democracy to be the civil face of dictatorship, and now you have revealed the true meaning of democracy from your point of view. Your democracy is telling us: Either stand with us and help us to bomb and destroy Afghanistan, or stand with the terrorists."

Bakry elaborated on his point, and he spent fifteen minutes trying to explain to Haddad, the host, the obstacles facing Muslims in Britain. However, at one point Haddad interrupted, "You have asked that Muslims be trained on carrying weapons, and your group has failed in finding any Arab or Islamic country to serve as its base. Britain was the only country that hosted you and your group. Now you are accusing Britain of fighting political Islam, while you are free to say whatever you want." Haddad is nothing if not an equal opportunity provocateur.

Bakry backed off: "We are suffering from discrimination in Britain." Toward the end of the program, Haddad pointed his pen toward Clerk and said, "You know that there is a feeling of frustration and social marginality among the Muslims in Britain. There is some sort of discrimination against them, and this affects their loyalty to your country." Clerk surprised Haddad and Bakry by saying, "There is some truth to what you [Haddad] have described. But other minorities in Great Britain have the same claims. We expect a draft for a new law that will put an end to this kind of discrimination."

Haddad, Al-Kasim, and the hosts of other Al-Jazeera talk shows have one professional characteristic in common: They are not biased to one side or the other. They try to provoke their guests, energize the discussions, and instigate debates—often to the breaking point—without taking one side or the other. In doing so, their main objective is to present all points of view for viewers and let *them* decide. Most other talk shows on Arab TV offer little more than top-down dictation.

FUNDAMENTALISM VERSUS SECULARISM

Despite these practices, some media scholars and professionals continue to accuse the Al-Jazeera network of promoting the views of Islamic fundamentalists and helping the movement win converts. Those critics also accuse the hosts of being radicals and Islamic fanatics, of being "anti-imperialists" who tailor programs to suit an Arab audience whose political bitterness they share and nourish. An extended and concentrated look at Al-Jazeera and its talk-show hosts indicates otherwise. To critics, it can be argued that spreading the ideas of Islamic fundamentalists is *not* Al-Jazeera's intent. In fact, it is very likely that Al-Jazeera's management is conscious of Islamic fundamentalism, and it has dedicated programs to the topic. Yet Al-Jazeera is open to nonsecular thinking as well, for many among its audience are conservative Islamists. Most of its journalists, however, are secular.

Several examples illustrate this argument. In one episode of *The Opposite Direction*, Yusif Al-Karadawi, a prominent Islamic religious figure in Qatar, was put in the position of defending his faith to Sadeeq Jalal Al-Azm, a prominent Arab secularist thinker and professor of philosophy at the University of Damascus. Al-Karadawi's defense was met by Al-Azm's scorn and derision; the latter ridiculed religious thought, mocked the prophets, claimed that Islam is a "backward" religion, and praised Kemal Ataturk (the founder of modern Turkey) for banishing Islam from his country. In the ensuing debate, host Al-Kasim never took sides; he kept his poise and never showed any emotions that would reflect his bias toward one guest or the other. Never before has such a well-known secularist like Al-

Azm had the chance to go toe-to-toe with a religious cleric on television. After this episode aired, cassette tapes of the broadcast sold for up to $40 on the black market in several Arab cities.

Commenting on this episode in the *Harvard International Journal of Press/Politics* article, Al-Kasim said, "Some would argue that it is high time that we 'de-iconize' many of the thoughts and sacred myths that have dominated the Arab world for decades. My show is providing a forum for people to present this argument, as well as for the opposite side to defend against it. And for the first time in many years, Arab citizens have the opportunity to judge for themselves. Nonetheless, religious preachers all over the Arab world have condemned my program, calling me a raving secularist."

It can be argued convincingly that Al-Jazeera's talk-show hosts try to follow suit with the channel's motto: "The opinion and the other opinion." It might be that this motto has discouraged several guests from even appearing on the network's talk shows, especially when they see long-held ideologies and sincere beliefs questioned and challenged by aggressive opponents and relentless interrogator-hosts. It might also be that the network motto has led some governments to prohibit citizens from appearing on Al-Jazeera talk shows. Al-Jazeera's managing director, Mohammed Jasim Al-Ali, said during a 2000 interview with the editor of the online journal *Transnational Broadcasting Studies* that on some occasions guests would change their minds at the very last minute and not appear on the air. "It happened that one of the guests was arrested by his country's authorities for doing nothing, only so he would not be able to show up for Al-Jazeera's program," explained Al-Ali. "Others were denied travel by their countries' authorities, or had their telephone lines disconnected." He also stated that in some countries Al-Jazeera's studio telephone lines were disconnected while on the air. "We do face such difficulties, but we stick to our stance and try to be balanced and fair as much as possible," he asserts.

In many cases, the formula of controversy and provocation has infuriated guests. Needless to say, making an appearance on one of these shows is not for the timid. Flailing arms, belligerent shouting, and frequent interruptions make for an adrenaline rush—in the studio *and* in living rooms. This is one of the reasons why many have accused these talk shows of being pure sensationalism.

Al-Kasim said in the May 17, 1999, issue of the Kuwaiti newspaper *Al-Watan* that he still remembered an especially humorous incident during an episode on democracy. According to Al-Kasim, the guest, who was hiding from Islamic fundamentalists, wanted to disguise himself using an artificial mustache. "Ten minutes into the program, the guest got too angry, and he started shouting to the point where he removed the mustache from his face and threw it on the ground. At this point, I couldn't hold myself from laughing," said Al-Kasim.

Al-Jazeera's motto seems to have encouraged its anchors and producers to select guests who represent the two extremes of an issue. This occurs often with the producers of *The Opposite Direction*, who routinely pick a guest from the far left and another from the far right; a knee-jerk liberal to debate an ultraconservative; or perhaps a U.S. flag-waver and an anti-American radical. Is there room for a middle ground? It's surely a positive that a program like *The Opposite Direction* presents dissenting views, but do the guests have to be absolute polar opposites?

Why not have a secularist, a cleric, and a moderate—all of whom would strongly state their cases but without the naked vehemence? The staff and hosts of Al-Jazeera believe that for a program like *The Opposite Direction* it is essential to invite two extremes to generate heated debates, to grow more provocative, to elicit ever-more extreme reactions from featured guests. Make no doubt, the real winners are Arab viewers, whose understanding of the issues is enhanced by exposure to two extremely conflicting points of view.

Yet Al-Jazeera doesn't confine its on-air fireworks to shows that host polar opposites. The weekly Wednesday show *Bila Hodoud* (Without Frontiers) often invites a guest to discuss one issue in current affairs—politicians, party leaders, intellectuals, experts, Islamic scholars. On the October 31, 2001 episode the topic was Malaysia's stand on the war in Afghanistan. The guest was Abdel Hadi Owang, the prime minister of Tringano Sultanate in Malaysia, an Islamic country. The host of *Without Frontiers*, Ahmed Mansour, may appear calm and pleasant on-screen, but the provocative, accusatory questions he often asks can make guests literally jump from their chairs.

During this episode, Owang was unruffled to start. He described the feelings and emotions of Malaysian people and offered that his country is opposed to the war in Afghanistan because, as he said, it killed innocent civilians. Mansour, in response, provoked Owang with the question, "Do you think the U.S. listens to no one? Do you think the U.S. takes the law into its own hands and acts like a rogue, outlaw state?"

At this point Owang opened up and started shouting, saying that the U.S. decision to launch a war in Afghanistan was illegal because the U.S. administration did not present any evidence or witnesses proving Afghanistan's involvement in terrorism. "There are hidden religious objectives behind the U.S. military campaign. There needs to be a discussion of the impact of Zionism on the Western public opinion. Israel should be included in the terrorists' circle because of its policies in the Palestinian territories," Owang insisted. Mansour seemed surprised by the outburst and suggested, "How could the U.S. have hidden religious objectives when it is a secular, nonreligious country?" Owang, as if he didn't expect Mansour's question, hesitated: "We have heard George W. Bush state that this war is a 'crusade' against the Islamic world."

Mansour explained that the term "crusade," as it was used by Bush, did not mean that it was a war against the Islamic world. He also added that Bush apologized for using that term, that the president explained how he hadn't meant to imply this was a war against Muslims but against Osama bin Laden and the Taliban regime that harbored the Al-Qaeda terrorist network. Mansour also highlighted the fact that Bush's decision to undertake military action in Afghanistan was supported by an overwhelming majority of the American public.

At the end of the episode, Mansour added that one of the "unintentional" though positive aspects of the current crisis in Afghanistan is the growing interest of the Western countries in Islam, as the West tries to learn about Islam's true tenets and teachings. "There is a very high demand for translated books on Islam in the Western countries," said Mansour. Owang agreed with his host.

There is no question that misunderstandings and misperceptions pervade the Arab world when it comes to the United States and the war on terrorism. Even some of those hostile to bin Laden have grown wary of the U.S. bombing campaigns; this may widen the gap between the United States and its Arab allies. For its part, Al-Jazeera offers a free worldwide forum to address Arab and the Muslim worries and, when it suits, tries to change some of these misperceptions. This is what Mansour did to Owang when he explained that the United States does not have a religious purpose in the war in Afghanistan. This is also what Al-Jazeera attempts when it hosts U.S. and other Western guests on its talk shows. We know of no Arab TV network other than Al-Jazeera that has accomplished this.

One of Al-Jazeera's popular programs is *Serri Lel Ghaya* (Top Secret), a documentary-style program that investigates in-depth issues too sensitive or veiled in secrecy. A recent episode hosted by the Egyptian Yosri Fouda, Al-Jazeera's London bureau chief, investigated the 1999 crash of Egypt Air flight 990. The plane, a Boeing 767, crashed off the coast of Nantucket Island, Massachusetts, en route to Cairo from New York on October 31, 1999, killing all 217 aboard. Fouda investigated the allegation that an Egyptian copilot on that flight could have committed suicide, a preliminary conclusion by the National Transportation Safety Board (NTSB), which passed the Egypt Air file to the Federal Bureau of Investigation, an indication that the crash would be treated as a criminal matter. The NTSB's preliminary conclusion angered Egyptian officials, who rejected the suicide theory as mere speculation without concrete evidence. In a 2001 article published in the online journal *Transnational Broadcasting Studies,* Fouda explained that "for three months after the horrible incident, Egypt's 20 or so TV channels did absolutely nothing while some Western sources used the world media to spread premature conclusions. Only when my program [*Top Secret*] managed to prove the technical impossibility of the suicide theory did Egyptian media tentatively applaud Al-Jazeera." The episode that undermined the suicide theory made front-page headlines in newspapers throughout the Arab world.

In the newest Al-Jazeera talk show, *Oula Horoub Al-Qarn* (The First War of the Century), aired weekly every Wednesday and hosted by Tunisian-born Mohammed Kreishan, the subject for the November 1, 2002, episode was the development of Arab and international positions toward the U.S. strikes on Afghanistan. Participating in the debate were the veteran French journalist and former ambassador Eric Rouleau (a fluent Arabic speaker); Mohammed Abdel Kader Jasim, editor-in-chief of *Al-Watan* newspaper in Kuwait and the Arabic edition of *Newsweek*; former U.S. diplomat Marc Ginsberg; and Azzam Al-Tamimi, head of the Institute of Islamic Political Thought in London.

The discussion challenged Kreishan's ability to moderate owing to the panelists' contrary points of view. Rouleau, who is as entertaining as he is convincing, made the point that although there are many Muslims living in France the majority of French people don't know much about Islam: "Unfortunately, bin Laden is trying to change a military and political confrontation to a religious confrontation, and some Muslims in France believe that this is a war against Islam." Responding to Rouleau, Al-Tamimi launched a robust attack against U.S. policies in the Arab world, saying he believed that the Western message gave the impression that this war is absolutely against Islam. "It was horrifying for the Muslims from the very beginning," he asserted. "[President] Bush's announcement that Afghanistan is just the first target that might be followed by Iraq and other Islamic countries was an indication that this is a war against Muslims. There is a huge ocean separating between the West and the Islamic world. The West wants to take revenge, while the Muslims consider this war to be unfair."

Jasim, in what appeared to be an attempt to mollify Al-Tamimi, responded that nobody has the right to speak on behalf of the whole Islamic world, which doesn't have one specific position. "I disagree with the accusations printed in some U.S. papers that state the Islamic teachings of the Quran are the reason behind terrorism. These kinds of accusations put a nonreligious war in a religious context," he said.

Jasim added that Arab governments have been supportive of the U.S. position in this war but that the situation is changing: "There was a mixture of fear and happiness among the Arab people; fear of the U.S. military response and happiness that the

U.S. was finally hit by someone. These mixed popular emotions have put the Arab regimes in a bad situation. They had to choose between backing America or standing with their own people." The "fear" Jasim referred to was caused by the Arabs' shock at the magnitude of the September 11 terrorist attacks, which claimed the lives of thousands of people in a single morning. This led many Arabs to believe that the United States would seek revenge by waging a wholesale war in Afghanistan and possibly other countries in the Middle East.

Ginsberg seemed to agree with Jasim's remark that Arab governments have been in a hard position since the September 11 attacks. "There is reasoning behind our policy of 'either with us or against us,'" he said. "I think that Washington is looking for a certain degree of cooperation, not hindrance of its policies or carelessness about the death of American civilians. The American public knows that there might be some questions about the American position with regard to the current crisis. And this makes it essential and important that we have continuous dialogue with our friends in the Arab region."

Al-Jazeera thus occupies a unique position in the Arab world. It weathers criticism from around the world but strives to maintain its independence as it unflinchingly presents all positions on topics of current importance. It could be argued that the United States might be able to strengthen its support throughout the Middle East by participating more freely with Al-Jazeera. The best example goes back to Osama bin Laden, that is, when he started his propaganda war against the West in general and the United States in particular. The U.S. point of view needs to be heard in the Arab world to balance perspectives on the war. The occasional appearance by U.S. officials on Al-Jazeera for fifteen-minute speeches is a start; it would be more effective if those officials agreed to be guests on Al-Jazeera's talk shows, to debate with opponents and to respond—live—to Arab concerns. Episodes of *The Opposite Direction* and other talk shows that featured U.S. and Western political and diplomatic experts have made good impressions on Arab viewers. When we talked with Al-Jazeera viewers in the United States and in the Arab world, they told us that such U.S. participation is exactly what they want to see. Boycotting the network, or pretending it isn't there, would demonstrate a lack of concern by U.S. officials for the Arab public at large. Hence, both the network and its talk shows present a rare and profitable opportunity to air official U.S. points of view to the Arab world. Will they seize that opportunity?

Interested U.S. officials would be wise to educate themselves about Al-Jazeera. Its talk shows are more akin to boxing rings, sometimes literally. The network is accused of being sensationalistic at the expense of genuine dialogue. Some claim that Al-Jazeera broadcasts little more than empty controversy devoid of substance, further stretching its credibility among Arab states. Stephen Wu, in a fall 1999 article for the *Harvard International*, stated that "such an occurrence [ignoring the network] would be a tragedy, given the minor revolution that Al-Jazeera has started." Today it comes as little surprise that several Arab stations emulate Al-Jazeera and broadcast programs similar to its talk shows.

One thing is certain: The popularity of Al-Jazeera and its talk shows is a testament that the Arab world is prepared to embrace meaningful discussion on contentious issues. And although the network's hosts can be criticized for their studio etiquette, they are steadfast in their position that this indeed is the best way neglected issues get discussed. They wear the accusations like badges of honor.

Al-Jazeera's studio hosts believe these debates are a microcosm of others throughout the Arab world today and reflect the existence of a true public sphere. What characteristic, one might

ask, is more emblematic of democracy than debate? Although
Al-Jazeera should not—and all signs point that it will not—shy
from controversy and provocation, it must be mindful of its responsibilities, of its unique role as the trailblazer for a liberal
media voice in the Arab world.

6

HERO OR HERETIC? AL-JAZEERA AND ARAB GOVERNMENTS

The night of January 27, 1999, was frigid in Algiers, the capital of Algeria. Temperatures often drop below freezing during winter in this mountainous country in North Africa, despite its location along the Mediterranean Sea. In a small apartment, all nine members of a large middle-class Algerian family huddled in their living room near a fireplace. They gathered around their TV set, waiting anxiously for the beginning of one of the controversial talk shows on Al-Jazeera. The topic that evening addressed the brutal civil war in Algeria, ongoing since 1992. Fought between Islamic fundamentalists and military authorities, the war has claimed more than 100,000 Algerians, many of whom had their throats cut in front of their families. The murdered victims include writers, journalists, and intellectuals. Massacres have destroyed entire villages, their inhabitants slaughtered wholesale. This Algerian family lost two members in the war.

The lawlessness that has characterized Algeria's civil war has kept serious investigative reporting at bay. Algerian journalists can barely function in this environment of violence, fear, and uncertainty. And given the propaganda that the Algerian authorities produce, it is difficult to get any information, much less truthful news reporting.

Many Algerian families were waiting for the Al-Jazeera talk show that evening. The much-hyped episode was advertised on the network a week in advance of its broadcast. The guests were two Algerians: one a dissident diplomat and exiled journalist, the other a leftist representative of the government. Ten minutes in the debate turned ferocious. The guests argued passionately, shouted, pointed fingers—all aired live. Suddenly there was a power outage, not just in the family's home, and not just in the neighborhood, but throughout the city of Algiers. That outage was not coincidental; it was intentional. The Algerian government decided to cut electrical power in several major cities, including the capital, to prevent the Algerian viewers from watching this one program.

Such a reaction was nothing new. In fact, Qatari diplomats have received some 450 official complaints from Arab states about Al-Jazeera since the network was established more than five years ago. Practically every Arab state has found something objectionable at one time or another—and that has helped to make Al-Jazeera the most popular satellite news network in the Middle East. Some Arab officials even claimed that programming has crossed acceptable boundaries by criticizing officials or bruising Arab sensitivities. Hardly a day goes by without an Arab state complaining that a program on Al-Jazeera resulted in slander, loss of national prestige, or hurt feelings.

According to Douglas Boyd, professor of international communications at the University of Kentucky and a Middle East media specialist, "Possibly the biggest impact [of Al-Jazeera] regards the realization that political leaders can no longer be protected by government-owned or inspired media." In many cases today, local and regional political agendas are no longer tailored by government leaders. Instead, it is Qatar-based Al-Jazeera—and the other services that now mimic its format—that influence those agendas. "Corruption, lack of political will, Islamic conservatives, lack of democratic institutions, etcetera, are now on the table," explains Boyd. He asserts that the primary indication of Al-Jazeera's impact can be judged in the past few years by the reaction of Kuwait, Saudi Arabia, the Palestinian Authority, Morocco, and Jordan, all of whom have closed Al-Jazeera's local offices. "Of course, that only makes people want to view more," Boyd adds.

Hafez Al-Mirazi, Al-Jazeera's Washington, D.C., bureau chief, in July 2001 criticized the actions of some Arab governments (specifically Qatar's Gulf neighbors, Bahrain and Saudi Arabia) who have gone so far as to deny visas to Al-Jazeera reporters. Other countries have closed down Al-Jazeera bureaus or recalled their ambassadors to Qatar to protest programming that was critical of their regimes.

SAUDI ARABIA AND THE POLITICS OF BROADCASTING

A spokesman for the Saudi embassy in Washington challenged Al-Mirazi's assertions, at least as they related to his country. "As far as Al-Jazeera not being allowed in Saudi Arabia, this is the first I've heard of it," said Nail Al-Jubeir, the embassy's deputy director of information, in July 2001. "Foreign reporters can come [to Saudi Arabia] and cover issues, but they cannot have established bureaus. It has nothing to do with Al-Jazeera. In fact, whenever we have an event here in Washington, we call Al-Jazeera." Al-Jubeir added that Al-Jazeera has its positives and negatives, but it has "set the standards" for news reporting from the Arab perspective.

However, the powerful Saudis, who conform to the strict Wahabi version of Islam, are said to be irate that such freethinking, freewheeling programming invades any home with a cheap satellite dish. Saudi officials, it seems, sense that their dominance of regional news media has weakened and is being eroded by the growing popularity and influence of Al-Jazeera. During the

1990s, several pan-Arab publications and broadcast outlets were founded or acquired by Saudi businessmen with links to the Saudi royal family. These media were noticeably devoid of content that was critical of the Saudi regime; Al-Jazeera broke Saudi Arabia's virtual lock on the international Arab media.

Saudi officials have publicly criticized the network, which has emboldened the Saudi press itself to launch fierce attacks on the network. Al-Jazeera's gutsy programming, which covers issues of Islam, the Prophet Mohammed, and the Quran, has elicited anger among Saudi writers and intellectuals. A prominent Saudi cleric wrote on March 14, 1998, in a daily Saudi newspaper (which happens to share the same Arabic name as Al-Jazeera), "How come Al-Jazeera officials allow the attacks on the Islamic religion and the Holy Quran to be aired live to Arab viewers? How dare Al-Jazeera programs host an atheist to talk about our sacred religion and make fun of it in the name of freedom? Can you imagine what the impact of all that would be on the Arab and Muslim children? Can you imagine its impact on the viewers who are not well-informed about the Islamic religion and culture?" The cleric praised a recent decision by the Arab States Broadcasting Union (ASBU) to reject Al-Jazeera's application for membership.

Such rancor is not limited to columnists. An editorial in the *Al-Jazeera* newspaper on January 7, 1999, commented: "Simply speaking, the poisonous ideas that are conveyed via the Western satellite channels are easy to handle because the [Arab] viewer knows the thought they are trying to convey in advance. However, when this poisonous thought is conveyed via an Arab satellite channel, it becomes all the more dangerous because it is concealing itself behind our culture."

Saudi authorities have adopted several subtle tactics to pressure Al-Jazeera. In the spring of 1999, the Saudi government reportedly asked Al-Jazeera's Saudi-owned advertising agency,

Tihama, not to place ads with the network and urged other local advertisers to follow suit. Moreover, Saudi officials allegedly intimidated the one Saudi member of Al-Jazeera's staff into leaving the network in 1999. In July 1999, Saudi authorities banned all satellite transmissions at public coffeehouses in Riyadh, the Saudi capital, apparently to keep Al-Jazeera from the public eye. This move followed a broadcast in which Abdullah Nefaisi, a Kuwaiti intellectual, criticized monarchical rule in the Gulf states and attacked the Saudi clergy for ignoring issues like royal corruption. "Political freedom in the [Arabian] Gulf?" Nefaisi scoffed. "It doesn't exist."

The Saudi interior minister, Prince Nayif bin Abdel Aziz, said in an interview with the Kuwaiti newspaper *Al-Rai Al-Aam* (The Public Opinion) on February 3, 2000, that Al-Jazeera's programming is excellent and accurate, but—as an offspring of the BBC—it serves up "poison on a golden platter." And a recent issue of the Saudi newspaper *Ukaz* attacked Al-Jazeera, accusing it of "fomenting hatred and arousing grudges in the Arab world." *Ukaz* also accused the network of "exercising racial discrimination and inflicting harm on the peoples and states of the Arab Gulf, particularly Saudi Arabia and Kuwait."

Thus far, Qatar has stood firm. "I think [Arab] people are not used . . . to hear things which they don't like, especially the top people, including me. However, democracy started. Either the leaders like it or they don't like it. Either you open the door or they break the door. It's a matter of time, in my opinion," said Sheikh Hamad bin Jasim Al-Thani, Qatar's foreign minister, during an interview with CBS's *60 Minutes* aired in May 2001. The foreign minister receives most of the complaints about Al-Jazeera, and he refers all of them to the network's managers.

However, there is a limit to how far Al-Jazeera will go in provoking Saudi Arabia, a much larger nation that historically has had domineering and subversive dealings with tiny Qatar. When

Amnesty International issued its 1999 report "Saudi Arabia: A Secret State of Suffering," Al-Jazeera was the only Arab network to cover it. However, Al-Jazeera did not follow up on the report—and its contents indicated that investigative reporting would have uncovered additional atrocities against human rights. Yet compared to all the other Arab news agencies, Al-Jazeera's limit in covering dangerous issues remains much higher.

Al-Anwar, a Lebanese newspaper, reported in its January 17, 2002, issue that Saudi Crown Prince Abdullah bin Abdul Aziz launched a scathing attack against Al-Jazeera in the presence of Qatar's emir, Sheikh Hamad bin Khalifa Al-Thani, at a summit of the six-nation Arabian Gulf Cooperation Council (GCC) held in Oman at the end of December 2001. Prince Abdullah accused Al-Jazeera of "discrediting the GCC countries, harming its members' royal families, threatening stability in the Arab world, and encouraging terrorism," *Al-Anwar* reported without giving sources. *Al-Anwar* also reported that other GCC leaders chimed in and pointed out that Al-Jazeera had run into trouble with several Arab governments. The emir of Qatar, meanwhile, kept an embarrassed silence, according to the Lebanese paper, which has good contacts in the oil-rich Gulf.

CLASH OF EMIRATES: QATAR AND KUWAIT

Kuwait has been openly critical of Al-Jazeera as well. The network is often attacked for what many in Kuwait see as a favorable bias toward Iraq. Moreover, Al-Jazeera's talk-show hosts regularly invite Iraqi official and nonofficial figures, something to which Kuwaiti officials object. Kuwait went so far as to accuse Al-Jazeera of supporting Iraq at Kuwait's expense. On a talk show that aired in April 1997, the editor-in-chief of one prominent Kuwaiti newspaper debated the editor of a London-based Palestinian publication about Iraqi suffering under UN economic sanctions. During the debate, both guests criticized the Kuwaiti regime for its endorsement of the sanctions, in effect since Iraq invaded Kuwait in August 1990. After the program aired, the Kuwaiti information minister flew to Qatar to submit an official complaint to his Qatari counterpart about Al-Jazeera. The Qatari emir explicitly told the Kuwaiti minister that Al-Jazeera is autonomous and that despite state funding for the network, he would not interfere.

Perhaps the emir inspired the Kuwaiti minister, because after this incident the Kuwaiti press changed its tone. In fact, Kuwaiti television adopted an Al-Jazeera-inspired style, increasing the number of talk shows and hosting members of the Iraqi opposition. Faisal Al-Kasim, host of Al-Jazeera's *The Opposite Direction*, in an article published in a recent issue of the French newspaper *Le Monde*, added that many state-owned Arab television have started to copy his program's style despite the criticism leveled by Arab regimes. "They even imitate the shape of my table, but they have a long way to go before they match the content," he said confidently.

However, relations between Al-Jazeera and Kuwait inexplicably changed again. In early June 1999, the Kuwaiti government closed the network's office in Kuwait. On June 19, Kuwait's then information minister, Youssef Al-Sumait, cited violations of professional ethics and issued a decree prohibiting Al-Jazeera reporters from covering stories in Kuwait. According to the Kuwaiti News Agency, "Media activity or any other activity by [Al-Jazeera] would not be allowed in the State of Kuwait and that the journalistic and media work permits of all those working at the Al-Jazeera office in Kuwait or those who cooperate with it had been revoked."

The ban came in response to a June 1999 broadcast of Al-Jazeera's live program *Al-Sharia wal Hayat* (Islamic Law and Life). During the broadcast, a viewer who identified himself as an Iraqi national living in Norway phoned in and railed against Sheikh Jaber Al-Ahmed Al-Sabah, the emir of Kuwait. In response to a guest who had asked that God save Sheikh Jaber, the caller reportedly said that God should not be asked to save a man "who embraces atheists and permits foreign armies to enter Kuwait."

Al-Sumait said Al-Jazeera was banned and its bureau in Kuwait was closed because it had the "audacity to attack" the emir and the state of Kuwait: "While understanding much of the embarrassments caused during live broadcasts, the repeated encroachment, more than once, makes Al-Jazeera directly responsible for this unacceptable insult against the symbol of Kuwait." In an interview with the Kuwaiti News Agency on June 20, 1999, Al-Sumait blamed the presenter "for not even trying to stop the caller or apologize for viewers."

Al-Jazeera had but a single correspondent in Kuwait and expressed regret over the Kuwaiti ban, adding that the insults could not have been prevented on the live program and that they were subsequently deleted from a rebroadcast of the show. Moreover, Al-Jazeera's board of directors suspended the show's host in a move widely seen as an appeasement of Kuwaiti anger. However, the network's managing director denied that the host's removal had anything to do with the Kuwaiti incident. Despite this official denial, some Al-Jazeera staff considered the incident to be the network's first concession to an Arab regime. One staffer said in an interview with a Qatari newspaper that some talk-show hosts cut telephone callers short before they say anything controversial because of the problem with Kuwait.

On July 29, 1999, Kuwait's new information minister, Saad bin Tiflah Al-Ajami, announced that the ban had been lifted, and he reopened the Al-Jazeera bureau. "Dealing with [Al-Jazeera] is important and necessary," Al-Ajami said in an interview with a

Kuwaiti reporter in August 1999. "For the sake of Qatar, we will welcome Al-Jazeera."

Kuwait's issues with Al-Jazeera did not end with this incident. On October 10, 2001, a Kuwaiti court ordered Al-Jazeera to pay a Kuwaiti lawyer U.S. $16,237 for accusing Kuwaitis of killing Palestinians and Iraqis at the end of the 1991 Gulf War. Salah Al-Hashem, the lawyer who represented twenty-two Kuwaiti plaintiffs, filed suit in September 2000, demanding provisional compensation for what he described as "devastating moral harm caused to all Kuwaitis." Al-Hashem said that during a political program on August 4, 2000, Al-Jazeera interviewer Samy Haddad claimed that Kuwaitis used acid to torture and kill a group of Palestinians, Iraqis, and fellow countrymen suspected of collaborating with the Iraqis. "We gave them the chance to prove it or apologize. They failed to do both. So we sued them," he said.

Atrocities and killings were reportedly committed in the first days after Kuwait's liberation from the Iraqi occupation in 1991, before Kuwaiti government forces entered the emirate and restored order. "Yes, there were some atrocities that we don't deny. But, no one, including Iraqis, had ever claimed that acid was used. This is a flagrant and totally baseless accusation," Al-Hashem said. He added he spoke to network officials who promised to take action: "Four weeks later we saw nothing and we decided to proceed with the case."

Al-Hashem has claimed that no TV network can afford to accuse a nation or its people of a crime without providing proof. "We consider this a Nazi-like accusation that not even the Iraqi government leveled." He added that any damages from Al-Jazeera would be donated to the National Committee for Kuwaiti Detainees in Iraqi jails and POWs. "This case is not about money, it's about the principle," Al-Hashem told Kuwait's *Al-Qabas* newspaper in late October 2001. Al-Jazeera has appealed the guilty verdict, and its officials refuse to comment on the case.

THE ANTI–AL-JAZEERA FAN CLUB

Qatar's neighbor Bahrain has joined the GCC countries in criticizing Al-Jazeera. In July 1999, Bahraini authorities expelled Hamid Al-Ansari, a former Al-Jazeera talk-show host, in response to a show he had hosted earlier in the year during which a caller criticized the emir of Kuwait on the air. Al-Ansari, a professor at Qatar University, had arrived in Bahrain to present a lecture and take part in a seminar. Although Al-Ansari was no longer working for Al-Jazeera at the time, the Bahrainis, who have a tendency to hold grudges against Al-Jazeera and Qatar, expelled him. Speaking to the Associated Press in late July 1999, a Bahraini official justified the expulsion by saying, "We are one Gulf family, where respect for each other is the rule. On this basis [Al-Ansari] was banned from giving the lecture."

The critical stance among Gulf countries toward press freedom was reflected in the meetings of the GCC information ministers during the 1999 GCC summit, held in Bahrain. The summit adopted a decision that seemed to criticize Al-Jazeera without specifically identifying it. The decision called on Gulf states to take a unified position toward individuals and media institutions that slander GCC states.

The GCC was not the only organization to issue a formal position toward Al-Jazeera's programming. Earlier, the Arab States Broadcasting Union, which monitors the performance of Arab networks, has been very critical of Al-Jazeera. When the ASBU rejected Al-Jazeera's December 1998 application for membership, it gave the network six months "to conform to the code of honor of the Arab media," which "promotes brotherhood between Arab nations." Al-Jazeera did not conform, and news of the rejection hit the wire services and the Internet like wildfire.

The Qatari newspaper *Gulf Times* noted in January 1999 that even other Arabic TV networks that "offer only nudity" were allowed to join the ASBU.

In his comment on the ASBU's decision, Mohammed Jasim Al-Ali, Al-Jazeera's managing director, said in a fall 2000 interview with the online journal *Transnational Broadcasting Studies*, "We tried to join in the beginning. We would be an excellent addition to them as much as they could be a support to us. We are not losing anything by not being part of ASBU, though; there's no advantage for us. They are the ones losing by keeping us out. . . . Our work with Western television is just as important. We have good contacts with them; they contact us and ask about our coverage of the Arab and Islamic world, because they know we are very strong. They ask us to help, and we do."

Attacks against Al-Jazeera programs are not confined to the Gulf states. They arise as well from North Africa, where Morocco, located in the northwestern corner of the African continent, accused Al-Jazeera of leading a "hostile" campaign against its monarchy. As a result, Morocco recalled its ambassador from Qatar on July 20, 2000. "The Moroccan government has been lately noting with astonishment and regret the various stands and attitudes adopted by the brotherly country of Qatar, both at the political and at the media levels," said the Moroccan state-run radio network, quoting a foreign ministry statement. It gave no further details, but diplomats in Rabat, the Moroccan capital, said that there has been apparent discomfort among official Moroccan circles with Al-Jazeera broadcasts, mainly because of the coverage of Islamic fundamentalism and Moroccan-Israeli ties.

The Qatari foreign minister defended Qatar by stating that the views and programs broadcast on Al-Jazeera are not the Qatari government's views; therefore it should not jeopardize relations between the two countries. In a July 22, 2000, interview broadcast on Al-Jazeera, Qatar's foreign minister said, "If it's a question of press [freedom] . . . today's world does not fear the press, but views it as a helping hand in correcting mistakes if such mistakes existed. But this should not be a reason for tension in relations between states. . . . International television stations, newspapers, and magazines are covering the Arab world much more than what we write about ourselves. Why be embarrassed when an Arab television station tackles our concerns?" Morocco's King Mohammed ordered his ambassador to return to Qatar in October 2000, after the Moroccan king met with the Qatari emir, Sheikh Hamad bin Khalifa Al-Thani.

Libya, another North African country, recalled its ambassador from Qatar on April 24, 2000, following criticism of the Libyan regime in one of Al-Jazeera's programs. Participants in the debate, which aired in mid-April 2000, discussed the ministerial changes in Libya and criticized its system of people's committees, describing them as "a mere façade for [Libyan leader] Muammar Qaddafi to make all decisions." Following this incident, Al-Jazeera was sharply criticized by the Qatari newspaper *Al-Watan* (The Nation), which said the network's "obsession with independence and freedom has sometimes pushed it to exaggerate and has created many problems for the station and for Qatar."

On May 2, 2000, the official Qatari News Agency (QNA) reported that the Qatari foreign minister expressed regret over the Libyan decision. "His Excellency expressed hope that the brothers in Libya would reconsider their decision regarding the withdrawal of the Libyan envoy to Doha," according to QNA.

THE THIN LINE BETWEEN LOVE AND HATE

Some of the Arab governments' arguments with Al-Jazeera have dissipated, replaced by curious love-hate relationships. Qaddafi, who protested one program featuring Libyan dissidents, called in to another program to talk about Arab nationalism and appeared twice as a guest on other programs. Yemeni President Ali Abdulla Saleh has denounced Al-Jazeera, yet also stated that he can't wait to appear on one of its shows.

These curious relationships crystallized during coverage of Iraqi President Saddam Hussein, who regularly pushes Al-Jazeera to cover his annual birthday speech in early May. After Al-Jazeera covered Saddam's sixty-third birthday celebrations in 2000, it received a protest note from Baghdad that described the coverage to be "too pro-American." A letter sent to Al-Jazeera's officials by the director of Iraq's information ministry on May 2, 2000 said, "Al-Jazeera followed a logic and even a way of expression that was purely American and this was by no means a matter of chance. It seems Al-Jazeera does not want to see Iraqis celebrating, but wants to see the people of Iraq living with disaster and suffering and even dying of hunger." Officials at Al-Jazeera refused to comment, saying only that Iraq had sent them numerous protests in the past about various programs it regarded as "anti-Iraqi."

AL-JAZEERA AND THE ARAB-ISRAELI CONFLICT
These spats pale in comparison to the barrage Jazeera has weathered from its coverage of the Arab-Israeli conflict. Jordan, one of the countries directly involved in the conflict, closed Al-Jazeera's news bureau in its capital, Amman, in November 1998. An Al-Jazeera commentator, in a piece on Jordan's peace treaty with Israel, had described Jordan as "an artificial entity" populated by "a bunch of Bedouins living in an arid desert." In the same program, a Syrian guest accused Jordan's late King Hussein of collaborating with Israel to deprive Syria of water resources. The guest, delving into history, described how the state of Jordan was established for Israel's benefit.

The Jordanian authorities found this to be an intolerable insult that could not go unpunished. On November 5, 1998, the

Jordanian information ministry decided to cancel the accreditations of Jordanian and non-Jordanian correspondents working for Al-Jazeera. The director-general of the Jordanian Press and Publications Department, in an interview with Arabic *News.com*, later that month said that the decision complied with its Publication Law concerning foreign media correspondents, citing Al-Jazeera's "deliberate insults against the Jordanian people and political system." The Jordanian news agency Petra characterized the Al-Jazeera broadcast as a "scathing attack." After apologies from Qatar, the Jordanian decision was rescinded, and the Al-Jazeera bureau in Amman was reopened.

Al-Jazeera's coverage of the Arab-Israeli conflict has played better in Palestine, where the network enjoys great popularity among Palestinian officials. Palestinian Authority President Yasser Arafat was quoted in the Kuwaiti newspaper *Al-Watan* on January 26, 1998: "I consider Al-Jazeera to be a badge of honor for Qatar. I believe it is an important and respectable channel."

However, in 1999 Arafat complained to the Qatari government about an Al-Jazeera interview with Sheikh Ahmed Yassin, the spiritual leader of the Palestinian opposition group Hamas, in which Yassin accused Palestinian officials of murdering opposition members. The mainstream Palestinian media, which are controlled by Arafat's Fatah movement, have not conducted interviews with Yassin or leaders of other Palestinian opposition groups.

On March 21, 2001, Arafat's Palestinian Authority temporarily closed the Al-Jazeera bureau in the West Bank city of Ramallah because of a promotional trailer for a documentary series about the Lebanese civil war that contained an unflattering image of Arafat. The image showed a picture of Arafat with a shoe hanging from it—a sign of disrespect. Al-Jazeera's correspondent in Ramallah, Walid Al-Omari, said in a broadcast that armed members of a Palestinian security service entered the office and demanded that part of a preview for the documentary war be removed. "When the change was not made, we were informed about the closure of the office," Al-Omari said in an interview with Reuters on March 22, 2001.

The Palestinian reaction was not exactly a government decision, a Palestinian official in Ramallah told the *New York Times* on March 22, 2001. Rather, the official said, one of Arafat's senior aides took it upon himself to rush, perhaps overzealously, to Arafat's defense by shutting down the network's office.

Visitors to the Al-Jazeera office in Ramallah said Palestinian security officers kept curious onlookers at bay. Hanan Ashrawi, a member of the Palestinian National Council, called the closure of the office "unfortunate" when she was interviewed on Al-Jazeera in late March 2001. "I am trying with many colleagues and others not only to reopen the office, but to make sure this doesn't happen again," Ashrawi said. An official statement was issued by Al-Jazeera following the closure: "The Palestinians' actions sought to change the tone of a television program by resorting to force, something all free media reject."

At a training course for Palestinian journalists held in March 2001, Marwan Kanafani, a spokesman for Arafat, lamented the lack of professionalism in the Palestinian news media. He blamed officials for manipulating the news media and the government for the fact that 80 percent of Palestinians get their news from non-Palestinian sources—Al-Jazeera and "even enemy news sources," that is, the Arabic-language Israeli news programs. According to a report by the *New York Times* on March 22, 2001, Kanafani said, "Any action which prevents anyone from, or punishes anyone for speaking out, is more dangerous than the speech itself, regardless of its nature. . . . A state that cannot tolerate differing opinions, cannot convince the world of its steadfastness on other more dangerous issues."

Arafat ordered the reopening of the Al-Jazeera office just two days after its closure, after he received a delegation from Al-

Jazeera. The International Committee to Protect Journalists had also complained to Arafat for closing the bureau, calling it a "crude attempt at censorship that violates basic international norms for free expression."

Yet with every dramatic action a government has taken against Al-Jazeera, its popularity among Arab audiences appears to grow. With every attempt to reprimand or silence the network, satellite subscriptions and website traffic increase.

TAKING ISSUE IN LEBANON

But even progressive Arab states have taken issue with Al-Jazeera. In February 2000, Lebanon, which has more press freedoms than most of the Arab world, issued a vehement protest against Al-Jazeera when it interviewed Roger Hatem, known as the "Cobra." Hatem is a former member of the Christian Lebanese Forces militia and the former bodyguard of Eli Hobeika (who was killed in January 2002), the then-intelligence chief of the Lebanese Phalange militia responsible for the massacre of Palestinian refugees in camps at Sabra and Shatilla in September 1982. Hatem accused his former boss of a long list of murders, including that of Hatem's infant daughter. He also gave a verbatim account of the reprimand Hobeika received at the time from Ariel Sharon.

The interview sparked a furor in Lebanon. Hobeika, who over the years was known as little more than a puppet politician in the Syrian government, was forced to break his silence for the first time on Al-Jazeera. Never before in the history of the Arab media has a politician been forced to respond point by point to such serious personal accusations. It set a powerful precedent.

AL-KASIM UNDER FIRE

Throughout its stormy history, then, Al-Jazeera has been attacked on every level. Serious accusations have been leveled at the Al-Jazeera board of directors, and bureaus have been shut down; network talk show hosts and commentators might as well don flak jackets before going on the air. It is not surprising that Faisal Al-Kasim, host of The Opposite Direction, receives most of the criticism.

Al-Kasim, one of eleven children born to a poor peasant family in the Jebel Arab region of Syria, was always fascinated by the media. Now, more than forty years old, he has achieved stardom. As a youth of fourteen, he visited Damascus Radio, a dream of his, and he spent seven years with the Arabic service of BBC radio, probably the most widely received source of news and views in the Arab world.

Although Al-Kasim is relatively unknown outside the Arab world, within it he enjoys the celebrity status reserved for top leaders and entertainment celebrities. He is sometimes mobbed during visits to Arab countries; cities are perceptibly quieter just before he goes on the air. It happened in his native Syria when he hosted two protagonists who debated whether Syrian President Hafez Al-Assad (now deceased) was abandoning the Palestinian cause.

Al-Kasim was recruited to Al-Jazeera by the promise of freedom. Despite that freedom, or perhaps because of it, he is subject to harsh criticism, not only by Arab officials but also by Arab journalists. A Jordanian columnist quoted on August 8, 2000, in the French newspaper Le Monde expressed the wish of many Arab leaders when he said with regard to Al-Kasim, "This man's tongue should be cut out."

In an interview we conducted on December 2, 2001, with Al-Kasim, he said he has at least thirty-five indexes of news articles attacking him and his program; he has collected thousands of articles. "I have been blacklisted by most Arab regimes. Some Arab countries, such as Jordan, have used much of their resources to fight Al-Jazeera and attack me personally," he told us. A columnist in the Kuwaiti newspaper *Al-Watan* compared Al-Kasim to Salman Rushdie, the renowned Muslim author despised in the Arab world for his alleged religious blasphemy. The columnist also accused Al-Kasim of "antagonizing Arab nationalism."

Al-Kasim and his program have also been attacked by hometown newspapers in Qatar. One columnist in the Qatari newspaper *Al-Raya* expressed anger at Al-Kasim for hosting guests that accused Iraqi officials of mistreating Kurdish minorities living in northern Iraq. "Al-Kasim ignored the fact that Iraq was the only country that allowed the Kurds to live on its lands and gave them the right of self-rule," the columnist claimed.

What hinders progress in the Arab world, according to Al-Kasim, is the ongoing absence of a free press. "The freedom of opinion in the Arab world is still buried in the stone ages. But I am certain this won't be the case much longer. Al-Jazeera offers a ray of hope. Some day a free Arab press may help to create real democracy in the Arab world."

Some Arab countries have gone so far as to personally punish Al-Kasim. Egypt deported Al-Kasim's thirty-year-old brother, Magd Al-Kasim, a well-known singer who lived and worked in Cairo. The decision to deport Magd was made on October 27, 2000, shortly after the Egyptian government accused Al-Jazeera of trying to discredit the country by broadcasting interviews with guests who criticized Egyptian President Hosni Mubarak for his softness toward Israel. The Egyptian security authorities who deported Magd declined to provide any reason; Magd was allowed to return to Egypt three months later.

The deportation of Magd Al-Kasim preceded a decision by the Egyptian musicians' guild to expel any member who works with Al-Jazeera. That decision, made in early November 2000, warned that "any singer, musician, or composer working with Al-Jazeera will be struck from the list of the union, which will stop dealing with this person permanently," according to an article in the Egyptian daily newspaper *Al-Akhbar* (The News). The guild's chairman told *Al-Akhbar* that his organization would stop dealing with people who work with "this Zionist and dubious channel, which has no other goal than to harm the reputation of Egypt and the Arab world."

CONTENT VERSUS EGYPTIAN TRADITION: JANUS IN THE DESERT

Egypt, the most populous Arab country and headquarters of the Arab League, has been the subject of several Al-Jazeera talk shows. Egypt's official position on Al-Jazeera has been ambivalent. Controversy erupted in government circles several times over Al-Jazeera programming that criticized the legacy of the late Egyptian President Anwar Sadat or that hosted Islamic militants who have been blacklisted by the Egyptian government. Several media barons from the state-owned press repeatedly called for the network's correspondents to be expelled from the country.

Al-Jazeera's willingness to tackle sensitive issues has driven the Egyptian government to prevent an invited guest from traveling to Qatar to appear on *The Opposite Direction*. Montasser Al-Zayyat, an Egyptian lawyer known for his support of Egyptian Islamists, was stopped at Cairo International Airport on September 1, 1997. He said in an interview with Agence France Presse the following day that the authorities stopped him because the show was going to discuss the aftermath of an announcement made by several prisoners on July 5, 1997, to stop the violent treatment of Egyptian Islamists behind bars. "I consider the decision to prevent me from leaving the country to be against the spirit of the Egyptian Constitution," said Al-Zayyat.

Some critics claim that Al-Jazeera harbors a veiled hostility toward Egypt. Such claims probably stem from the strained relations between Qatar and Egypt, particularly after Egypt led a 1997 boycott against an economic summit scheduled to be held

in Doha. Egypt went even farther, however, accusing some
Qatari officials of financing Islamist militant organizations
working against the Cairo-based government. The dispute esca-
lated into a war of words between the two countries until King
Fahd of Saudi Arabia intervened in December 1997. But a few
weeks later, Qatari authorities laid off about 700 Egyptian workers employed in the private and public sectors. Many had to
leave the country on short notice.

Almost a year later, Al-Jazeera managing director Al-Ali told
the *Al-Ahram* Weekly that the network does not aim to bring
out Egypt's negative aspects. "We merely give the opportunity
for the expression of opposing views with great impartiality," he
said, also pointing out that the majority of the network's 300
staff members are Egyptian.

One episode of *The Opposite Direction* broadcast in early
September 1998 triggered another angry response from
Egyptian officials. The show aired a debate on whether the
United States imposes its hegemony over Arab and Muslim
countries. It was hosted by a Kuwaiti university professor who
advocated the U.S. presence throughout the Middle East. His
adversary was a London-based Egyptian who was convicted in
absentia by Egyptian courts for crimes of terrorism and sentenced to death in 1997 for his involvement in a conspiracy to
bomb one of Cairo's popular tourist destinations. Egyptian security officials said the appearance of the convicted terrorist on Al-
Jazeera violated an Arab antiterrorism treaty signed in April
1998. "Allowing a person who had been condemned to death in
a terrorism-related case to enter an Arab country and appear on
a television program is a serious development that should be
confronted firmly," claimed an Egyptian security source claimed,
who spoke on condition of anonymity to the Egyptian English-
language newspaper *Al-Ahram Weekly*. "The spirit of the treaty

clearly prohibits terrorists from using the media to propagate their poisonous ideas." But, the source added, because the incident may have an impact on relations with other countries, it is better left for the politicians to handle.

The convicted terrorist, speaking to *Al-Ahram Weekly* newspaper on the telephone from London on September 17, 1998, said he entered Qatar legally. "I am free to go anywhere," he said. "Whenever I want to leave Britain, I do." But he refused to specify whether he received security guarantees before traveling to Doha (Al-Jazeera officials also refused to disclose whether security arrangements had been arranged). "We asked the authorities for an entry visa for him and we got it, but we are not authorized to discuss security matters," said a senior Al-Jazeera official in the *Al-Ahram Weekly* interview.

The incident was not the first of its kind. A year earlier, *The Opposite Direction* hosted another person who topped the list of London-based Egyptian terrorists. The Egyptian government took issue and accused Al-Jazeera of being anti-Egyptian.

Al-Jazeera's managing director, Al-Ali, defended the appearance of Islamist militants as an "exercise of impartiality in news coverage." He added in an interview with *Al-Ahram Weekly* in the fall of 1998 that "these people live in London freely. They left Britain for Qatar in broad daylight and returned in broad daylight. We do not work in darkness. We merely act as the Western media do. So why are we blamed?"

Yet Al-Jazeera is blamed nonetheless. In Egypt, as in most Arab nations, the media are operated by the government. "Our society is conservative. We have too many taboos, and we don't wish to shock the audience," said Hassan Hamed, vice president of the Egyptian Radio and Television Union's Satellite Channels Sector, in an interview with *Al-Ahram Weekly*. Hamed added, however, that Egypt's satellite channels do in fact "tackle serious

issues and hot events such as demonstrations." But why are politically sensitive issues, like Islamic militancy or terrorism, not
addressed? "Are these really issues?" Hamed asked.

Egyptian officials' negative view toward Al-Jazeera is not always shared by the Egyptian public, which by all accounts is
watching Al-Jazeera as much as its Arab counterparts. In fact,
Al-Jazeera's correspondent in Cairo, Hussein Abdel Ghani, also
an Egyptian, has been stopped by people on the streets while on
assignments and has been commended for his courage in tackling sensitive issues. The editor of a weekly opposition newspaper in Cairo was quoted in the *Middle East Times*, an Egyptian
English-language newspaper in April 1998: "They [Al-Jazeera
reporters] make interviews with everyone, from everywhere,
some you like, some you don't. We should not be so sensitive to
this."

The relationship between Egypt and Al-Jazeera entered a new
phase in April 2000 when Sheikh Hamad bin Thamer Al-Thani,
the chairman of Al-Jazeera's board, signed a contract under
which the network would open production and broadcast offices
within a "free media production zone" located in Sixth of
October City, just outside Cairo. At the Cairo press conference
to announce the new offices, Al-Jazeera's board chairman said
that the deal would not compromise the network's hard-hitting
editorial policy. Egyptian officials promised there would be no
hindrance of Al-Jazeera's work within the zone.

Egypt's new media city, sometimes called "Hollywood on the
Nile" (although it is located in the desert), was established and
financed by the Egyptian government to enhance domestic TV,
film, and video production and to attract private and international production houses. It represents Egypt's bid to entice the
Europe-based satellite networks to Cairo and to restore its status
as the media leader in the Arab world. "There is an economic
factor to the media-making business in Egypt, and everyone is

trying to be number one now," said Mohammed Gohar of Video Cairo, an independent media production company that used to host Al-Jazeera's Cairo bureau.

Commenting on Al-Jazeera's new Egypt deal, managing director Al-Ali, in the spring 2000 issue of the online journal *Transnational Broadcasting Studies*, said, "We've been expanding in Cairo, with more freedom to operate here in the country. It used to be blocked out; if you wanted to film, you needed permission, you needed to write letters, you were denied permission. After the resolution of our recent problems, they've been making it easier, not censoring the programs. The cost of media production is also dropping, especially if we build our own facilities here [in Cairo] and link directly to the home in Doha." Al-Ali added that Al-Jazeera has been receiving invitations from other Arab governments to open offices in their countries. "We should soon have independent offices in Yemen, the Sudan, and Kuwait," he predicted.

The question asked by many of the journalists at the Cairo press conference was, What's the trade-off? Would Egypt's hospitality blunt Al-Jazeera's critical edge? Most observers privately speculated that Al-Jazeera had struck an inside deal that would downplay Egypt's outmoded traditions and reduce the presence of convicted militants on network programming. Egyptian officials denied such allegations. "We'll allow all sorts of media to work there, but we have regulations that should be respected," said Abdel Rahman Hafez, head of the Egyptian Radio and Television Union. Hafez referred to a "code of ethics" agreed to by the Arab League whereby Arab countries honor informal agreements not to criticize one another in the state media.

The chairman of Nilesat, the official Egyptian satellite network, Amin Bassiouni, was quick to add that the code of ethics was not obligatory, little more than a commitment to respect ethics and ideals like objectivity and truth. "We have a code of ethics, but we have only one tenet which is 'one opinion and the other,'" Bassiouni said, echoing Al-Jazeera's official slogan. He repeatedly stressed that there would be no censorship in the free zone.

The Egyptian minister of information, Safwat Al-Sherif, who signed the agreement with Al-Jazeera, endorsed Bassiouni's statement and added in an interview with *Al-Ahram Weekly*, "We have willingly chosen a difficult path, a challenge. The free zone means that there is no censorship. What they [Al-Jazeera] will say from Egypt, they have been saying from Qatar, and can say from anywhere else. The communications revolution has eliminated barriers. We decided to enter this age with open hearts and minds."

One media commentator pointed out that Egypt may hope that Al-Jazeera will temper its criticism of the Egyptian government owing to its new offices in the media zone; but there are no guarantees. The media zone in fact needs the prestige of a network like Al-Jazeera (thus far the first and only major foreign investor; the deal is worth about U.S. $400 million). Egypt cannot afford to alienate its first wealthy tenant.

One of Al-Jazeera's talk show hosts, Ahmed Mansour, was quoted in *Al-Ahram Weekly* as saying that he had personal assurances from Al-Jazeera that the Egyptian government placed no conditions on the network: "Al-Jazeera will not change its approach, or it will cease being Al-Jazeera and die," he said.

Another Al-Jazeera reporter, Hussein Abdel Ghani (chief of Al-Jazeera's Cairo bureau), said in the same *Al-Ahram Weekly* issue, "We [Al-Jazeera] have been described as the stone that stirred the stagnant waters, creating currents and waves in the Arab media. . . . Some said we are like a matchbox that started a fire that hasn't been extinguished yet . . . I would like Al-Jazeera to be described as a flower that is blooming among other flowers."

Egyptian officials remain unconvinced by Al-Jazeera's good-intentioned rhetoric, as they continue to hurl accusations. In an interview with CBS's 60 Minutes aired in May 2001, Mohammed Abdul Monem, a former spokesman for the Egyptian president, said he believed that Al-Jazeera was subversive and trying deliberately to destabilize Arab governments. "They [Al-Jazeera] are undermining us. They are undermining Egypt, undermining Saudi Arabia, undermining all the Arab countries. They are separating the Arab world. It's no good," he said. Another Egyptian official, Nabil Osman, head of Egypt's State Information Service, tried to downplay the popularity of Al-Jazeera among Arab viewers in an interview with the *Washington Post* (December 4, 2001): "It's a tabloid, no more than a tabloid. And tabloids, by the way, sell in the millions," he said.

Top officials in the Egyptian government have also expressed dissatisfaction with Al-Jazeera's coverage of the most recent Palestinian Intifada and accused the network of fostering Arabs' anger by airing footage of Palestinians clashing with Israeli forces. Since the start of this Intifada in September 2000, Al-Jazeera has featured political figures who have been critical of Egypt's role in the peace process.

Egyptian fury peaked when Al-Jazeera crews in the West Bank and Gaza provided footage in late October 2000 of angry Palestinians burning Egyptian flags in protest of the Arab summit held in Egypt earlier that month. On October 26, 2000, Safwat Al-Sherif, Egypt's minister of information, told the *Good Morning Egypt* TV program that Arab television "should not broadcast nonsense." Al-Sherif complained: "I want to tell officials in charge of Al-Jazeera that this is unacceptable to Egypt and the Egyptian people. . . . Egypt has offered the souls of its martyrs. Its president brings the Arab nation together, seeks to stop the Palestinian bloodshed and responds to all international calls for mediation, and after all that, this noisy campaign is waged." He also threatened to close down Al-Jazeera's new facilities in Cairo. "I hope Al-Jazeera stops attacking Egypt, otherwise [we will] forbid the channel from having studios and correspondents in Egypt, and even ban this channel from broadcasting by satellite," he warned.

The minister shifted his position and accusatory tone, no doubt because such a reaction would destroy the credibility of Egypt's free media zone and decrease its appeal to potential foreign clients, Arab and non-Arab. In an interview with the Cairo weekly magazine *Rose Al-Youssef* later that fall, Amin Bassiouni, the chairman of Nilesat, was asked why the government didn't retaliate against Al-Jazeera and yank broadcasts off the air. He responded that the relationship between Nilesat and Al-Jazeera was motivated by commercial implications more so than political ones.

Earlier that year *Rose Al-Youssef*, known for its coverage of political scandals, devoted an entire section to attacking Al-Jazeera. One of the articles accused Al-Jazeera of conspiring against Egyptian national interests and cooperating with the Israeli press to create a "deep divide" between Egyptian and Palestinian officials. The article stated how the Israeli press "claimed that Arafat had reduced the number of his visits to Cairo because he felt the Egyptian president hadn't been helping the Palestinian Intifada." It also mentioned that Al-Jazeera had helped enforce that claim through talk shows and its coverage of the Intifada. The article included a strong message that encouraged readers not to trust Al-Jazeera, which the writer described as "a suspicious channel that is antagonistic to the Arab regimes."

Another article in *Rose Al-Youssef* ("A Broadcaster from Egypt . . . Is Against Egypt") singled out host Ahmed Mansour, who hails from Egypt, as anti-Egyptian and a member of an extremist

Islamic group. Mansour, who hosts the talk show *Without Frontiers*, dismissed the article and said he wasn't part of any political position.

The Egyptian newspaper *Al-Ahram* (The Pyramid, an Arabic-language paper different than the English-language weekly cited above) joined the chorus of criticism when one of its reporters wrote a column in late October 2000 that accused Al-Jazeera of being unethical and biased. "Al-Jazeera forgets, or pretends to forget, the mission of media, and does not abide by the rules and ethics of dialogue. It shows a sort of media adolescence, and we should look for the real purpose of its attempts to distort the image of Egypt and to break the bonds with the Arab states," he wrote.

The Egyptian public's opinion of Al-Jazeera is not all one-sided. A handful of Egyptian journalists have declared their opposition to the anti–Al-Jazeera media blitz. Salama Ahmed Salama, the respected columnist and former managing editor of *Al-Ahram*, said in the English-language *Al-Ahram Weekly* in late October 2000, "Al-Jazeera threw a stone in the stagnant waters of the official and traditional media, regardless of whether those who attack them like it or not." Salama acknowledged that some of Al-Jazeera's commentators were biased against Egypt, but he insisted that "Egyptians are over-sensitive and don't like criticism." The problem, according to Salama, is that Egyptian media are not capable of responding to criticism with rational argument and can respond only with insults.

Al-Jazeera's chief editor, Salah Negm, dismissed the criticism that Al-Jazeera has been targeting Egyptian officials. In an interview with the *Los Angeles Times*, he said Arab leaders have to realize that Al-Jazeera is not going to "carry water" for their regimes. Negm said that the same people who accuse Al-Jazeera of inciting violence also characterize the network as pro-Zionist when it interviewed then–Israeli Prime Minister Ehud Barak and other Israeli leaders. "Everyone here understands that news values rules. We'll be out of business in no time if we feel the need to be sensitive to this king or that government," said Negm.

Arab governments' criticism against Al-Jazeera will probably continue, but Gohar of Video Cairo predicts that it will matter less and less as the fight for media preeminence in the region leads to the triumph of professionalism. "I think the battle will come down to professionalism—who will do a better job." In the Arab world right now, that is Al-Jazeera.

IS QATAR THE REAL CULPRIT?

Although the Qatari government denies any influence over Al-Jazeera broadcasts and editorial policy, most official Arab complaints are directed to the Qatari government, not the network. Because Al-Jazeera is a new phenomenon in the Arab world, and because Arabs are not accustomed to an independent Arab network free of government control, many refuse to accept that Al-Jazeera truly operates on its own. They simply cannot separate Al-Jazeera from the Qatari government.

There is no question that state sponsorship impacts the objectivity of Al-Jazeera coverage of events within Qatar, although not as much as one might expect. And there is no question that sponsorship of Al-Jazeera has helped the tiny Gulf emirate achieve a level of regional and international influence disproportionate to its military and economic strength. Al-Jazeera, arguably, is better known than its host country. The running joke is that Al-Jazeera is a country with Qatar as its capital.

However, Al-Jazeera does not function as an instrument of Qatari foreign policy, as it should not. Qatar's foreign policy remains wholly separate and is characterized by cordial and open ties with neighbors. This appears to contradict Qatar's sponsorship of Al-Jazeera, which regularly broadcasts interviews with other countries' political dissidents, reports on their dismal human rights records, and holds open debates on religious practices.

The question is this: Given the vital role played by satellite television in weakening authoritarian regimes, why hasn't Qatar suffered a backlash in its relations with other Arab states? The reason probably lies in the Qatari government's lack of interference in the network's affairs. The government absolves itself of any charges, saying it has nothing to do with the contents on Al-Jazeera. According to Al-Ali, the network's managing director, in a September 1998 interview with *Al-Ahram Weekly,* "We just use Qatar as a base for the channel. But we have our own policies and views that focus on professional requirements. We deal with any Arab issue the same way we deal with Qatari issues. . . . Our channel does not represent a specific country or government; we merely act as the Western media do." He asked, "Why aren't they blamed when they act similarly?"

Needless to say, Al-Jazeera has succeeded by overcoming the incompatible media expectations of Arab regimes and the Arab publics they rule. Its ability to criticize virtually every state's instruments of power has made it the marketer and primary conduit for mass distribution of dissenting voices in the region. This situation has placed Arab governments in an unenviable position that prevents them from being too vocal in criticizing Al-Jazeera. Most governments are more concerned, and rightly so, with the negative coverage that could ensue if they boycotted Al-Jazeera. Instead, many Arab governments grant Al-Jazeera access to sources and facilities in an attempt to appease the network and court favorable coverage. Regardless, most governments in the region recognize that they will be held accountable for their policies in domestic, regional, and international respects.

The future of Al-Jazeera's relationship with Arab governments ultimately will be decided by two factors: the durability of Qatar's democratic experiment, and the fruition of Al-Jazeera's plans to commercially succeed. However, given the current conditions in the Middle East, it seems that Al-Jazeera will continue to be a thorn in the side of many Arab regimes.

7

AL-JAZEERA
SCOOPS THE WORLD

When Deborah Bassett switched on the television set in the living room of her Florida apartment at 12:30 p.m. on October 7, 2001, she watched the first U.S. attacks on Afghanistan. Many of the pictures carried Arabic-language graphics. The live images from the Afghan capital, Kabul, framed by the Al-Jazeera logo in red Arabic letters—and, most stunning of all, a videotaped statement from suspected terror mastermind Osama bin Laden—was being aired on the Al-Jazeera network, whose very name was news to millions of Americans like Bassett.

"I thought it [the bin Laden video] was sent directly to CNN, but then I noticed some strange logo in the top right corner of the screen, and I knew later that it was an Arab channel called Al-Jazeera that delivered the tape to CNN," said the twenty-nine-year-old Bassett, who neither heard of Al-Jazeera nor saw bin Laden before that day. "I was in a state of shock that I was actually seeing the person responsible for the deaths on September 11. But I think, seeing him personified the force behind terrorism, I feel that it is important for people to be able to make some sense out of what happened. I am glad they [Al-Jazeera] were able to get the footage."

IN THE RIGHT PLACE AT THE RIGHT TIME

Al-Jazeera's grainy footage of a black sky with firefly flickers of white light, together with its exclusive bin Laden video, represented some of the most significant news on a day when the American TV media struggled to monitor the rapidly unfolding events during the first hours of war. In fact, it was that very day—one marked by images of war action in Afghanistan, the video cloaked in a surreal green haze—that heralded Al-Jazeera's breathtaking rise to international acclaim.

A little more than a decade ago, in 1991, when the United States launched the bombardment of Iraq in the Gulf War, it was the Baghdad-based CNN crew who announced the onset of the war when Bernard Shaw suddenly declared, "Something is happening outside." But when British and U.S. planes started bombing Afghanistan, Al-Jazeera was the only TV network operating from Kabul, with its permanent, live, twenty-four-hour satellite link. Its Qatar-based anchorman, Mohammed Kreishan, was talking on camera when a voice came through his earpiece. "Mohammed, you're now on CNN . . . and BBC . . . and Sky News." This time, Al-Jazeera was in the right place at the right time. No wonder Al-Jazeera has been dubbed the "Arab world's CNN" since its inception.

But Al-Jazeera's exclusive footage from Kabul was not its only scoop that evening. The network soon boasted its second exclusive of the night: a videotaped speech from Osama bin Laden. This bin Laden video, which first broadcast over Al-Jazeera and then rebroadcast by CNN and other U.S. and European networks, provided America's most wanted man with his most visible platform to date. He used it to deliver his distorted view of Muslim history and the jihad [holy war] against the Western world.

Different explanations about how Al-Jazeera obtained the video circulated, including one that insisted it was tossed from a speeding car. However, Tayseer Allouni, Al-Jazeera's former reporter in Kabul, provided the only cogent explanation at the time. Shortly after his return to Qatar once the Northern Alliance took control of Kabul, Allouni said that Al-Jazeera did not go out of its way to obtain the tape. "I was covering the start of the bombings from the roof of our building in Kabul when one of our staff came running at me and said, 'Someone associated with bin Laden delivered this tape to us at the gate.'" Allouni previewed the tape and immediately called Al-Jazeera's Doha headquarters. The network's executives recognized quickly the exclusive story they had in their hands and, without viewing even one second of the tape, directed Allouni to run the feed immediately. "We trust our reporters," one of Al-Jazeera's producers said in an interview with *The Guardian* on October 9, 2001.

Al-Jazeera's chief news editor, Ibrahim Helal, issued a starkly contrasting statement, however. He claimed that the network actively solicited a taped message from bin Laden through Afghan contacts with direct links to bin Laden's Al-Qaeda terrorist network. "After American investigators started talking about bin Laden, we contacted our correspondent in Kabul [Allouni] asking if we could get any reaction at all from Al-Qaeda. He told us that we could get a reaction any time. Fifteen days before we received this tape, he told us: 'Expect a reaction.'" Helal also denied the rumors that Al-Jazeera received the tape before the September 11 attacks, only to embargo it until afterward. "It happened just by chance that it arrived immediately afterwards. A couple of hours after," Helal said during an interview with the *London Sunday Telegraph* on October 14, 2001.

In this now infamous video—which appeared to have been shot inside a cave during daylight hours—bin Laden, eerily calm, soft-spoken, with a long, gray beard, was framed by barren rock and a solitary rifle. He was flanked by three lieutenants: Ayman Al-Zawahri—his operations chief and the leader of the Egyptian Islamic Jihad—and two leading members of Al-Qaeda.

On the tape bin Laden, dressed in white and beige robes and an Afghan-style white turban, started his chilling speech: "God has hit America, and He has destroyed its greatest buildings, and thanks be to God, America has been filled with fear from north to south and east to west." He alluded to years of U.S. air strikes against Iraq, economic sanctions, images of Israeli tanks rolling into Palestinian towns—each listed by name.

While bin Laden impressed some Muslim viewers with his deceptively simple phrases, he frightened others with his apocalyptic vision of a religious war between Muslims and non-Muslims. "These events have split the world into two camps," he said, "the camp of the believers and the camp of the infidels. It is the duty of every Muslim to make sure that his religion prevails. The winds of faith and the winds of change are blowing against the infidels who occupy the land of the Prophet Mohammed, may peace and God's blessings be upon him."

Bin Laden ended his speech with a threat to the United States: "To America and its people, I say a few words: I swear to God, who raised the sky without pillars, that America and those who live in it will not be able to dream of security before we live it on the ground in Palestine, and before all of the infidel armies leave the land of the Prophet, may peace and God's blessings be upon him."

In the same broadcast, bin Laden's deputy Al-Zawahri vowed that the "tragedy of Al-Andalus" would not be repeated. He was referring to a period in history widely considered to be the Islamic golden age, in Andalusia, Spain, which ended when Muslims were driven out of Europe by Christian armies during the fifteenth century.

Many Middle East experts said that the video was carefully staged. Bin Laden was fully aware of the importance of the propaganda battle that would accompany the military actions. "This is language that can really reach the people, especially in the

[Arabian Gulf], where the tension is very high," said Fahmi Howeidi, an influential Islamic political writer for the Egyptian newspaper *Al-Ahram* during an interview with the *New York Times* on October 9, 2001. "Here you have a simple man who presents himself as someone who left behind millions of dollars to defend Muslim dignity," he added. "He has become the symbol now of challenge to the West."

However, bin Laden's Arabic statements, aired by CNN with its own simultaneous English translations, were "butchered" by translators, according to linguistic experts. "The translations were very poor; bin Laden was using very sophisticated theological and legal language, but the translators were neither linguists nor theological scholars. There is a real problem here," said Bernard Haykel, a professor of Islamic Studies at New York University in an interview with *National Post Online* on October 9. He said the CNN translator "was putting his own spin on it, selectively translating."

Another linguistic expert, Nabil Baradey, an English-Arabic translator based in the United Arab Emirates, was quoted in the same *National Post Online*, "The simultaneous translation omitted a great deal, and used the wrong terms, and it seems to me that the interpreter was not a professional one at all." English wire services also provided written versions of the bin Laden text, translated by their own Arabic-speaking staff in the Middle East, drawing from local television broadcasts.

Regardless of whether the English translations that accompanied bin Laden's broadcast speech were accurate, the entire episode transformed Al-Jazeera into a world-renowned media outlet virtually overnight.

Edmund Ghareeb, a specialist on Middle East media and a political communications professor at American University in Washington, D.C., remarked that it was no accident that bin Laden and Al-Qaeda chose Al-Jazeera as their mouthpiece. "They wanted to have access to a major news network that is going to reach across borders. And this, to an extent, is what Al-Jazeera is, what CNN is. These are news channels that cross international boundaries and present in this globalized world, new access," Ghareeb said in a televised interview with PBS's *NewsHour*.

Inside the Al-Jazeera studios—a heavily guarded compound in Doha—there is great pride. "We never expected to achieve global celebrity," said Sheikh Hamad bin Thamer Al-Thani, chairman of Al-Jazeera's board. "Any organization that was able to obtain such a scoop would not hesitate to accept it; broadcasting videos of bin Laden is no different from CNN's broadcasting speeches of Saddam Hussein during the 1991 Gulf War." Tawfiq Taha, an Al-Jazeera news anchor in Doha, added that "this is our chance . . . to be number one as CNN was number one in the Gulf War."

The excitement produced by Al-Jazeera's airing of the bin Laden video extended beyond studio management to the Qatari community at large. Abdullah Khalid, an Al-Jazeera satellite engineer in Doha, said, "Everybody feels proud and happy here because this channel is becoming famous and we will become famous too." For Helal, the chief news editor, the network was simply doing its job. "If we can reach Osama, or Osama can reach us, it is just journalism. . . . You have to know what the other side looks like; you have to listen to him. If I put myself in the other camp, in the West, even politicians in the West need to know him [bin Laden]; they need to know what Al-Qaeda thinks. We are giving them a great chance to get to know the other side of the story," he added in an interview with the *Washington Times* on October 15, 2001.

BIN LADEN'S EXCLUSIVES

The bin Laden tape that was released on October 7, 2001, was merely one of several exclusive broadcasts. Al-Jazeera was the first network to conduct a televised interview with bin Laden, which took place in an undisclosed location in Afghanistan in 1998 by the network correspondent in Pakistan. Al-Jazeera aired that interview on June 10, 1999; it is not clear why the interview was not aired earlier. Still, it was the first time Arab viewers heard and saw bin Laden himself speak.

In the ninety-minute interview, bin Laden declared that every American male would be his target and added that it was the duty of Muslims to free their lands from what he called "American occupation." He spoke of himself mostly in the third person: "As to what he [bin Laden] wants, what we want and demand is the right of any living being. We want our land to be freed of the Americans. God equipped living creatures with an instinctive zeal, and they refuse to be dominated."

During the interview, bin Laden denied he was behind the attacks on U.S. embassies in Kenya and Tanzania in 1998, which killed more than 200 people and injured hundreds more. Yet he stated he admired those who had carried out attacks on U.S. bases in Saudi Arabia in 1995 and 1996.

Al-Jazeera scored another exclusive with its coverage of bin Laden's son's wedding in the southern Afghan city of Kandahar on January 9, 2001. During the wedding, attended by Afghan officials and Arabs living in Afghanistan, bin Laden's son, wearing a traditional white Arab headdress, was shown sitting on a carpet between his father, who was wearing a white turban, and another man believed to be the bride's father, a senior aid to bin Laden. Al-Jazeera said the bride and groom were both born in Pakistan when their fathers were fighting in neighboring Afghanistan.

Months later, on October 5, 2001, Al-Jazeera followed up this coup with broadcast footage of bin Laden, standing and unsmiling, accompanied by his closest collaborator, Al-Zawahri. Both men wore white robes and turbans, surrounded by several men armed with assault rifles, their faces covered with checkered khefiyyas (Arab scarves). At least three sport utility vehicles equipped with floodlights were parked in the background. An encampment of three or four squat cement huts and several sand-colored tents surrounded the group. Parched, rugged mountains, lit by slanting golden rays of either early morning or late afternoon sun, loomed behind them. The terrain and arid mountains suggested that the footage was shot in Afghanistan, bin Laden's base since 1996. Dozens of fighters wearing camouflage uniforms stood at attention, and a crowd of cheering supporters looked on. At times bin Laden glanced toward the camera, but his face remained unmoving. Al-Jazeera said the footage was believed to record a celebration of a union between bin Laden's Al-Qaeda network and Al-Zawahri's Jihad group. It also marked the graduation of a group of newly trained fighters into Al-Qaeda, the network reported.

On October 9, 2001, Al-Jazeera broadcast a taped statement by a spokesman of Al-Qaeda, delivered to the network by one of the group's associates in Kabul. "It is every Muslim's duty today to wage jihad against the United States," according to the statement, read by Al-Qaeda spokesman Suleiman Abu Geith. "You must fight if you are able-bodied; there is no excuse. The time is now. This is the word of God." Abu Geith, a Kuwaiti recently stripped of his citizenship, said that the United States and Britain should withdraw from Afghanistan or the "land would burn with fire under their feet, God willing." The message was similar to bin Laden's earlier statement, which interpreted the battle between the United States and Al-Qaeda as one waged between Israel and the West against the interests of Muslims.

Once Abu Geith's statement aired, Al-Jazeera broadcast a panel discussion that included Edward Walker, former U.S. assistant secretary of state for Near East affairs, and a Muslim cleric. The panelists analyzed the statements released by Al-

Qaeda and discussed the Islamic position, which does not agree with the actions of bin Laden and his followers.

QUESTIONS FOR BIN LADEN

A major development involving Al-Jazeera and CNN took place on October 17, 2001, when representatives of Al-Qaeda invited the networks to submit questions. CNN submitted six questions, including whether bin Laden or his followers had weapons of mass destruction and whether he was behind the September 11 attacks. Al-Jazeera submitted twenty-five questions of its own later that week. According to Al-Jazeera's managing director, Mohammed Jasim Al-Ali, Al-Jazeera faxed the questions to its bureau in Kabul, where Al-Jazeera correspondents read them over the phone to contacts with whom they had previously spoken, men who identified themselves as representatives of bin Laden. "To communicate is very difficult. We haven't a fixed time or date when we will get a tape," Al-Ali said during an interview with the *New York Times* on October 27, 2001.

CNN took pains to avoid the appearance of secret access to bin Laden. CNN's news group chairman called competitors to tell them about the questions submitted to bin Laden, promising to immediately share both the questions and the answers with other news outlets. The network also stated on the air to its viewers that it had submitted questions and hoped for bin Laden's reply.

No responses were ever received from Al-Qaeda. However, information surfaced that on October 21, 2001, Tayseer Allouni, the Al-Jazeera correspondent in Kabul, was invited by bin Laden to conduct an interview. According to an Al-Jazeera statement to the Associated Press that was made on February 2, 2002, "Allouni was told he must cover an important event. He was blindfolded and taken by armed men to interview bin Laden."

Yet Al-Jazeera never aired that October 2001 interview, and according to a *New York Times* story of December 2001, the network went so far as to deny that its correspondent had ever even conducted such an interview. CNN, however, obtained the videotaped interview from an independent source and aired excerpts on January 31 and February 1, 2002.

According to Al-Jazeera executives, the primary reason it decided not to air the interview was that bin Laden intimidated Allouni and refused to respond to many of his questions. In the above-mentioned statement to the Associated Press, Al-Jazeera explained that "the correspondent [Allouni] received a list of questions, and only a few of them were the ones CNN and Al-Jazeera submitted." It continued: "The interview, in which Allouni was subjected to intense psychological pressure, made it difficult to accomplish it professionally." Furthermore, Al-Jazeera officials decided not to air the interview because "the circumstances under which it was conducted did not represent the minimum limit of objectivity and professionalism."

Helal, Al-Jazeera's chief news editor, said in an interview with the *New York Times* in November 2001 that he had been contacted personally by Fox News. A Fox spokesman reported in the October 18, 2001, issue of the *Los Angeles Times* that Fox told Al-Jazeera: "If Mr. bin Laden agreed to a customary interview, Fox would like to be considered." However, Fox said it would conduct the interview on its own terms: "The only way we would do it is if we could have a sit-down interview with bin Laden and we were allowed to ask follow-up questions." Of course, a few days after Fox's request, Al-Jazeera scored the interview—but it was never aired or distributed to CNN or any other U.S. news network.

However, the U.K. and U.S. governments secretly obtained copies of the interview, which turned out to be the only TV interview conducted with bin Laden after September 11. Chief news editor Helal said in an interview with the *New York Times* in early November 2001 that he did not know of any interview turned over to those governments. But later he added that he had several videos of bin Laden, possibly including a taped interview, that were not broadcast because they were deemed not newsworthy or of poor technical quality.

On November 1, 2001, Al-Jazeera received a faxed statement from bin Laden in which he appealed to Muslims to overthrow their U.S. allied governments and install fundamentalist regimes. There was no mention of the Al-Jazeera or CNN questions.

BIN LADEN AND AL-JAZEERA VISIT AGAIN

Bin Laden made yet another contact with Al-Jazeera through a videotaped statement that aired on November 3, 2001. Bin Laden appeared on the videotape wearing a headdress and a military camouflage jacket, an automatic rifle propped at his side. "The United Nations is a crime tool," he said. "We are being slaughtered every day, but the United Nations does not move. Today, without any evidence, the United Nations is peddling resolutions in support of America against the weak [Afghanistan], who just emerged from a massive war by the Soviet Union."

Al-Jazeera editors reported that the tape was delivered to their Kabul bureau by someone associated with Al-Qaeda. The date and location of the recording were not given. Al-Jazeera waited a few days before airing the videotape, marking a shift in its assessment of bin Laden's newsworthiness. Chief news editor Helal told the Associated Press a few days later that bin Laden's nineteen-minute videotape "wasn't news," so the network held it (but he refused to confirm for how many days). The broadcast of this video was followed by a panel discussion that included a U.S. political analyst. "We wanted to put it within the context of a relevant panel discussion . . . because we are not a platform for anybody," said Helal.

The previous month, Al-Jazeera's managing director had explained the network's standard practice regarding "unsolicited" news items. "We don't just take any tape that comes to our offices or to the network and put it on air. Before that, we have a meeting to discuss how we should treat the news, and not be subject to the propaganda from a party or organization or group, Osama bin Laden or others. . . . We try to find the right people to talk to us on air. . . . To air statements without any comments, without any opposing statements or viewpoints or analysis, that's when it's propaganda."

Al-Jazeera used the broadcast of that bin Laden tape as an introduction to a long discussion about bin Laden's message. Christopher Ross, a former U.S. ambassador to the Middle East, criticized the speech for the first fifteen minutes of discussion. "The war is not against Islam; it is against the perpetrators of terrorist crimes. The terrorists are twisting facts and forging history. They openly call for violence and murder and insist on making this war a religious war," he said, speaking in fluent Arabic.

Many in the Western world heard parts of the chilling messages bin Laden delivered on this videotape. CNN linked to Al-Jazeera when it broadcast the November 3, 2001, tape. Following the feed, other U.S. networks picked it up and aired it. Compared to Al-Jazeera's ninety-second clip, CNN initially aired only five seconds without sound. It cited two bin Laden quotes criticizing Muslim nations belonging to the United Nations. Although CNN's first broadcast of that tape was brief, the network re-aired it many times in its entirety, with translations and analyses after the network had the opportunity to break down the dialogue, secure translations, and provide background.

Bin Laden's most recent message was delivered yet again through Al-Jazeera. By December 2001, the campaign against the Taliban had succeeded; the regime was defeated, and a new interim coalition government was established in Afghanistan. With U.S. Marines and Afghan forces combing mountains and caves for bin Laden, Al-Jazeera made world headlines on December 27, 2001, when it released a thirty-three-minute video thought to have been taped around mid-December. Although it did not confirm the whereabouts or even the survival of bin Laden, it nonetheless confirmed that Al-Jazeera remained squarely in the world media spotlight.

Station officials stated that the video was mailed to their Doha offices by an air courier service from Pakistan. They said the tape went unnoticed for two days before realizing it was from bin Laden. This time Al-Jazeera generated some additional media buzz by releasing a three-minute clip the day before it aired the complete video. For twenty-four hours, the world waited. This video carried less weight than the earlier ones, but Al-Jazeera seemed determined to get the most out of it. In the tape, bin Laden appeared pale and tired, wearing a combat jacket with a Russian-made submachine gun propped beside him. In this tape, bin Laden, who seemed to have lost much weight, condemned the West for excessive bombing of Muslims in Afghanistan. "The latest events have proved important truths," he said. "It has become clear that the West in general and America in particular have an unspeakable hatred for Islam. Terrorism against America deserves to be praised because it was a response to injustice, aimed at forcing America to stop its support for Israel, which kills our people." Western officials dismissed the video as the "same propaganda" that bin Laden had spewed in the past. Immediately after the broadcast, Al-Jazeera hosted three panelists—a former U.S. ambassador to Pakistan and two Arab political analysts—to comment on the tape.

Critics have continued to assert that Al-Jazeera is being used in a willful sort of way, that it is acting as instrument of propaganda for bin Laden and Islamic extremists. Some have gone so far as to claim that Al-Jazeera is acting as bin Laden's news partner. These people know little about Al-Jazeera. They may know little of Al-Jazeera'a short but illustrious history, much less its tireless pursuit of covering every angle of any given story. Al-Jazeera's coverage has been the same before and after the September 11 terrorist attacks. In addition to the statements from bin Laden and associates, the network routinely broadcasts speeches and press briefings by U.S. officials, translating them into Arabic for its viewers. In fact, Al-Jazeera correspondents booked at least six hours a day of satellite time from Washington to the Arab world. In essence, Al-Jazeera is an unofficial two-way communications channel between the Arab and Western worlds. The Arab world tunes in for information, and foreign networks tune in for material and footage.

THE WESTERN RESPONSE

After Al-Jazeera broadcast the bin Laden–Al-Qaeda statements, many in the West quickly clued in to the seriousness of the propaganda machine that bin Laden had created. British Prime Minister Tony Blair was the first Western leader to act, requesting an interview with Al-Jazeera in order to explain to the Arab and Muslim worlds the reasons for attacking Afghanistan. Political observers said Blair understood the need for a rapid rebuttal, a technique his Labor Party had refined so successfully in Britain.

On October 9, 2001, Samy Haddad, host of the Al-Jazeera talk show *More Than One Opinion*, interviewed Blair live for almost thirty minutes at Downing Street. Blair, who studied the Quran during his summer holiday, warned that if bin Laden's forces prevailed they would impose fundamentalist Islamic regimes across the region. "I don't believe that anybody seriously wants to live under that kind of regime," said Blair, who was quoted in *The Guardian* on the same day: "This is not about the West versus Islam. Decent Muslims, millions of them in European countries, have condemned these acts of terrorism in New York and elsewhere in America with every bit as much force as any of the rest of us." Blair was questioned vigorously on many issues, from the creation of a Palestinian state and the West's ongoing support of Israel, to the continuing economic sanctions against Iraq, to the abandonment of Afghanistan by the West in the wake of Russia's 1989 defeat and departure.

Al-Jazeera officials were gratified that Blair agreed to be interviewed by the network. "It was at his [Blair's] request and we were glad for it. He wanted to address the same viewers, especially Muslims, who watched bin Laden's tapes," Ahmed El-Sheikh, chief of Al-Jazeera's news desk, told the Egyptian newspaper *Al-Ahram Weekly* on October 11, 2001.

It seemed that the Blair interview prompted U.S. officials to request airtime on the network. U.S. Secretary of State Colin Powell gave a brief interview six days after the September 11 attacks. Afterward he told Agence France Presse, "I've given an interview on Al-Jazeera and I would hope to do so again in the future."

Shortly thereafter, Condoleezza Rice, the U.S. National Security Advisor, appeared on Al-Jazeera to explain the bombing of Afghanistan and to appeal for peace between Israelis and Palestinians. "We believe that the policies that the United States is pursuing are ones that are good for the Middle East as a whole," she said during the October 15 interview. Although Rice told the interviewer that the United States had no plan to review U.S. policies in the volatile Middle East, she echoed comments issued by U.S. administration leaders that favored Palestinian statehood. Rice defended the UN sanctions against Iraq and claimed that Iraqis led a better life in areas where the United Nations administered its so-called oil-for-food program than in areas where Iraqi President Saddam Hussein controlled the program. Rice also reemphasized that the campaign against terrorism was not aimed at Islam; the hijackers were mostly Arab Muslims, and Afghanistan is a non-Arab Muslim state.

Before she taped the interview with Al-Jazeera, Rice answered questions from White House reporters in Washington. She was asked why so many top administration officials had agreed to appear on Al-Jazeera. "We do think it is important that we get our message out to Arab publics, and we know this is a network that is very popular with Arab publics," she said. Rice added that she would not appear on Al-Jazeera if she did not respect it.

The day after Rice's interview, U.S. Defense Secretary Donald Rumsfeld appeared on the network. He blamed Taliban antiaircraft fire for some of the civilian casualties: "It kills people on the ground when it comes back down." He added that the United States had approved $320 million in aid for Afghanistan and that U.S. troops were stationed abroad at the request of foreign governments for only as long as those governments approved. "This effort is not against the Afghanistan people, it's not against any race or any religion. It is against terrorism and terrorists and the senior people that are harboring terrorists," Rumsfeld said.

Middle East analysts noted that U.S. officials finally were addressing Arabs directly. Mindful of the Arab public's unfavorable position on the war in Afghanistan, many of these analysts pushed for a stronger explanation from Washington. Veteran Egyptian TV anchor and media expert Hamdi Qandil told the Associated Press on October 17, 2001, "This [U.S. officials' interviews with Al-Jazeera] shows that for the first time, the Americans admit that they must address the people, not just the rulers. Their friendship with the Arab governments is not enough."

AL-JAZEERA IN AFGHANISTAN

The main reason for Al-Jazeera's rocket ride to fame in the Western world may be its on-the-ground coverage of the war in

Afghanistan. It was the only broadcast network permitted in Kabul in September 2001 (the Taliban had ejected all other foreign journalists from Afghanistan after the September 11 terrorist attacks). Only two Al-Jazeera correspondents remained on site.

Two years earlier, Al-Jazeera had applied for and was granted permission from the Taliban to open two bureaus in Kabul and Kandahar. "At the same time permission was granted to us, it was also granted to CNN, Reuters, and APTN (Associated Press Television Network)," managing director Al-Ali said. "The others didn't move in, because they didn't consider it [Afghanistan] very important and didn't see much news coming out of there. But for us it was important, because Afghanistan is an Islamic country," he added.

Since its arrival in Afghanistan at the end of 1999, Al-Jazeera correspondents have covered the northern regions of the country, where Northern Alliance troops were based. "We planned to open an office in the north, but it's very, very difficult to get people in to those areas. But we were there, covering both sides, the North and the Taliban," Al-Ali said.

Chief news editor Helal explained further, "A year ago, we sent Mohammed Safi—who before coming to Al-Jazeera was a correspondent for Abu Dhabi TV in Pakistan, and had good connections with the Northern Alliance—into northern Afghanistan. He got exclusive interviews with everybody—including more than half an hour with Massoud [Ahmed Shah Massoud, the assassinated Northern Alliance leader], which was unprecedented for an Arab journalist."

However, after Massoud was killed on September 9, 2001—by two Algerian suicide-terrorists posing as journalists, a bomb hidden in their camera—it became all but impossible to get an Arab reporter into northern Afghanistan. Still, according to Al-Ali, Al-Jazeera invited many leaders of the North, such as Foreign

Minister Abdullah Abdullah and the Uzbeki leader Abdel Rashid Dostam, to appear on its programs.

A major reason for Al-Jazeera's success in getting exclusives from Afghanistan was due to the experience of its two correspondents in Kabul and Kandahar. Allouni, Al-Jazeera's bearded Kabul correspondent, who usually appears on camera dressed in a khaki vest, explained during a November 22, 2001, interview on Al-Jazeera that his experience between 1992 and 1996 as a reporter in Afghanistan directly impacted his ability to get the story ahead of any other news agency. Allouni added, however, that he faced constant problems with the Taliban's infamous Ministry for the Suppression of Vice and the Promotion of Virtue, for it prohibited the use of TV cameras. "I tried to convince them that we are a satellite network, not a newspaper, and thus our use of the camera was essential; and after lots of efforts, we were able to get their permission to use a camera, but with restrictions," said Allouni, who was arrested and imprisoned several times by Taliban forces for using the camera in restricted sites.

WHEN THE WORLD'S ATTENTION FOCUSED ON AL-JAZEERA

Al-Jazeera made headlines in March 2001 when the world braced itself as the Taliban ordered the destruction of two colossal statues of the Buddha that date to the fifth century. Al-Jazeera filmed the event. It alerted the world to the Taliban regime, which not only restricted citizen rights but also flagrantly disregarded international pressures to save these historically important religious monuments. Little did the world know that this desecration of Buddhist icons would be followed by violent events on a global scale, as well as a string of compelling news firsts for Al-Jazeera aired from the mountains of the once-neglected Afghanistan. The network's unique position in Afghanistan and its lengthy 1998 interview with bin Laden, which it rebroadcast with English subtitles not long after the September 11 attacks, would grab the world's attention.

Al-Jazeera broadcast the only pictures of Afghan demonstrators attacking and setting fire to the empty U.S. Embassy in Kabul on September 26, 2001. It made headlines again a few days later with a report that Al-Qaeda had captured three U.S. Special Forces operatives and two Afghan-U.S. citizens near the border with Iran. Both the Taliban and the U.S. government denied it; however, Al-Jazeera stood by its report, saying that a member of Al-Qaeda had called its bureau in Pakistan to provide details of the capture.

When the U.S. bombs started falling on Kabul in October, Al-Jazeera reporter Allouni ran for the rooftop of the Al-Jazeera bureau. He set up a spotlight, taking care not to make it too bright. Then he proceeded to give a live report. "I don't want to be a target myself, otherwise you'll be without news," he said jokingly in an interview with the Associated Press. "The city's power has been cut; I'm in the dark and will become a sitting duck if the missiles zero in on me."

Al-Jazeera's exclusive footage from Afghanistan was hardly free of controversy. Its graphic footage of young children bruised and bandaged in Kabul hospital beds, mothers wailing and lamenting the loss of families, elderly men lying helpless in tents, bodies laid out on stretchers, homes reduced to rubble—all were devastating for many viewers. "There were some very painful images of civilians who suffered from the bombing, but the network's editors preferred not to air them for humanity's sake," Allouni explained during his November interview on Al-Jazeera. Although Allouni suggested that the footage had been edited before being aired, the images were still too distressing for wider consumption. U.S. officials feared that the images would compromise Arab and Muslim support for the antiterrorist campaign. One image showed a dead child with a pronounced bullet hole in his head. Footage of this sort was seen as counterproductive to the pursuit of bin Laden and Al-Qaeda. U.S. networks chose not to purchase or rebroadcast this footage.

Al-Jazeera's wide-ranging coverage may have raised hackles among members of the Taliban and other fundamentalist groups inside Afghanistan, but it enthralled the rest of the world. In fact, CNN relied on the retransmission of Al-Jazeera's images from Kabul and Kandahar in its coverage of the war and its more frightening aspects. Commenting on Al-Jazeera's exclusive footage, ABC News anchorman Peter Jennings said during an interview on PBS's *NewsHour* in October 2001, "We are listening to live broadcasting from Kabul via an Arabic reporter through an Arabic television company based in the Persian Gulf in Qatar, which has been a real window on the world for people all over the region."

Al-Jazeera's popularity has skyrocketed in the U.S. and the world media. Suddenly, offers from news organizations around the world began pouring in to Al-Jazeera, as did the requests for information. Journalists from various news outlets crowded Al-Jazeera's newsroom, director's office, e-mail in-boxes, and telephone lines with requests for interviews, requests for resource-sharing, and questions about the controversial footage and videotapes, some hoping to make deals, others wanting to cover Al-Jazeera as it covered the news. The hype turned Al-Jazeera into an overnight sensation and made it a household name. Some U.S. TV shows devoted major segments to lampooning Al-Jazeera. One episode of NBC's *Saturday Night Live*, broadcast on December 1, 2001, opened, "It is now 11:30, and if you are not watching Al-Jazeera, we are live from New York, it's Saturday Night!" The *Brain Trust*, a newspaper of political satire and the British equivalent of *The Onion*, ran a spoof about Al-Jazeera in its November 16, 2001, issue. The headline read that popular comedian and actor Bill Cosby had signed a $1.2 million contract to host talk shows, game programs, and occasional made-for-TV movies on Al-Jazeera. The article poked fun at Mohammed Jasim Al-Ali, the network's managing director, as well as its now-famous reporter in Afghanistan, Tayseer Allouni. The online version of the publication even allowed commentary about the article, with phony responses from Al Sharpton and Oprah Winfrey.

For Arab-speaking audiences without satellite subscriptions to Al-Jazeera, many visit the network's website at aljazeera.net. Abdulaziz Almahmoud, the chief editor of the website, reported that the daily hit count rose from pre-September 11 levels of about 1 million to an astounding 7 million.

With so much traffic on the network's website, Ghida Fakhry, Al-Jazeera's New York City correspondent, commented during a radio interview with the Foreign Policy Association in October 2001 about the stunning growth in the network's popularity: "There have been more people willing to speak to us, I think, and approaching us. Just general interest in finding out more about the station. You've had numerous stories run in the different newspapers and TV stations about Al-Jazeera."

U.S. NETWORKS OBJECT TO THE AL-JAZEERA–CNN DEAL

Since the beginning of the war in Afghanistan, Al-Jazeera frequently aired prepackaged reports and live shots from its Kabul-based reporter, Allouni, and, by videophone, from its other Kandahar correspondent, Youssef Al-Shouly. It soon grew obvious to Al-Jazeera and CNN management that some kind of affiliate relationship would be mutually advantageous. Days after the September 11 attacks, the two networks negotiated deals to exchange footage and resources. Originally, CNN would receive six-hour exclusive rights to Al-Jazeera footage and remote access to news-breaking locations like Kabul through the Al-Jazeera correspondent. In return Al-Jazeera would receive access to northern Afghanistan through a CNN correspondent, professional assistance with crews and equipment in other Afghan cities, and access to CNN's syndicated news feed. In addition, CNN shipped a satellite uplink facility for both networks to use.

The relationship between Al-Jazeera and CNN began in January 2001 when Ghida Fakhry began filing stories for CNN's *World Report.* Then in June 2001, Fakhry accompanied Al-Jazeera's vice chairman to CNN's annual World Report conference, the first meeting between the two networks' top executives. That led to a visit by the head of CNN's news-gathering operations to Al-Jazeera's Qatar headquarters, a visit that paved the way for the deal that was signed by the two networks at the start of the war in Afghanistan.

Once the war started and the media frenzy hit full stride, the exclusivity arrangement between Al-Jazeera and CNN came under fire when rival U.S. networks, unhappy with the deal, started using Al-Jazeera footage and criticizing CNN. The Associated Press reported in October that Al-Jazeera's managing director, Al-Ali, faxed a letter to several U.S. networks the day before the U.S. strikes on Afghanistan that stated the network had established an "exclusive relationship" with CNN; any network that violated that agreement would "be held legally responsible and could face prosecution in a court of law."

Several networks cited fair use, which they contended allowed widespread use of broadcast material during times of national emergency. "These were the only pictures from an area where the United States was beginning a war. There was no question we would use them," said Dianne Brandi, vice president of legal affairs at Fox News in an interview with the Associated Press on October 7, 2001.

Fox and ABC didn't even bother checking with CNN. CBS and NBC executives did, however, and were told CNN was enforcing its agreement with Al-Jazeera. Both networks used the video anyway. "The American public's interest was served today [October 7, 2001] by putting its right to be informed above petty competitive issues," said CBS spokeswoman Sandra Genelius, also in an interview with the Associated Press. According to NBC news spokeswoman Barbara Levin in an interview with the *Boston Globe* on October 8, 2001, "When America was attacked on September 11, the networks put competition aside and responsibly served the public and shared footage. When America struck back, CNN chose a different path despite a request that they make their material available." Another network spokesman, ABC's Jeff Schneider, was quoted in the same Boston Globe interview: "We just felt there was an overwhelming natural interest in showing these important images to the American people, which outweighed any commercial agenda CNN was trying to pursue in this hour of national emergency. We expect this will be worked out to everyone's satisfaction."

CNN spokesman Matthew Furman declined to respond to these criticisms, but he added (in the same *Globe* interview) that "given what's going on right now and the seriousness of events, we have no plans to enforce our limited exclusivity with Al-Jazeera." After the bin Laden video was aired by several networks on October 7, 2001, CNN chairman Walter Isaacson said to the Associated Press on the same day, "I'm not going to worry about it [the arrangement with Al-Jazeera]. The biggest issue right now is not to worry about the competition, but to worry about covering this the best that we can."

Al-Jazeera officials, for their part, sent stern letters to the U.S. networks on the day after the U.S. strikes on Afghanistan, threatening to take legal action if the networks continued to use footage that was exclusive to CNN for the first six hours after Al-Jazeera's transmission. However, they did not press their claims. Instead, they acknowledged that the network had, after all, become the network of the moment and that all the major U.S. networks were fighting to get Al-Jazeera footage.

The recent upsurge of success has started to pay off financially for Al-Jazeera, as revenues from subscriptions and footage fees have increased. The network's managing director, Al-Ali, said in many recent interviews that Al-Jazeera has charged as much as $250,000 for a three-minute clip from the 1998 bin Laden interview. He would not say how much CNN and other media outlets were being charged for the right to the most recent clips, although he said it was less than $1 million. "We're making good money," he said to the *New York Times* on October 12, 2001. The BBC directly paid Al-Jazeera for the footage it used during the first day of the U.S. strikes on Afghanistan. But since then, BBC had been receiving Al-Jazeera footage from other news agencies. Al-Jazeera also reported that it saw an "exponential increase" in subscription orders for its cable-based service in the United States and Australia.

Al-Jazeera's many commercial deals include one it signed in October 2001 with the U.K. network Sky Television that would make its broadcasts available to Sky's digital viewers in the United Kingdom and Europe. In the United States, Viacom engaged in talks with Al-Jazeera, though no agreement was confirmed. And a few days after the start of U.S. strikes in Afghanistan, ABC News reached a nonexclusive agreement with Al-Jazeera that entitles each network to use the other's facilities and footage while covering the war on terrorism.

In his October 2001 interview with the online journal *Transnational Broadcasting Studies*, Al-Ali referred to Al-Jazeera's deal with CNBC to put together an Arabic-language business news network. "We haven't decided when it will be launched, because we haven't signed the last agreement. But we've signed a memo of understanding, about a month ago. Top CNBC executives came here to meet with us. The plan is for a network starting with six hours of transmission which will gradually increase to 24 hours," he said.

If Al-Jazeera is to hold on to its sudden global success, such financial deals are essential, especially because it is trying to gain financial independence from its host country, Qatar.

AL-JAZEERA SCOOPS THE ARAB WORLD

Al-Jazeera's rocket-ride to fame in the Western world is only part of the story, however. Time and again, it scoops other Arab news networks on breaking stories. Al-Jazeera's first exclusive news story from within the Arab region was in December 1998, when U.S. and U.K. air forces mounted raids against Baghdad over four nights. Saddam Hussein chose to announce his survival and speak directly to the Arab world on Al-Jazeera. On January 5, 1999, Al-Jazeera scored another coup when it broadcast, before even the Iraqi media, Saddam's Army Day speech in which he called on Arabs to overthrow their leaders if they allied with the United States. Al-Ali told BBC News on January 7, 1999, "The American CNN and British BBC were also considered . . . but Saddam preferred Al-Jazeera for its credibility and wide audience in the Arab world. . . . Our station refuses to be any regime's propaganda instrument."

But the major news story that established Al-Jazeera regionally as a respectable, popular, and independent Arab network was its coverage of the second Palestinian Intifada in September 2000. Provocative live shots—of Palestinian youths throwing rocks at Israeli soldiers and of Israeli troops bombing Palestinian cities in retaliation—made an impact on Arab viewers. No other Arab news network moved quickly enough to capture such images. Although it is overwhelmingly sympathetic to the Palestinian position, Al-Jazeera has not shied from presenting views that serve Israeli interests, and Palestinian violence showcased on Al-Jazeera has often worked in Israel's favor. For instance, the network was the first to broadcast footage of Palestinians firing mortars at Israeli communities, demonstrating aggression precipitated by some Palestinian groups.

Even if Al-Jazeera's coverage of the Intifada is not utterly impartial and balanced, its relentless broadcasts of the Israeli-Palestinian conflict have been a critical component to its success in the Arab world. "The crisis here is enormously important to the Arab world at large," explained Walid Al-Omari, Al-Jazeera's correspondent in the West Bank city of Ramallah. "And, of course, violence sells."

THE BOMBING OF THE KABUL BUREAU

Al-Jazeera's Kabul bureau was destroyed by a U.S. missile on November 13, 2001, hours before Northern Alliance troops entered the Afghan capital. Al-Jazeera headquarters in Doha temporarily lost contact with Allouni, the local correspondent who resided in the two-story building.

Allouni was missing for more than a day after he left the bureau, but he called Al-Jazeera headquarters November 14, 2001, to say he was safe and near the border with Pakistan. He added in a later interview broadcast on Al-Jazeera that he and the rest of the ten-member Kabul staff left the bureau only minutes before the attack. He fled the city shortly before midnight and said he witnessed "scenes that . . . I'm sorry . . . I couldn't describe to anybody." Allouni, himself an Arab, was concerned about Northern Alliance reprisals against Arabs in Kabul after their leader, Massoud, was killed by Arab assassins who posed as journalists. Kabul fell into complete chaos as the ruling Taliban forces abandoned the capital just hours ahead of the advancing Northern Alliance tanks.

Allouni said he was assaulted as he fled the Afghan capital amid the Taliban retreat. He would not say who attacked him and the rest of the Kabul office staff. They were saved by tribesmen who also retrieved their equipment, he added. Allouni returned to Qatar to receive medical treatment for a slipped back disc. He said he plans to return to Afghanistan. Al-Shouly, Al-Jazeera's correspondent in Kandahar, also decided to leave Afghanistan for his own safety.

With its two key reporters out of action, Al-Jazeera was temporarily reduced to airing footage from other TV networks. However, plans were made to send more reporters to the Afghan capital. "We have a new team led by three journalists who are en route at this moment for Pakistan from where they hope to go into Afghanistan," managing director Al-Ali told Agence France Presse on November 14, 2001.

During his interview with Al-Jazeera in November, Allouni was asked by Algerian anchorwoman Khaduja bin Guna whether he thought the bombing of the Kabul bureau was intentional. Allouni responded simply, "Our location has always been known to them." Entire shows on Al-Jazeera were dedicated to discussing possible U.S. intentions to deliberately eliminate the Al-Jazeera bureau. And naturally, the event fed advocates of conspiracy theories, especially those who claim that the United States will use its power to undermine any opposition.

AL-JAZEERA AND CNN: PARTNERS NO MORE

On January 31, 2002, Al-Jazeera announced it was severing its relationship with CNN. Al-Jazeera made the decision after CNN broadcast, that same day, excerpts from the exclusive interview that Tayseer Allouni had conducted with bin Laden on October 21, 2001, one month before the Taliban regime collapsed. Al-Jazeera had never aired the interview and even denied its existence; its officials were not aware of CNN's intention to broadcast the tape.

According to a *New York Times* article published on February 1, one day after the renunciation of the CNN partnership, Al-

Jazeera executives denied initial knowledge of the interview. According to the article, after U.S. and Middle Eastern officials who had viewed the videotape confirmed that it was conducted by the network, Al-Jazeera executives said they would not air it because it did not meet the network's standards and was not newsworthy.

CNN felt otherwise. "Once that videotape was in our possession, we felt we had to report it and show it because it is extremely newsworthy," said Eason Jordan, CNN's chief news executive. "And we really were dumbfounded as to why Al-Jazeera would decide not to air or even acknowledge the existence of the videotape."

Jordan said CNN worked "very hard to establish and maintain and grow a very, very good relationship with Al-Jazeera, but this is a tough spot." He said the Arab network "has some very tough questions to answer. Among them, why was the interview not ever televised, why did Al-Jazeera initially deny the existence of the tape, and what other tape does Al-Jazeera have, or did it have, that had never been acknowledged or televised. Clearly a lot of interesting material has fallen into Al-Jazeera's hands."

Transcripts from this bin Laden interview have been circulating among U.S. officials and intelligence organizations since early November 2001. U.S. officials refused to discuss the circumstances surrounding the videotaped interview publicly to avoid jeopardizing the method by which it was obtained. When asked about the videotape, however, one U.S. official told the *New York Times* on February 2, 2002, that Al-Jazeera tried to be "responsible" in what it does and doesn't broadcast. CNN announced on January 31, 2002, that it obtained the tape "independently" from a nongovernment source. CNN also claimed that it did not know about the interview until a *New York Times* story on December 12, 2001, revealed the interview's existence.

British Prime Minister Tony Blair was evidently aware of the interview's existence when he first referred to it during a November 2001 speech before the British Parliament. In that speech, he quoted at least one translated excerpt that supported the West's case that bin Laden was responsible for the September 11 attacks.

Al-Jazeera officials have refused to appear on CNN to discuss the bin Laden interview, and they refused to say where the interview was conducted. However, Al-Ali issued the following statement on January 31, 2002: "Al-Jazeera denounces the fact that CNN resorted to such illegal ways to obtain this tape. Al-Jazeera would have expected CNN to use its judgment and respect its special relationship with Al-Jazeera by not airing material that Al-Jazeera itself chose not to broadcast. Al-Jazeera does not feel it is obligated to explain its position and its reasoning of why it chose not to air the interview. Al-Jazeera will nonetheless respond to CNN's airing of the interview using its own means in its own way. Furthermore, Al-Jazeera will sever its relationship with CNN and will take the necessary action to punish the organizations and individuals who stole this video and distributed it illegally."

In response to Al-Jazeera's statement, CNN stated that "it did nothing illegal in obtaining this tape, and nothing illegal in airing it. Our affiliate agreement with Al-Jazeera gives us the express right to use any and all footage owned or controlled by Al-Jazeera without limitation."

In a phone interview with Al-Ali on February 2, 2002, he added, "We [Al-Jazeera] never denied having this interview. But we said in our interviews with Reuters, AP, and others that we have tapes and interviews from bin Laden that we decided not to air because we thought they were not newsworthy." Al-Ali refused to comment on the decision to sever his network's agreement with CNN, stating that everything was expressed in Al-Jazeera's formal statement.

However, Al-Jazeera issued a follow-up statement to the Associated Press on February 2, 2002, in which it expressed "bewilderment" at CNN's position. It said CNN obtained the tape in an "unknown way and aired it without Al-Jazeera's approval and without explaining the circumstances of the interview." Kabul correspondent Allouni, who gave several exclusive interviews to Al-Jazeera after returning to Qatar, never mentioned the October 21 interview of bin Laden.

During that one-hour interview of bin Laden, Allouni seemed to establish a professional rapport and, as CNN pointed out, even interrupted the Al-Qaeda leader to ask questions. When bin Laden was asked about U.S. accusations that he was involved in the September 11 attacks, he replied that the charge is "unwarranted." But he later added, "If inciting people to do that is terrorism, and if killing those who kill our sons is terrorism, then let history be witness that we are terrorists."

During the interview, bin Laden ridiculed White House concerns that other on-camera statements he issued after September 11 carried hidden messages. "They made hilarious claims. They said that Osama's messages have codes in them to the terrorists. It's as if we were living in the time of mail by carrier pigeon, when there are no phones, no travelers, no Internet, no regular mail, no express mail and no electronic mail. I mean, these are very humorous things. They discount people's intellect," he said.

In answering a question about the anthrax attacks in the States, bin Laden said, "These diseases are a punishment from God and a response to oppressed mothers' prayers in Lebanon, Iraq, Palestine, and everywhere."

The rift between Al-Jazeera and CNN made headlines on the latter network on January 31 and February 1, 2002, but it was not even mentioned in Al-Jazeera's news bulletins. Although the

squabble continues, this recent development has raised fundamental questions that as of yet remain unanswered, and hence
troubling to followers of the Arab world's broadcasting leader. Al-
Jazeera's logic in deciding not to broadcast the interview is impossible to follow, and its refusal to respond to criticism makes it look
all the more suspicious. For its part, CNN is in the unenviable position of having to explain how it acquired the tape and whether
airing it was a violation of the mutual agreement it had with Al-
Jazeera.

OSAMA BIN LADEN AND AL-JAZEERA

Today Osama bin Laden is a global media figure to say the least,
perhaps unmatched in TV broadcasting's short history. As
bombs fell on Afghanistan, a new men's cologne hit the markets
in neighboring Pakistan, named after the man himself. The label
reads "Osama bin Laden," and just below is a smiling portrait of
the Al-Qaeda leader. Elsewhere, in the streets of old Cairo, a
street vendor laughs as he explains to an unconvinced passerby
the difference in flavors between the types of dates he offers for
sale. The priciest dates were marked "bin Laden," the mediocre
ones "Bush," (named after U.S. President George W. Bush) and
the cheapest "Sharon" (named after Israeli Prime Minister Ariel
Sharon). For many of these people, as well as Americans, bin
Laden's name will be forever linked to Al-Jazeera after the network aired that six-minute videotape on the first day of U.S. military strikes in Afghanistan.

It is one thing to broadcast a videotape of bin Laden, but it is
another thing entirely to support him. In an article in the
November 18, 2001, issue of the *New York Times Magazine*,
Middle Eastern scholar Fouad Ajami argued that Al-Jazeera used
its power in the pan-Arab media sphere to represent bin Laden,
making him out to be a hero. However, it needs to be noted that
the U.S. networks did exactly as Al-Jazeera did. They aired the

very same footage that Al-Jazeera aired: images of bin Laden seated on the ground, another of him firing a rifle, another of him clad in military fatigues. On any given day during the early days of the conflict, the same footage could be seen on all networks—Al-Jazeera, Fox, CNN, ABC—down even to local TV news shows.

Any news that covers bin Laden engenders immediate interest from practically any audience. He is the critical element that drives the media's rhetorical and sensational construction of the war today. Some people in the United States now know more about the life of bin Laden than they know about top U.S. government officials.

The mistake, however, is to assume that bin Laden is more than a celebrity—that he is a star or hero—because Al-Jazeera has given him so much airtime. Instead, he is as much a selling point for Al-Jazeera and its host country, Qatar, as the Gulf War was for CNN and the United States. The truth is that although Al-Jazeera has filled headlines in the Arab world since its inception in 1996, the events of September 11 and the network's exclusive access to bin Laden created a formula that made Al-Jazeera a household name. Such access has proven to be financially rewarding as well. Al-Jazeera, like the other Middle Eastern private media, is hoping to sustain itself through independent revenue sources, not government handouts. Right now, bin Laden news clips drive network viewership and advertising sales. But with the rush of success comes a harbinger of caution.

Al-Jazeera earned many of its exclusives prior to September 11, but its coverage of bin Laden surely overshadows those achievements. At some point bin Laden will become old news. Will Al-Jazeera be old news, too? It seems unlikely. Instead, the network's ability to uncover meaningful stories, conduct investigative journalism, and provide cutting-edge news has established and confirmed its integrity to a critical and cautious West.

8

Al-Jazeera and the West:
The Love-Hate Relationship

A U.S. State Department official tunes into Al-Jazeera everyday to watch its programs; he is only one among many U.S. government employees who do so. "We recognize it [Al-Jazeera] as a powerful voice with a wide viewership in the Arab world. It is a media outlet of importance in the Arab world," he said. Before the U.S. air strikes against Afghanistan started on October 7, 2001, his statement could be taken as general opinion among the many diplomats, consultants, lobbyists, and officials in Washington, D.C. who watch Al-Jazeera. Al-Jazeera has become well-received, perhaps due to its free style of programming. All that seemed to change after October 7. The debate over Al-Jazeera's coverage and editorial choices soon raised many questions about the duty of free media during times of crisis and war, not just in the Middle East but also across the globe.

The American Perception of Al-Jazeera

U.S. diplomats formally complained to top Qatari officials that Al-Jazeera was giving too much airtime to anti-U.S. activists, especially the suspected terrorist Osama bin Laden. U.S. officials also complained that Al-Jazeera provided airtime to experts hostile to U.S. policy. These complaints came after the network, which at one point was the only TV network in Taliban-controlled territories, aired several messages from bin Laden and other Al-Qaeda leaders. "It [Al-Jazeera] is an important station in the Arab world; our concern, however, is that they give an undue amount of time and attention to some very vitriolic, irresponsible kinds of statements," U.S. Secretary of State Colin Powell said during an interview on ABC's *Good Morning America.* The *New York Times* reported that Powell, who was interviewed on Al-Jazeera a few days after the September 11 attacks, had asked the Qatari emir, Sheikh Hamad bin Khalifa Al-Thani, during their Washington, D.C. meeting on October 3, 2001 to "tone down" Al-Jazeera's inflammatory rhetoric. The emir said he would consider the U.S. complaints as "friendly advice." He added in a joint news conference with Powell following that meeting that Qatar "heard from this administration, as well as previous U.S. administrations, on this issue. Parliamentary life requires you have free and credible media, and that is what we are trying to do."

U.S. officials' dissatisfaction with Al-Jazeera's coverage of the Afghan crisis drew angry responses from the station and other advocates of a free press, who together claimed that the United States was trying to muzzle one of the most independent voices among the Arab media. "We learned media independence from the United States, and now the American officials want us to give up what we learned from them," Al-Jazeera's managing director, Mohammed Jasim Al-Ali, said during a phone interview on December 10, 2001. "Our critics tend to forget that bin Laden is one side in this war that we need to present to our viewers. How would our news be balanced without presenting both sides?"

The International Press Institute sent a letter to Colin Powell on October 8, 2001, stating that any attempt by one country to curtail the news reporting of an independent TV network based in another country is "an infringement of editorial independence and has serious consequences for press freedom." This was just one of many letters sent in support of Al-Jazeera's coverage and editorial license. However, U.S. State Department officials defended the Bush administration's position, claiming that Washington had no influence or control over what Al-Jazeera— or any other network, for that matter—broadcasts. In a phone interview, a department spokesperson said that Secretary Powell does not maintain policy positions on the media. "The particular issue that came up with Al-Jazeera was that its repeated broadcast of unedited bin Laden tapes tended to provide a platform for bin Laden to spread his inflammatory messages," said the spokesperson, who spoke on condition of anonymity. "We have the right when we see something that we disagree with to express our opinion, whether it is about foreign or domestic media," he added.

The State Department's concerns came one week after U.S. officials attempted to prevent an interview with Taliban leader Mullah Mohammed Omar from being aired on *Voice of America*. "Considering the fact that U.S. taxpayers pay for this [VOA], we don't think that the head of the Taliban belongs on this radio station," said U.S. State Department spokesman Richard Boucher during an interview with the *Washington Post* on October 7, 2001. One hundred and fifty VOA journalists signed a petition protesting the State Department's move. They were backed by the Washington Post—and they won. The interview was aired on September 28, 2001, as scheduled.

The White House backed the State Department when it objected to the October broadcast of bin Laden's videotaped messages. National Security Advisor Condoleezza Rice criticized Al-Jazeera for the broadcast on the grounds that the video, among other things, could be used to send coded messages to terrorists in so-called sleeper cells in the United States and elsewhere to

kill Americans or prepare for their next attack. After a conference call with Rice, executives of the five major U.S. networks—
ABC, CBS, CNN, NBC, and Fox—agreed not to broadcast
videotaped remarks from bin Laden or his aides in their entirety
without first carefully reviewing them. They also agreed to avoid
repeatedly broadcasting excerpts from these tapes. "We'll do
whatever is our patriotic duty," said Australian-born U.S. citizen
Rupert Murdoch, owner of Fox News, in an interview with the
Guardian on October 15, 2001. Rice also appealed to the editors
of leading U.S. newspapers not to publish full transcripts of the
bin Laden messages.

However, Rice's reference to coded messages did not convince
many journalists. Gerard Baker, a *London Times* columnist,
wrote, "It seems improbable that 'sleeper' units of the Al-Qaeda
terrorist network in the U.S. would be sitting glued to ABC
World News Tonight on the off-chance that they might get a signal from their leader." Howard Rosenberg, a columnist for the
Los Angeles Times, wrote, "Journalists have an obligation to their
nation, but also to a free flow of information, as much as that is
possible during war. Americans have the right to see for themselves whom they are fighting, for example, and watching bin
Laden and others vow further violence provided at least a
glimpse into the soul of terrorism."

Even technical experts and specialists doubted that the bin
Laden tapes would include any high-tech visual cues or hidden
messages. "There are so many easier ways for him [bin Laden] to
communicate with his allies that are completely plausible," said
Bruce Schneier, an Internet security specialist, in an interview
with the *Los Angeles Times*. Schneier said terrorists can keep in
touch, for example, by using free and anonymous e-mail accounts that can be used a few times and then discarded.

Professional journalism or media organizations joined the fray
and expressed opposition to the calls for Al-Jazeera to stop air-

ing the bin Laden videos. Reporters Sans Frontières (Reporters Without Borders), a London-based international advocacy group for media freedom, denounced the White House request to suspend the broadcast of bin Laden's speeches as "censorship." Robert Menard, the group's general secretary, was quoted in the *Guardian* as saying that the United States was "joining the many authoritarian regimes in the Middle East who have little respect for freedom of the press, in their criticism of Al-Jazeera." Menard added that "information pluralism must be respected in all circumstances."

Nevertheless, Ari Fleischer, the White House press secretary, was quoted in several U.S. publications as saying, "At best, Osama bin Laden's message is propaganda, calling on people to kill Americans. At worst, he could be issuing orders," thus reaffirming Rice's conjecture.

But it didn't stop there. Other critics accused Al-Jazeera of outright collusion with bin Laden. Zev Chafets, reporting in his *New York Daily News* column, claimed that "Al-Jazeera is the favorite network of bin Laden. It provides him with an unedited forum for his calls to jihad [holy war]. Al-Jazeera is far from legitimate. It is an Arab propaganda outfit controlled by the medieval government of Qatar that masquerades as a real media company."

In response, Al-Jazeera's Washington bureau chief, Hafez Al-Mirazi, told the *New York Post* that the tendency of "thugs" like bin Laden to seek out specific media should not necessarily undermine the station's reputation for journalistic integrity. "It's the same reason that the Unabomber would send a letter or fax to the *New York Times*; it's a matter of credibility with the audience," said Al-Mirazi.

Moreover, Al-Jazeera's chairman of the board, Sheikh Hamad bin Thamer Al-Thani, said in an interview with the *Washington Times* on October 15, 2001, "I am not in a position to know whether there is a message in any videotape we receive. Our target is to do things professionally from a journalistic point of view. We leave security concerns to security people. If we have scoops, we will cover them."

One news analyst, who spoke on condition of anonymity, told *Middle East News Online* in mid-October that he opposed what he described as "vacuous" attacks on Al-Jazeera. "When there is no freedom of the press in a country, that country is vilified and accused of being oppressive and undemocratic. Yet when a particular country makes a great effort toward freedom of expression and democracy, you find those who advocate taking action to have it silenced," he said.

Meanwhile, despite the uproar, Al-Jazeera officials seemed willing to listen to the U.S. pleas. "There have been comments from the United States and we have listened to them. If there are errors, which is possible in any journalistic work, it will be normal to rectify it," the Al-Jazeera chairman told the Associated Press on October 11, 2001. However, he also vowed to continue airing bin Laden's taped messages and said the network would continue "to follow the same professional path that it has followed since its launch as a media outlet with a margin of liberty in the Arab world." This prompted one diplomat stationed in Doha to claim in an interview with Agence France Presse that the issue "risks harming Qatar, whose leaders do not seem to be able to take stock of the deep anger of the United States."

The United States reported further frustration with Al-Jazeera's coverage of the war after the network ran footage of Afghan casualties along with a barrage of images that included wounded children, whom Al-Jazeera correspondents on the scene claimed were injured by U.S. bombs. U.S. officials argued that such images fed Arab wrath toward U.S. military activities and encouraged anti-American sentiments throughout the

Middle East. On several occasions, U.S. Secretary of Defense Donald Rumsfeld described Al-Jazeera's coverage as propagandistic and inflammatory. He also accused the Arab network of manufacturing footage of dead civilians. Al-Jazeera, as it had many times before, defended its journalistic integrity and the public's right to view these images.

"Talking heads just can't compete with powerful images; the images touch emotions, and people in this part of the world [the Middle East] react according to their emotions," a Western diplomat in Washington told the *New York Times*. After several weeks in the fall of 2001 of watching TV footage of U.S. missiles streaking across the skies of Afghanistan and civilians in bloody bandages, many Arabs have become skeptical about the war's aim.

The *San Francisco Chronicle*'s correspondent in Cairo, Egypt, Frank Viviano, conducted several interviews with Egyptians who followed Al-Jazeera's coverage of the war. "No way the U.S. military should do this," one Cairo shopkeeper told the *Chronicle* on October 8, 2001. Another Egyptian, a businessman from Cairo, in the same issue asked, "In killing this one man, bin Laden, can you justify what will happen to men, women, and children in Afghanistan? What he has done to America is a violation of Islam. But what of the harm that America has done to innocent people here?"

Al-Jazeera journalists have insisted time and again that they are simply striving to cover the war from both sides. "Because we aim to be objective, we have to show those graphic images," said Ibrahim Helal, Al-Jazeera's chief news editor, in a November interview with the Associated Press. "Do you think we invented them?" In fact, the network has exercised some discretion in showing images from Afghanistan, and Helal said the network aired less than a quarter of the shots of dead bodies in the footage it received.

Still, Al-Jazeera's Afghanistan correspondents often added personal commentary. For example, one Al-Jazeera reporter told viewers that Afghan civilians had nowhere to hide because the "U.S. strikes no longer distinguish between one place and another." Even their soiled tents could be targeted, he said. What U.S. networks referred to as the "war on terrorism," Al-Jazeera referred to as "so-called terrorism" or "the U.S. war on what they called terrorism."

Chief news editor Helal explained to the Associated Press that Al-Jazeera believed the World Trade Center and Pentagon attacks were terrorist acts, but recent measures taken by the United States could not be described as targeting terrorism. "We cannot consider them acts against terrorism; those measures included arresting innocent people, threatening many countries, and bombing civilian places," he said.

William Rugh, a former U.S. ambassador to the Middle East and now head of AMIDEAST, a nonprofit organization devoted to promoting U.S. relations with the Arab world, said Al-Jazeera's coverage is a reflection of the broader public discussion in the Arab world. "They [Al-Jazeera reporters] are not deliberately anti-American any more than the private and public debate is anti-American in the region," he explained to the Associated Press on November 7, 2001. Marda Dunsky of Northwestern University's Medill School of Journalism, a former correspondent in the Middle East, told the Associated Press that even in the United States, where objectivity is emphasized, the audience can color the coverage. "We report things from the American point of view," she said.

Bridget Foley, an associate producer at CBS's *60 Minutes*, told New Jersey's *Newark Star-Ledger*, "There are many criticisms of Al-Jazeera's objectivity. You could argue that Al-Jazeera is too pro-Mideast or pro-Arab, but our news organizations are all pro-Western. That's who we are, and that's who they are. We can see the whole world from just an American perspective, and say that everybody should see it that way. But I think we'd be mistaken to do that."

U.S. officials' accusations against Al-Jazeera have not been limited to the content of war footage from Afghanistan. Several officials have accused Tayseer Allouni, the former network correspondent in Kabul, of bias and sympathy for the Taliban regime. Some critics have gone so far as to suggest that Al-Jazeera's superb access in Kabul was because Allouni was a long-time Taliban supporter, not because its reporters were braver than others. Allouni denied vehemently that he had any sympathy for the Taliban. In fact, he said Taliban leaders sometimes harassed him for not having a long-enough beard and for using TV cameras. Allouni added that he tried, like any reporter, to establish rapport with Taliban sources to get access to restricted areas. "I had good relations with some Taliban leaders and bad relations with others. But my relationship with them had not exceeded the professional lines of objectivity," he said.

These kinds of accusations might sound familiar to some readers, because CNN has been hit with variations on this theme since its inception in 1980. Americans—especially conservatives—have complained that CNN considers itself a world news entity first and an American company second. In truth, CNN's international division does not use the term "foreign" because CNN claims that it does not represent any specific nation, including the United States, in its coverage. Complaints against the Atlanta-based network intensified during the Persian Gulf War in 1991, when CNN correspondent Peter Arnett was branded a traitor to U.S. interests and journalism for reporting live from Baghdad, the Iraqi capital, and filing exclusives on Iraqi President Saddam Hussein. For CNN and Al-Jazeera, such complaints come with the territory—and for both networks that territory reaches across the globe.

In an interview conducted in December 2001, Al-Jazeera managing director Al-Ali described the similarity: "When CNN was the only foreign network allowed in Baghdad during the Gulf War, it was accused of being Iraq's mouthpiece; in Afghanistan, we were the only foreign network in the Taliban-held territories, and we were accused of being Taliban's mouthpiece." He added that there is "a professional jealousy on the American side because now we [Al-Jazeera] stand shoulder-to-shoulder with the major American networks." He went on to say that Al-Jazeera has been accused of being a CIA agent, an Israeli agent, Saddam Hussein's agent, and most recently, a Taliban agent. "This shows that we present all the sides. We must be doing something right."

Joel Campagna, program director for the Middle East at the New York-based Committee to Protect Journalists, a media watchdog group, said Al-Jazeera is well-respected in the Arab world, even by moderates. "Is it a biased channel? Sure. But every channel has at least a slight bias. I believe that they do their best to air all points of view," he said in an interview with the *Atlanta Journal-Constitution*. Howard Kurtz, host of the weekly CNN program *Reliable Sources*, also praised Al-Jazeera in a recent show: "My sense is that while they [Al-Jazeera] cover this conflict from an Arab point of view, they have a sense of journalistic balance that is all too rare in that part of the world."

Some critics claim that Al-Jazeera's bias against U.S. policy is demonstrated by the roster of guests who appear on its programs. Most guests are opposed to U.S. policy, and its critics say that Al-Jazeera has not provided equal opportunities to U.S. officials. However, Faisal Al-Kasim, host of Al-Jazeera's talk show *The Opposite Direction*, countered, "Those critics don't seem to have been watching Al-Jazeera regularly; almost all our programs have somebody to defend the American position."

Al-Jazeera has also carried news conferences by U.S. officials live, most with simultaneous Arabic translation. Moreover, its Washington bureau chief, Al-Mirazi, said during an interview on WNYC Radio that he's been begging U.S. officials to give interviews to Al-Jazeera to help the U.S. point of view. He even told U.S. officials, "Exploit us! You know, please, come, come talk to us!"

Most Arab journalists and media observers acknowledge that the United States needs to directly address the Muslim world. U.S. officials could help that effort by appearing more frequently on Al-Jazeera. "Obviously, they [U.S. officials] rethought their position; they went to Al-Jazeera to deliver their message to the Arab world," Hussein Amin, a professor of TV journalism at American University in Cairo, told the *San Francisco Chronicle* on October 20, 2001. Still, such appearances are rare. According to Amin, it could be difficult to change Arab public opinion. And without consistent participation in the political dialogue in the Middle East, Washington's chance of conveying its message is slim. "But they have to keep trying; they have to keep knocking on the door," Amin explained.

And yet the challenges persist for U.S. officials, even when they do appear on Al-Jazeera. For example, when Al-Jazeera interviewed Condoleezza Rice, many of the questions centered on Israel. Although Rice was invited to discuss the U.S. position on the war in Afghanistan, Al-Jazeera advertised the interview before it aired by playing up her remarks about the Israeli-Palestinian conflict. Al-Jazeera ran more than a dozen promos highlighting Rice's demands that Palestinians halt the violence in Israel and her defense of U.S. policy in Iraq, comments that are likely to upset Arab viewers. The ploy worked. Hamdi Qandil, a veteran Egyptian TV anchor, told the Associated Press on October 16, 2001, "America has already lost . . . before the whole interview was aired."

Al-Jazeera officials attempted to deflect claims that the network deliberately influenced Arab audiences before broadcasting
the interview. They explained that the network received the tape
in the morning and needed time to translate it and edit it to fit
into the thirty-minute weekly program *Exclusive Interview*,
which airs after midnight in the Middle East. Al-Jazeera news
editor Ahmed Al-Sheikh maintained that the West was getting a
fair chance to present its case to Muslims and Arabs. Oraib El-
Rantawi, director of the Jerusalem Center for Islamic Studies in
Amman, Jordan, said in an Associated Press interview that U.S.
officials' arguments would have been more convincing "if they
were accompanied by some crucial solutions for problems in the
region, especially the Palestinian issue." Reda Helal, an
Egyptian columnist, also told the Associated Press that the
West's public relations campaign should have preceded the military campaign. Then, "the United States and the West would
have been able to win the struggle over the Arabs' hearts and
minds."

Diverging perspectives and reactions persist on both sides—
the Middle East and the United States—as to the exact nature of
Al-Jazeera's objectivity and biases.

EUROPE AND AL-JAZEERA'S COVERAGE
IN AFGHANISTAN

Many European TV networks have also been relying on war
footage from Al-Jazeera. However, the European response has
been more favorable compared to the U.S. response. Like the
Bush administration, however, European governments urged
networks to restrict the broadcast of the bin Laden videos. And
like the Americans, Europeans argued that the tapes could contain coded messages to activate terrorist cells. But the BBC described its doubts about such speculation. "We simply don't

know. Our government . . . simply said that it is a possibility," said Richard Sambrook, director of news at BBC, in an interview with CNN in late October. "It would be a pretty inefficient way of sending out a message because the original twenty-five-minute message from bin Laden was cut down to about a minute by the Al-Jazeera network, and then cut down more by broadcasters like ourselves, and then voiced over in English, so it's pretty difficult to see how it could get through intact," he added. A spokesman for Tony Blair said the issue of what to air was an issue best left to the networks themselves. "We will leave it to them," he said in an interview with the BBC. A spokeswoman at British Independent Television News told CNN, "We will take each item on its merit."

Across the English Channel, the French media seemed more divided. Most French TV stations said they would not broadcast the complete bin Laden tapes, showing only newsworthy segments. At the same time, French newspapers ran a campaign supporting Al-Jazeera's coverage. An October 11 editorial in the newspaper *Liberation* deemed the U.S.-requested restrictions "unwise." The editorial framed its argument against the TV images of September 11: "The present conflict was born on live television. It is not so much a confrontation of two powers but of two worldviews, and its true battlefield is first and foremost that of public opinion. Instead of berating Al-Jazeera," it added, "we should ponder that mutations like the Taliban are precisely the fruit of state censorship of the media in the Arab world." It concluded: "To defend media freedom is to refuse to censor the media, even during times of war."

Spanish media seemed more willing to align with free speech and freedom of the press. Barcelona's *Avui* newspaper reported that media freedoms are in safe hands in America. In its October 12, 2001, issue, the paper stated, "Americans defend such rights and freedoms as an inalienable part of their make-up as a nation." Madrid's *El Mundo* agreed: "The freedom of information remains sacred in the United States." The latter paper noted that Spanish TV networks agreed to form a committee to decide how the Al-Jazeera footage would be broadcast yet told President Bush that they were "not prepared to exercise censorship nor to deprive the public from relevant news. The networks take the view," the paper stated, "that the free flow of information is a key element in enabling the citizens to form an honest opinion."

German networks supported Al-Jazeera. In an interview with CNN on October 10, 2001, Perphes Volker, the director of the Middle East program at the German Institute for International and Security Affairs in Berlin, said, "It seems that Al-Jazeera has become a main channel for communication between two enemies with no other means of communication. I think that Western leaders should use Al-Jazeera in the same way as bin Laden did. It is a free, uncensored channel, which is quite extraordinary for the Arab world. And instead of putting pressure on Al-Jazeera to stop sending certain messages, I think the wisest path was the one British Prime Minister Tony Blair took, when he addressed his message to the Arab world over Al-Jazeera."

The Austrian news media compared Al-Jazeera to CNN. The Vienna newspaper *Der Standard* in its October 10 issue described Al-Jazeera as ensuring "a near equality of arms in the battle of the airwaves" between the United States and the Middle East. "While during the Gulf War the whole world was served news brewed by CNN for western-northern palates," the paper stated, "this time, another voice has loudly interrupted the proceedings." The paper suggested that Western leaders should accept Al-Jazeera's influence and grant it interviews. "Washington should shower Al-Jazeera with offers of interviews with U.S. officials or respected Muslims who can counter the anti-U.S. propaganda."

THE U.S. INFORMATION BATTLE IN THE MIDDLE EAST

The United States has learned that war in Afghanistan must result in more than military victory. The United States has discovered that the more important battle is being waged over information. An unnamed U.S. State Department official recently told CNN, "We are getting hammered in the Arab world." Many U.S. officials stated that Al-Jazeera, with its popularity and influence among Arab viewers, has overwhelmingly won the first round in the information battle in the Middle East. The ongoing obstacle facing the United States is the misguided perception that Al-Jazeera is the enemy itself or at least a conspirator. Yet a handful of U.S. officials have finally recognized that Al-Jazeera is a mere vehicle for information, a vessel through which ideas and opinions are disseminated and discourse is forged.

There is no question that Al-Jazeera has prompted U.S. officials to exert more effort to communicate with the Arab people. "I don't think it has always been important to reach out, but in this particular case, public diplomacy plays an increasingly important role; people are going to choose sides based on what they hear or who they believe; it's part of the war on terrorism," an unnamed senior Bush official told the *Boston Globe* on October 21, 2001.

Although U.S. officials have chosen to appear on Al-Jazeera to communicate the U.S. point of view to ordinary Arabs, some experts have cautioned not to expect success too soon. "Our leaders have been saying all the right things, but there are certain misperceptions that, even with the most diligent public relations efforts, are difficult to dispel," said Paul Pillar, a former CIA counterterrorism official, in an interview with the *Los Angeles Times* on October 18, 2001.

The damage to the U.S. image was perpetrated throughout the Middle East decades ago, mostly due to general misunderstandings and misinterpretations between the Arab and Western cultures. "In the middle of a crisis, America can't expect to change ideas that have taken root over decades. That takes years to happen," according to Shibley Telhami, professor of government at the University of Maryland, from an interview with the Associated Press on October 18, 2001.

Part of the problem stems from the cautious approach the U.S. government maintains when midlevel State Department diplomats grant interviews. There is always the possibility of mixed messages, and only a few officials are cleared to speak about U.S. policy, even though the Arab world needs to hear from as many as possible. "For a long time, U.S. administrations not only ignored Al-Jazeera, but shunned them," Edward Walker, a former assistant secretary of state for Near East affairs, told the *Boston Globe*. "They discovered they were losing the battle of public opinion—a big brilliant discovery; but the problem has been that those senior U.S. people are not talking to the audience; they are talking like they're giving the message to Congress, or the *Washington Post*, or *Boston Globe*, so the message doesn't convey," he added. And Walker should know—he appeared on one of Al-Jazeera's talk shows in the aftermath of the U.S. strikes on Afghanistan.

The issue is not who is delivering the message or when the message is being delivered; the issue is whether the message can connect with Arab viewers and whether they identify with its content. To deliver the message effectively requires deeper understanding of the Arab mentality and awareness of its cultural

and religious intricacies. In an attempt to address these deficien-
cies, the Bush administration chose Charlotte Beers, a former
executive at the J. Walter Thompson advertising firm, to be the
new undersecretary of state for public diplomacy and public affairs. Beers, who was sworn in on October 2, 2001, has been as-
signed to sell the American image to the Arab and Muslim
worlds. Beers, who intends to go after younger and more receptive Muslims, recently told the London Daily Telegraph, "It's a
battle for the eleven-year-old mind."

But words might not be enough in the information battle. "If
[the Prophet Mohammed] came down to do the PR campaign
for the U.S., he would fail," said Osama Siblani, publisher of
Arab American News in Dearborn, Michigan, when he was interviewed in the San Francisco Chronicle. "You cannot win with
words; you have to win with actions." He recommended greater
U.S. action to end the Palestinian-Israeli conflict and to lift the
sanctions against Iraq.

Siblani's comments make sense and would resonate among the
Arab population, since winning over Arab audiences through the
media alone may itself prove futile. In many respects, the worldwide Arab community genuinely mistrusts the United States and
its policies. The entire community is disenchanted with what is
perceived as empty rhetoric from U.S. officials aimed at the
Palestinian cause. That disenchantment drives the perception of
a double-standard in Washington policy toward Israel and the
Palestinians, something that has persisted for more than fifty
years. The growing distrust has been exacerbated by the absence
on Arab news networks of U.S. officials arguing on behalf of
their government policies and actions. Siblani may thus be correct in stating that the Arab community can be swayed in favor
of U.S. policy only if it sees a more evenhanded approach to the
Israeli-Palestinian conflict. Nonetheless, any action must start

with some meaningful gesture, and perhaps the best way to begin dispelling this animosity is to open channels of dialogue.

The action that the State Department has taken to persuade the Arab world of U.S. global intentions is to craft a "public democracy" campaign under the aegis of the Advertising Council, a New York-based nonprofit group that develops advertising strategies for national causes. Charlotte Beers told *Newsday* in mid-October 2001 that she would consider buying airtime on Al-Jazeera to deliver the U.S. message to the Arab audience. "If I have to buy time on Al-Jazeera, I would certainly consider it," she said in an interview with the Associated Press on October 15, 2001. However, some advertising executives and media analysts were skeptical about the administration's strategy. Jeff Odiorne, chairman of Odiorne Wilde Narraway and Partners, a San Francisco advertising firm, in an interview with the *Chicago Tribune*, asked: "Can you imagine being an eighteen-year-old Arab kid, going to religious school and being taught to hate Americans, and we put on a pasty, sixty-year-old white guy to tell you that what we are doing is just?"

The one proven strategy came to light when U.S. diplomats who know how to present the U.S. point of view and relate to Arab viewers first appeared on Al-Jazeera. This worked for Christopher Ross, a former U.S. ambassador who speaks fluent Arabic, and it could work for others. According to Al-Kasim, host of *The Opposite Direction*, Ross's charisma and ability to choose the right words made a big difference with viewers. "At the end of the day, it all boils down to the better speaker. The better speaker will win the battle, whether he is American or non-American," Al-Kasim said in a phone interview on December 10, 2001.

Unfortunately, there are not many U.S. officials who have mastered the Arabic language. And even those who do speak Arabic have not really made the effort to connect with the Arab world. "Public diplomacy . . . has been a critical missing link in the U.S. policy toward the Islamic world; the basic reason we're not very effective is we don't even try," said Edward Walker, the former assistant secretary of state, in an interview with the London-based Arabic newspaper *Al-Hayat* in October 2001. President Bush should follow Prime Minister Blair's lead and appear on Al-Jazeera.

Still, Beers, the administration's spearhead in the information battle, believes she understands what it takes to send an effective message to the Middle East. "You'll never communicate effectively unless you walk in the shoes of your intended audience; and the communication we're about now is philosophical and psychological as well as factual; so we're in the position of having to speak to very distant, cynical—if not more hostile than that— audiences, and if we can't speak in their language, or start in some common ground, we're not going to have very effective communications," she said in an interview with the *Washington Post.*

It seems that the U.S. administration has been listening to Beers. In late November 2001, President Bush signed an initiative to start the Middle East Radio Network. Legislation authorizing this new broadcast service was passed immediately by the U.S. Congress; it is intended to update and improve VOA's Arabic programs. The broadcast service provides a twenty-four-hour Arabic news, information, and entertainment forum designed to appeal to the younger Arab audience and to counterbalance the growing wave of anti-Americanism in the Arab world. "The initiative for this new network predates September 11. It is not a direct response to Al-Jazeera, but there is a greater urgency for it now to tell the American story to the world and increase our ability to be heard in that region," said Gary Thatcher, Middle East project director at the International Broadcasting Bureau (IBB). According to Thatcher, there has always been a great need for the new network because VOA's Arabic service was limited to only nine hours per day. Douglas Boyd, a renowned scholar who has studied media in the Arab world for several decades, explained that "VOA has always had a problem in the Middle East because it is—like Arab local media—government operated." Although networks like the BBC and RMC-ME will always carry a good following, fewer Arabs are interested in knowing what the United States has to say through VOA. The budget for the new network, which is based out of Cyprus in the Mediterranean Sea, will be about $30 million and will begin broadcasting in June 2002 on AM, FM, and digital satellite.

IBB, the agency that controls the transmission for all U.S.-produced international broadcasts, has also been consulted by Congress about launching a new Arabic-language satellite TV station; authorizing legislation in the U.S. Congress had become a real possibility. Al-Jazeera has even played an indirect part in the proposed legislation. "After 9/11, we now realize the great influence of Al-Jazeera in the Arab world; had Al-Jazeera not existed, few American policy makers would have focused on the role of TV in shaping the Middle East public opinion," IBB's Thatcher explained. The estimated budget for the new network is about $50 million, and its primary purpose is to promote the American image in the Arab world. "We have to earn respect in every broadcast, using every word, every single day, and we expect the proposed channel to faithfully represent the U.S. culture," said Thatcher, who predicts great success for the TV channel should it become a reality. "The mere fact that the U.S. government is behind this channel is not going to be a big factor in the way it is perceived because the Arab viewers are used to the idea of government-sponsored TV systems. But because it represents the U.S. government, it has to be journalistically fair, responsible, and accurate." Thatcher added that he already has 150 résumés from broadcasters all over the Arab world who want to work for the new channel. "We will offer competitive salaries."

Douglas Boyd argues against U.S. funding of the TV initiative described by Thatcher, claiming it will not be effective, but he also suggested that the new entertainment-oriented radio "might help with the under–25 group that is now so large in the [Arabian] Gulf." A recent study by the Broadcasting Board of Governors reported that young people in each of the Arab countries range from 22 percent to 33 percent of the populations.

Although Thatcher correctly assesses that Arab audiences are accustomed to government-sponsored media, they are not naive about the intentions of the media and the information they disseminate (a good example is Israel's Arabic-language radio, recognized by Arab audiences as a partisan instrument of the Israeli government). Nonetheless, these new services are likely to be received especially well among younger audiences given the sway of American pop culture. Still, Arab viewers will always recognize the source and agenda behind the broadcasts.

Can hearts and minds be won over? In an area where animosity toward the West in general and the United States specifically is fostered by ideological and political differences, airing American superstars and popular shows will do little to resolve fundamental issues. There is strong likelihood that the new U.S. radio network will be seen as a way to sell Americanism through entertainment rather than by tackling the issues that plague the region, something that Al-Jazeera has already accomplished. One Egyptian journalist stated it best: "You can't use the Backstreet Boys to sell policies in the Middle East."

The success or failure of these new services will be years in the making, and Boyd emphasized the importance of recognizing local Arab networks and their unique ability to communicate with and consolidate Arab audiences. He argued that the United States "should take a positive view of Al Jazeera. A cornerstone of [U.S.] policy has been more freedom of information and less government media control. Now, to some extent, that is happening. The U.S. has at long last realized that we need people like Chris Ross speaking in Arabic on Al Jazeera."

Can new American networks stand up to Al-Jazeera and establish a measure of popularity and credibility among Arab viewers? The free market will determine that.

EPILOGUE

Everything continues to change after September 11. A different world emerged from the smoldering rubble of the World Trade Center towers. Today, questions of democracy, freedom of expression, civil liberties, and war pervade discussions in the public sphere—whether in the United States, the Middle East, or across the world. Along with the spiral of events that followed the attacks on New York and Washington, D.C., within the lightning-fast pace of world media, Al-Jazeera—a network whose operations and future will forever be inextricably intertwined with that momentous day—rose to almost meteoric prominence. Now the story of Al-Jazeera rests squarely at the center of any examination of Middle Eastern politics and public exchange of ideas.

Who would have imagined that a free and independent all-news channel would spring from the Arab world, where notions of a free press have been mostly unattainable? Who would have imagined that an Arab channel launched from a tiny Arabian Gulf emirate would scoop the world and become a major player and competitor alongside the colossal Western news networks? Incredibly, Al-Jazeera did it.

In some respects, the station seems to have ended the Western monopoly of global dissemination of information. The war in Afghanistan, described by U.S. President George W. Bush as the "first war of the new century," provided the stage on which

197

Al-Jazeera rocketed to worldwide fame. Major TV news networks, including CNN, were pushed to the sidelines, at least for a moment, to give way to what many observers now call the "Arab world's CNN."

When Osama bin Laden and Al-Qaeda leaders used Al-Jazeera to relay messages about the Afghan war, the United States found itself for the first time since the end of the Cold War competing fiercely to disseminate its own message about the conflict to the Arab and Islamic worlds. The Bush administration registered displeasure with Al-Jazeera's role in the Afghan conflict. U.S. officials accused Al-Jazeera of giving too much airtime to bin Laden and Al-Qaeda. Others went so far as to ask the Qatari emir to "tone down" Al-Jazeera's coverage of the conflict. In doing so, the U.S. administration seemed more determined to keep the enemy from airing its story, even though Al-Jazeera repeatedly offered U.S. officials the opportunity to air their side.

There is little doubt that if Osama bin Laden had chosen CNN instead of Al-Jazeera to deliver his messages, CNN would have aired them exactly as Al-Jazeera did. CNN would have seized the opportunity to scoop the world. In one of the biggest surprises that occurred after September 11, Al-Jazeera beat all competitors with its exclusive first look at Osama bin Laden—in his own words. Only much later, after months passed, CNN enjoyed a short-lived moment, when it exclusively broadcast an interview with bin Laden, taped by Al-Jazeera correspondent Tayseer Allouni. The irony is that Al-Jazeera arranged that interview, conducted and taped it, but chose not to air it.

Regardless of who would have aired the interview, it is very unlikely that anyone would have changed his or her opinion of bin Laden and Al-Qaeda. Still, Al-Jazeera did not put the bin Laden videos on the air without forethought or planning. Once they aired, Al-Jazeera provided context and put issues into perspective for its viewers through its talk shows, which invited Arab as well as Western panelists to interpret the bin Laden messages. Former U.S. ambassadors Christopher Ross and Edward Walker and other U.S. officials appeared on Al-Jazeera on more than one occasion and were given the opportunity to explain the U.S. position on the Afghan crisis and the bin Laden tapes.

It will behoove U.S. officials to keep up with Al-Jazeera's scoops. In November 2002, Al-Jazeera exclusively aired an audiotape in which bin Laden praised the more recent terrorist strikes on a French tanker in Yemen, attacks on American soldiers in Kuwait, and the deadly explosions in Bali, all of which occurred after the U.S. military campaign in Afghanistan. The tape, which was authenticated by counterterrorism experts, provided the first evidence after the U.S. bombing in Afghanistan that bin Laden was still alive.

The latest hard evidence that bin Laden is alive surfaced through another audiotape aired by Al-Jazeera in February 2003. In it, the Al-Qaeda leader condemned the U.S. efforts to launch a war on Iraq and urged the Iraqi people to engage in urban warfare and suicide attacks should the United States invade. He also tried to rally Muslims by drawing on his experience of surviving heavy bombardment in the Afghan mountains. Al-Jazeera aired a response to bin Laden's message from a senior U.S. State Department official, who said the recording showed that Iraq and Al-Qaeda "are bound by a common hatred." Although the bin Laden audiotape was not authenticated, U.S. officials said they believed the speaker on the tape was, in fact, bin Laden.

Although the U.S. administration repeatedly announced that there was no conclusive proof whether bin Laden was dead or alive, these tapes seemed to take Washington by surprise.

In this book we neither defend nor criticize Al-Jazeera's airing of the bin Laden tapes or its coverage of the Afghan crisis. Although we believe Al-Jazeera newscasters acted professionally, our objective has been to draw attention to the Arab world's urgent need for a free channel like Al-Jazeera, one that is modeled on Western journalistic principles and practices. Unlike the United States, where freedom of speech is a right guaranteed by the First Amendment of the U.S. Constitution, freedom of expression in many Arab countries is a privilege meted out stingily by governments to favored reporters whose stories prop up government positions. Al-Jazeera abolished this practice and thereby created a new direction that respects diversity in opinion—all opinions.

We have also tried to demonstrate that even though the Arab public does not always think or act in unanimity, in many ways it is connected to the same central social system. Arab audiences, like all audiences, are eclectic and in flux. Perhaps that is why Al-Jazeera presents much of its programming as nothing more than the mix of opinions. The basic premise at Al-Jazeera is that the "truth" on any subject can be reached only if all possible opinions are exposed and argued, usually exhaustively, sometimes to the point of on-air fistfights.

Al-Jazeera has generated anger and fear among Arab governments, for it has dared to give reporters the ability to uncover and report the news in an environment characterized by freedom of speech. And yet Al-Jazeera is criticized for what appears to be self-imposed censorship. One of the glaring flaws in Al-Jazeera's coverage is its sparing coverage of its host country, Qatar.

We directed this question to Sheikh Masha'al Al-Thani, the second Secretary at the Qatari embassy in Washington, D.C. He argued that "Qatar is a small country that does not have much going on. We cannot compare Qatar's domestic issues to the domestic issues of other bigger countries." In response, we would point out that domestic policies in Qatar are just as important as in any other country. We urge the Al-Jazeera staff to cover Qatari news using the same exacting reporting they apply to all countries in the Middle East. If Al-Jazeera refuses to champion freedom of speech in Qatar, then who will?

In early 2003, Al-Jazeera started to discuss sensitive political and military issues inside Qatar. Moreover, Qatari officials have cooperated more fully by discussing these issues through Al-Jazeera. One sensitive topic that was raised by Al-Jazeera was the use by the United States of Al-Udeid, the U.S. military command base in the Qatari desert, which has served as a primary staging area for military operations in Iraq. Many Persian Gulf countries besides Qatar have U.S. bases, but their regimes do not discuss the existence of these bases through their own government-controlled media. However, Al-Jazeera crews visited Al-Udeid and interviewed U.S. and Qatari army officials about the extent of military cooperation between the two countries. Many Arab critics accused Qatar of betraying the Arab cause by allowing U.S. troops to stockpile combat equipment at Al-Udeid. Months earlier in October 2002, Qatar's foreign minister, Sheikh Hamad bin Jassem bin Jaber Al-Thani, told Al-Jazeera that Qatar had not received a U.S. request to use Al-Udeid as a base for a strike on Iraq, but he said his country may approve such a request.

After 2002, the U.S. administration pressed the international community to implement a "preemptive" military strike against Iraq. After months of tumultuous negotiations at the United Nations, and inconclusive UN weapons inspections in Iraq, the United States, alongside a small number of allied nations, mobilized its armed forces on what would become a sustained attack on Iraq. Despite significant worldwide protest, U.S. forces pushed into Iraq from Kuwait. While some countries like Turkey did not allow U.S. forces to use their borders with Iraq to launch the military campaign, Qatar approved the U.S. request to use Al-Udeid as a base of military operations. In addition, Kuwait allowed the United States to use its soil as the main launching pad for coalition forces. While the Arab public—from Morocco to Oman—was fervently against the war, the few Arab governments that supported the U.S.-led war on Iraq came under increasing pressure from Arab media to justify such support. With its headquarters in the same city as U.S. Central Command, Al-Jazeera was poised to prove that its coverage was truly independent of Qatar's government censors. Surprising many of its critics, the network was one of the first to question its Qatari financial sponsor's political position with respect to Iraq and the U.S. military strike.

It came as little surprise that this war turned into a media spectacle. The newly globalized audiences braced themselves for the latest coverage from several television outlets. As we had predicted, Al-Jazeera once again was a focal point of a war, this time between the United States and Iraq. Alongside other Arab TV news networks, Al-Jazeera broadcast nonstop from Baghdad as well as other cities and towns in Iraq. Al-Jazeera's competitors Al-Arabiya (which started airing shortly before the onset of the war), the Lebanese Broadcast Channel, and Abu Dhabi Television all aired "exclusive" footage from battlefronts and residential locations. While all these networks gained considerable attention, Al-Jazeera emerged as the "go-to" station for war coverage in the Arab world and beyond. This prompted many Western media analysts to refer to this as the "Al-Jazeera effect."

Even as Western journalists broadcast every moment of the war live from the military front lines, so did Arab-language television corespondents report the war to their constituent audiences. The interpretation of war events was reported differently, and it came under scrutiny and criticism from both Western and Arab communities.

While American audiences scrambled for news leads from Al-Jazeera, other agencies and groups tried to silence the network.

At the same time, Internet search engines that monitor the most requested keywords recorded an astounding increase in the number of hits for Al-Jazeera, so many that it was ranked number one for the duration of the war. In fact, at one point "Al-Jazeera" received three times more searches than the keyword "sex." But in New York City, the New York Stock Exchange and NASDAQ both banned Al-Jazeera business reporters from airing live market reports from their trading floors. Neither organization had justified reason to take such actions, and when their spokespersons scrambled for a formal explanation, the apparent reason was cited as Al-Jazeera's "irresponsible" war coverage.

While European subscriptions to Al-Jazeera rose by 4 million, some U.S.-based groups took different action. Only one day after Al-Jazeera launched its English-language website, both the Arabic and English sites were hacked into and rendered inaccessible. In place of the active sites, visitors were diverted to a screen that displayed an American flag and the words "Let Freedom Ring." In other cases, visitors were routed to a pornographic site. Several Jewish groups in Canada took measures to block Al-Jazeera broadcasts there, accusing the network of "anti-Semitism," setting off a debate in the Canadian newspapers over freedom of the press.

One White House correspondent reported that President Bush was "furious" with Al-Jazeera, even as the Freedom of Expression Awards ceremony held in the United Kingdom acknowledged Al-Jazeera's war coverage by honoring the station with its prestigious Anti-Censorship Award.

Since the original publication of this book, we have been quoted in the media, describing the differences in perspectives between audiences in the Middle East and the United States, and we have commented about how these differences can predict the level of news coverage across regions. This notion, which we have de-

scribed as "contextual objectivity," came to the forefront in the
discussion of war coverage in Iraq. It had been widely reported
in the international press that audiences in the United States
were watching a different war from the rest of the world. Debate
reached its highest point in the United States when Al-Jazeera
rebroadcast footage of captured American POWs from Iraqi
Television. While this drew strong criticism and accusations
from U.S. officials, it also sent Al-Jazeera subscriptions skyrock-
eting, particularly when American networks refused to air the
footage. As Al-Jazeera showcased every possible angle of the
conflict, including the Arab "street," Iraqi civilian establishments, "embedded" reporting with U.S. forces, Iraqi press conferences, and U.S. Central Command war briefings, many
American networks were making decisions on what *not* to air.
The product was a more graphic war broadcast to the Arab
world and a more sanitized war broadcast to American audiences. Despite the differences in broadcast strategy, Al-Jazeera
won the respect of many journalistic establishments, with favorable articles appearing in much of the American and European
press. Once again, Al-Jazeera's ability to maintain a watchdog
role for every regime and administration won the admiration of
journalists and audiences alike.

Al-Jazeera's coverage of the war in Iraq didn't come without
sacrifices. The network was scolded by the administration in
Washington, and midway through the war the Iraqi regime
banned two senior Al-Jazeera correspondents from doing their
jobs—they were ordered to leave under accusations that they
were acting on behalf of the United States. Saddam Hussein's information minister, Mohammed Said Al-Sahhaf, accused Al-
Jazeera of being an instrument of the West and a conspirator with
the Americans. But perhaps Al-Jazeera's greatest loss occurred
when its senior correspondent, Tarek Ayoub, was killed during
the U.S. bombing of Al-Jazeera's Baghdad office, an event remi-

niscent of the bombing of Al-Jazeera's office in Kabul. Ayoub was mourned throughout the Arab world and lauded by Al-Jazeera as a martyr who died in the line of journalism.

On April 9, 2003, Al-Jazeera aired footage of U.S. Marine tanks in one of Baghdad's main squares. While scenes of Saddam Hussein's regime collapsing reverberated throughout the world, Al-Jazeera broadcast the surreal images to a perplexed and confused Arab audience, but it was not alone. Now, with so many Arab networks committed to news coverage and competing for airtime, Al-Jazeera has proven to be the hallmark of change throughout Arab media. Its efforts have yielded new competitors.

Despite the scrutiny brought on by the U.S. war in Iraq, we believe that Al-Jazeera is an unprecedented phenomenon in the Arab world, and we commend Qatar's emir for helping to launch it. However, we strongly suggest that additional steps be taken to grant the Qatari people (and all people in the Arab world) more meaningful civil rights and, ultimately, complete freedom of the press. Since the original publication of this book, the emir has taken some steps to push for democracy in his tiny state. In mid-April 2003, a legislative constitution was created for Qatar and posted on Al-Jazeera's website. While such a step is significant, the next five to ten years will prove definitively how far the emir is willing to move forward in making good on his promise of democracy. And as the network pushes toward financial independence, Al-Jazeera remains the emir's flagship and, after oil and gas, Qatar's most important export.

Democracy in some parts of the Arab world is virtually nonexistent. Now that Arab audiences have tasted Al-Jazeera, they are not willing to give up such freedom. For Arab viewers, free access to a news channel like Al-Jazeera is a significant step toward democracy and the continuing free discussion of political issues. In that context, Faisal Al-Kasim, an Al-Jazeera talk-show host,

said in a recent interview published in the *Guardian* newspaper
on February 7, 2003, "We used to discuss politics in the Arab
world in a very servile and frightened way. Now, for the first
time ever, we can raise our voices and shout. Why not?"

However, in attempting to represent diverse opinions, Al-
Jazeera has often relied on radically antagonistic perspectives.
Many viewers have requested that the station adopt a less sensationalistic approach in its programming and to exercise modera-
tion—especially on its talk shows. Although Al-Jazeera's management argues convincingly for its programming formula, a
middle ground needs to be established that reflects the Arab majority—whether their views are described as "nonextremist,"
"secular," or something else. Al-Jazeera must seek out guests
who reflect the prevailing public opinion, which in the Arab
world—contrary to popular belief in the United States and elsewhere—is truly moderate.

Al-Jazeera is not an extension or representative of any one
Arab regime. Much like CNN, the twin sources of Al-Jazeera's
success lie in capital investment and the free flow of information.
We are mindful that Al-Jazeera reflects and responds to cultural
traditions and expectations from its audience, but only in the
same way that CNN approaches stories from an American-
Western perspective. Al-Jazeera has managed to avoid the kind
of government cheerleading that became characteristic of some
networks, such as FOX News in the United States and Iraqi
Television. Al-Jazeera was accused of an anti-American bias for
its unflinching coverage of U.S.-inflicted casualties in
Afghanistan and then in Iraq. Yet when CNN and the other U.S.
networks showed virtually no images of Afghan casualties, and
comparatively little of the "collateral damage" in Iraq, they
weren't accused in Western circles of being anti-Arab. In analyz-
ing the networks' use of such images, we would like to pose a

question: How much is too much for Al-Jazeera, and how little is too little for American networks?

Critics have also accused Al-Jazeera of having a pro-Palestinian slant because its correspondents call Palestinian suicide-bombers *shuhada* (martyrs), not terrorists. To put it mildly, many Arabs view the Israeli occupation of Palestine as unfair, even illegal. Palestinians who are killed while fighting for freedom from occupation are subsequently portrayed as martyrs. Al-Jazeera reports this because it reflects the attitude and beliefs of its Arab audience. Now, however, there is increasingly heated debate among Middle Eastern clerics and intellectuals who question the logic of resistance movements that undertake brutal ambushes to kill innocent civilians. We take the position that attacks on civilians or civilian establishments are unacceptable and contradict any legitimate tenet of resistance. And we believe that Al-Jazeera should refrain from using such highly charged jargon. Yet at the same time we openly acknowledge that few networks are free of blame on this issue. U.S. networks, for example, do not use the term "assassination" in reporting on the Israeli policy of eliminating Palestinian leaders of groups like Hamas (the term they use is "targeted killings"). Moreover, there seems to be an unspoken agreement among U.S. networks when and whether to label an individual a "terrorist" or an "Islamic militant." The skeptical Arab public can see that the U.S. coverage of Middle Eastern events is not impartial. All networks should be accountable for their use of such terms and held to the same code of ethics and conduct in their pursuit of fair journalistic coverage.

Beyond obviously sympathetic word-usage, Al-Jazeera has tried to provide balanced coverage of the Israeli military operations against the Palestinians that started at the end of March 2002, when a Palestinian suicide-bomber attacked a hotel dining room in Netanya, killing nineteen people and wounding 134 others. In April 2002, Al-Jazeera started a new daily program called *Under Siege*, which discussed the repercussions of the Israeli attack on the headquarters of the Palestinian leader Yasser Arafat. Viewers of the program were given the opportunity to express their frustration against the Israeli practices in the Palestinian territories. So in a way, the program served as a "safety valve" for the public release of anger. We maintain that public outcry and discussion, even heated discussion, is much better than suppressing these feelings or expressing them through illegal or violent means.

It needs to be pointed out again that Al-Jazeera announcers avoid savage criticism or harsh commentary on the viewpoints of viewers or guests. And they have taken the extra steps to try to interview Israeli officials as well as show the devastation caused by the Palestinian suicide-bombings inside Israel. This is something that other Arab networks have not done in their ongoing coverage of the Palestinian intifada. In addition, Al-Jazeera anchors continue to get comments from senior U.S. officials through correspondents in Washington.

Still, Al-Jazeera has not shied away from reporting the ferocity of the Israeli practices against the Palestinians. Pictures of Al-Aqsa Mosque and the Dome of the Rock, eternal reminders of a Palestinian Jerusalem, appear frequently in introductions to several programs. Moreover, they feature scenes of the angry rallies held by Arab people against the routine Israeli incursions in the West Bank.

In its coverage of the Palestinian-Israeli conflict, Al-Jazeera has angered not only Israeli officials but also Palestinian officials. In early January 2003, a unit of the Palestinian intelligence arrested the Al-Jazeera correspondent in Gaza and detained him. The arrest was made in response to a live broadcast that included a phone call by a member of the Al-Aqsa

Martyrs Brigade, the military wing of the Fatah movement, who criticized what he called "the defeatist trend" in Fatah. Again, such remarks are not often heard on other Arab networks.

Earlier in this book and in our discussion of Al-Jazeera's role in post-9/11 coverage, we offered the concept of "contextual objectivity," wherein we describe the pattern of covering an issue objectively and thoroughly, but coloring it with the innate perspective of the reporting medium. We have attempted to articulate and capture the tensions between the view of audiences and the objective responsibility of reporters. While the term appears to be an oxymoron, it is not.

Contextual objectivity expresses the inherent contradiction between attaining objectivity in news coverage and appealing to a specific audience. This is one of the great struggles among networks today, never more so than during times of war. Contextual objectivity can be seen in every broadcast in every media outlet in the world, not just Al-Jazeera and U.S. networks. During times like these, how do networks strike a balance that provides audiences with a true representation of events even as they strive to appeal to and broaden their respective audiences?

If we apply the concept of contextual objectivity to Al-Jazeera's coverage of the Palestinian-Israeli conflict, we would easily recognize that Al-Jazeera is faced with two professional and persistent dilemmas that face broadcast news in general. First, prevailing notions and practices dictate that the news should be as comprehensive as possible, yet for other obvious reasons, it must also be selective. As just mentioned, Al-Jazeera has tried to provide comprehensive coverage of the conflict, but in the process it has focused on certain aspects, such as the Israeli atrocities in the Palestinian territories. The second dilemma is that news, while expected to convey objective, factual accounts, is also obliged to make those accounts meaningful to the audience. However, the addition of context and analysis almost inevitably involves the intrusion of opinion and directed points of view. Al-Jazeera has given context to every suicide-bombing and every Israeli response by interviewing political analysts and officials. However, since an overwhelming majority of the Arabs are opposed to the Israeli occupation of the Palestinian territories, this creates a prevailing perspective throughout Al-Jazeera's coverage of the conflict.

The other achievement of Al-Jazeera is its ability (if not mission) to unify Arab audiences everywhere: It has become the pan-Arab transnational channel. For the first time in recent history, Arab viewers across the world gather in front of their TV sets at the same time every evening to watch Al-Jazeera's news bulletins and talk shows. Al-Jazeera reporters, anchors, and talk-show hosts are transnational personalities themselves, hailing from all corners of the Arab world: Morocco, Egypt, Iraq, Palestine, Syria, and others.

Al-Jazeera management seems to understand the power of public opinion and the role it plays in formulating public policy. Al-Jazeera could take several steps beyond that, however. It could expand its influence far beyond the Middle East; it could seek a global audience; it could do better in presenting the West with free, uncensored versions of Arab views, opinions, and beliefs. Al-Jazeera recently decided to launch an English-language website tailored to a Western audience. The site, launched in the first half of 2003, was intended to be the first leg in the network's English-language plans that ultimately could include an English-language TV channel to be launched by the end of 2003. According to Joanne Tucker, the managing editor of Al-Jazeera's English-language website, "The website operation is like a halfway house to a full TV service. . . . We will be streaming audio and video, and we will have our own dedicated team of reporters, including correspondents in the field, who will be filing TV-style reports."

This is probably the best way Americans will be able to learn and comprehend the Arab perspective on events in the Middle East. In today's world, Al-Jazeera's reports are subject to the editing choices of Western editors, mostly resulting in incomplete or inaccurate translations. This needs to change. But the real challenge for Al-Jazeera's English services is whether they will be able to reach Americans and get them to watch. A powerful image would be useless if people don't log on or tune in to the station.

Al-Jazeera changed the way Arabs watch TV as much as the September 11 attacks changed Americans. It also familiarized Arab viewers with the popular saying "the pen is mightier than the sword"—suggesting that news media reporting without restrictions can have a greater impact than military might and repressive regimes. The network's distinctly Western approach collided with Arab governments, resulting in temporary closure of Al-Jazeera offices in Arab cities and putting more financial pressures on the station. This is understandable given the history of the region, though hardly acceptable. Al-Jazeera lost many of its commercial advertisers to pressure exerted by the Gulf Cooperation Council (GCC) member states, spearheaded by Saudi Arabia. A meeting of the GCC's ministers of information, held in October 2002, issued a call for boycotting any advertiser that bought time on Al-Jazeera. The Saudi firms, which constitute a key revenue source for Al-Jazeera, responded to the pressure and halted their advertising campaigns. Saudi Arabia went farther by recalling its ambassador to Qatar during the same month, in protest over Al-Jazeera broadcasts perceived by the Saudi officials as critical of the Saudi royal family. Moreover, the Saudi Arabian government refused to allow Al-Jazeera to cover the annual Muslim pilgrimage to Mecca, the hajj. Many other networks, including CNN, were allowed to broadcast from Mecca.

Contrast this with those U.S. officials who criticized Al-Jazeera for abiding by the rules of free speech and a free press. The 2000 edition of the U.S. State Department's *Human Rights Report* discusses, among many other issues, Qatar and Al-Jazeera. It states that "the privately owned satellite television channel Al-Jazeera operates freely." The U.S. State Department has found itself in the curious position of seeking to restrain the very same organization that it rightfully commends, an untenable position given that the *Human Rights Report* views a free media as an essential element of democracy.

Trying to vilify or censor Al-Jazeera thus sends the worst possible message to Arabs—that freedom of speech in the Arab world is a threat to the West. Al-Jazeera has been trying (and it often succeeds) to maintain the balance between its role as a free media outlet serving the public's right to know and its ethical accountability as a responsible news outlet that abides by a professional journalistic code of conduct.

The Afghan crisis and both wars in the Gulf demonstrated that information is a powerful weapon in modern warfare. Osama bin Laden recognized this and used Al-Jazeera to spread his message. Bin Laden might have opted for Al-Jazeera since it is the most influential and popular Arabic-language news medium broadcasting predominantly to Arab audiences. Similarly, top U.S. officials appeared on every single Western media channel to dispense their mission statement to the West.

Today, American officials need to intensify their diplomatic efforts to communicate with Arab people through Al-Jazeera and other Arab media channels. We know that this is critical given Arab news coverage of the war in Iraq. A primary source of Arab frustration and anger toward the United States is a perceived lack of empathy toward Arab pain and hardship. To help reduce that frustration, U.S. officials need to appear on Al-Jazeera and engage in direct dialogue with Arab people as they try to understand and respond to Arab fears and concerns. Al-Jazeera played a vital role in the U.S. war in Iraq given the advantage of its local resources. As in the recent past, few U.S. officials were entirely pleased with Al-Jazeera's coverage of the war. But as occurred after the Afghan war, and once the occupation of Iraq is over, U.S. officials may find that Al-Jazeera offered not only criticism but also the best avenue available to communicate the American point of view to Arabs everywhere.

The United States could express its position in the years after the war in Iraq, making the case for U.S. policy in the free market of ideas. U.S. officials could take a measured risk, appear on camera, and explain the U.S. position to potentially hostile audiences. An interview here or there by the administration's brightest, most articulate stars is not enough to alter generations of animosity, anger, and frustration toward U.S. policy in the region. U.S. officials need to devote more airtime specifically for Arab audiences to clarify policies. Working through U.S.-financed Arabic-language networks might be a good start, but this alone probably won't do the trick. A year has passed since the Middle East Radio Network (known as Radio Sawa, Arabic for Radio "Together") was launched. Embassy reports and e-mail messages from listeners have showed that Radio Sawa, which is heard in six Arab countries, has succeeded in attracting young Arab listeners to its highly popular, upbeat, disc jockey–style music programming. But young listeners, who are the target by Radio Sawa, may be ignoring the network's newscasts—the core of its public diplomacy mission. Echoing that thought, an editorial in the Egyptian *Al-Ahram Weekly* newspaper said "chances are [that] the Arab youth will split the strategy: take the U.S. sound and discard the U.S. agenda." Arab viewers trust Al-Jazeera, but they may not trust a network overflowing with U.S. ideology and money. There will always be questions—and rightly so. If the messenger is not trusted, the message will not be trusted.

If U.S. officials want to gain Arab support worldwide, they need to use a trusted messenger, and that is the Middle East's own: the credible, popular, and powerful Al-Jazeera TV news network. It's the smart bomb in the battle over information—and it's already winning Arab hearts and minds.

The opening salvo in this battle should be a consolidated effort to appeal to the Arab public, followed by a meaningful, consistent, and genuine U.S. commitment to issues that are most important to Arabs and Muslims. There is no doubt that an Arab public raised to distrust U.S. sincerity in the Middle East crisis fosters nothing by mutual animosity. Arabs need to see for themselves a sincerely impartial U.S. position on the Israeli-Palestinian conflict, in addition to genuine U.S. concern for the Arab position. A meaningful commitment from the United States to solve the Israeli-Palestinian deadlock will plant the seeds of mutual understanding and cooperation between the Middle East and the West.

What message would the United States be sending if officials in Washington neglect, boycott, or ignore Al-Jazeera? As the leader of the free world, the United States should acknowledge and work with the Middle East's most independent broadcast media outlet in the same way it works with networks like CNN, MSNBC, and BBC. In the free market of ideas, the U.S government could establish a conduit through which its officials share opinions and discussions with Arab peers. This could, in all likelihood, counter anti-U.S. sentiment, foster mutual trust, and dissolve the fanatic, self-fulfilling prophecies of the clash of civilizations.

The most dangerous misconceptions about Arabs and Americans are subliminal—they lurk beneath the surface of everyday discourse. Indirect, veiled messages can distort reality and persuade anyone listening that the differences between East and West are ideological, even innate and immutable.

Middle East scholar Fouad Ajami argued in his November 18, 2001, *New York Times* feature that hatred by the Arab Muslim world toward the West is deep-rooted and difficult to understand. But here we offer an optimistic view, one that assures mutual dialogue once all sides participate. With statements like "anti-Americanism is a potent force that cannot be readily dissolved," Ajami did little but distort reality. Instead, such remarks tell American readers that they cannot possibly understand the Arab world through Arab eyes (and, conveniently, that the Middle Eastern expert is the only one who can translate such Arab inscrutability).

Such irresponsible statements amount to doomsday scenarios, perpetuating the myth that the Arab world is blood-dark with hatred, a hostile people who reject Western ways regardless of intent or merit. But Arab audiences are not as impenetrable to U.S. media as Ajami suggests. We should not forget that the Western media campaign—led by CNN, no less—sold the first Gulf War to Arab citizens during the early 1990s; it's the same today, only more so. Mutual dialogue, situated in the public sphere and broadcast to Arab audiences, must therefore be sought out and engaged. Al-Jazeera is the one to lead this charge, and it stands ready to do so.

This freewheeling trendsetter in independent Middle Eastern TV news media has changed the landscape throughout the region. Today, Al-Jazeera is copied by major satellite and cable services from Egypt to Kuwait. If imitation is the sincerest form of flattery, then Al-Jazeera has enjoyed a flood of compliments. These other networks mimic more than its content, however—they copy its production, values, and style.

A few Arab channels have even geared up to try to challenge the primacy of Al-Jazeera by competing against it. The most ambitious endeavor to date is the launch by the Middle East

Broadcasting Center (MBC) of an Arab satellite channel owned by the brother-in-law of Saudi Arabia's King Fahd; it is a twenty-four hour news channel in Arabic to compete directly with Al-Jazeera, known now as the Al-Arabiya channel. It was launched in time for the war in Iraq. The new channel did compete with Al-Jazeera, especially when Al-Jazeera's news center in Baghdad was bombed.

Before Al-Arabiya's launch, MBC's director claimed in an interview with the *Washington Post* that "Al-Jazeera has dominated the scene for the last six or seven years. We're trying to provide an alternative." The launch of Al-Arabiya provides a measure of proof that that Al-Jazeera has enhanced public discourse in the Middle East. Another competitor is the refurbished and repackaged Abu Dhabi TV channel.

In a way, Al-Jazeera reflects the contradictions of its programming. Remember its motto: "the opinion and the other opinion." We acknowledge that the network is a force for democracy in the Middle East, but we should also point out its visible shortcomings. Even though Al-Jazeera sometimes falls short of its ambitious goals, it remains the most viable network of its kind in the region. Al-Jazeera has revolutionized the Arab Middle East, challenging censorship imposed by the government-controlled media and addressing any relevant issue, including weak democratic institutions, fundamentalism, state corruption, political inequality, and human rights violations.

Al-Jazeera may not be perfect, but it remains the first choice for Arab self-determination, political openness, and democracy. What the Arab world needs now are more media services like Al-Jazeera, not fewer. And so we close with a fitting expression, something of a personal proverb for an unsettled age: The only cure for what ails democracy is more of it.

NOTES

Except as noted, statements quoted in this book are from personal interviews or from presentations attended by the authors. Many of our citations are to Arabic publications, which we have transliterated.

CHAPTER 2

Page 28   Yosri Fouda, "Al-Jazeera: Here We Stand; We Can Do No Otherwise," *Transnational Broadcasting Studies Journal*, Fall 2001.

Page 28   Ali Al-Hail, "Civil Society in the Arab World: The Role of Transnational Broadcasting," *Transnational Broadcasting Studies Journal*, Spring 2000.

Page 29   Tawfik Mahroos, personal interview, November 15, 2000.

Page 30   Douglas Boyd, International Center Against Censorship Seminar, Cairo, February 1999.

Page 32   Joseph Straubhaar, "Beyond Cultural Imperialism: Asymmetrical Interdependence and Cultural Proximity," *Critical Studies in Mass Communication*, 1991, 8 (1).

Page 32   Marwan Kraidy, "Transnational Television and Asymmetrical Interdependence in the Arab World: The Growing Influence of the Lebanese Satellite Broadcasters," *Transnational Broadcasting Studies Journal*, Fall/Winter 2000.

Page 32   Yosri Fouda, "Al-Jazeera: Here We Stand; We Can Do No Otherwise," *Transnational Broadcasting Studies Journal*, Fall 2001.

Page 33   Ali Al-Hail, "Civil Society in the Arab World: The Role of Transnational Broadcasting," *Transnational Broadcasting Studies Journal*, Spring 2000.

Page 34   Hafez Al-Mirazi, personal interview, July 20, 2001.

Page 40   Christian Miller, "Arab Satellite TV Station a Prime Battlefield in Information War," *New York Times*, October 12, 2001.

Page 41   Hafez Al-Mirazi, personal interview, July 20, 2001.

Page 41   S. Abdallah Schleifer, "A Dialogue with Mohammed Jasim Al-Ali, Managing Director, Al-Jazeera," *Transnational Broadcasting Studies Journal*, Fall 2000.

Page 43   "Egyptian TV Fights Arab Rivals with Tepid Glasnost: A Plethora of Political Debates, Talk Shows, and Social Comment Is Now on Air After Years of Drab Propaganda," Reuters, June 6, 2001.

Page 43   Ibid.

Page 43   Ibid.

CHAPTER 3

Page 46   Abdullah Al-Hajj, personal interview, November 10, 2001.

Page 47   S. Abdallah Schleifer, "A Dialogue with Mohammed Jasim Al-Ali, Managing
           Director, Al-Jazeera," *Transnational Broadcasting Studies Journal*, Fall 2000.
Page 47   "Kaifa Yanzor Al Ra'y Al Aam Al-Arabi Wal Ajnabi Ila Qanat Al-Jazeera?" *Al-
           Sharq*, November 20, 2000.
Page 48   "Qanat Al-Jazeera Al Akthar Horreyya Baina Al-Fadaeiyyat Al-Arabia," *Al-
           Watan*, May 5, 2000.
Page 49   "Istitla'a Al-Jazeera," *Al-Watan*, May 17, 1997.
Page 49   Muhammed I. Ayish, "American-Style Journalism and Arab World Television:
           An Exploratory Study of News Selection at Six Arab World Satellite Television
           Channels," *Transnational Broadcasting Studies Journal*, Spring/Summer 2001.
Page 50   Brian Whitaker, "Battle Station," *The Guardian*, October 9, 2001.
Page 50   Jian Al-Jacuby, "Interview with 'Inside Al-Jazeera,'" *60 Minutes II*, CBS, October
           10, 2001.
Page 51   Dan Williams, "A Real Newsmaker," *Jerusalem Post*, September 2, 2001.
Page 52   Brian Whitaker, "Battle Station," *The Guardian*, October 9, 2001.
Page 52   Frank Viviano, "Arab World Glued to TV Sets—Streets Appear Calm but Anger
           at U.S. Lies under Surface," *San Francisco Chronicle*, October 8, 2001.
Page 52   Walid Al-Omary, Interview with *60 Minutes*, CBS, May 2001.
Page 53   S. Abdallah Schleifer, "A Dialogue with Mohammed Jasim Al-Ali, Managing
           Director, Al-Jazeera," *Transnational Broadcasting Studies Journal*, Fall 2000.
Page 54   Sharon Waxman, "Arab TV's Strong Signal: The Al-Jazeera Network Offers
           News the Mideast Never Had Before, and Views That Are All Too Common,"
           Washington Post, December 4, 2001.
Page 54   Ibid.
Page 56   "Shrine to Legendary Egyptian Diva," *BBC Online News*, December 28, 2001.
Page 57   Walid Al-Omary, Interview with *60 Minutes*, CBS, May 2001.
Page 58   Francine Kiefer and Ann Scott Tyson, "In War of Words, U.S. Still Lags
           Behind," *Christian Science Monitor*, October 17, 2001.
Page 63   Frank Viviano, "Arab World Glued to TV Sets—Streets Appear Calm but Anger
           at U.S. Lies under Surface," *San Francisco Chronicle*, October 8, 2001.
Page 64   Arab American citizen in Baltimore, personal interview, July 30, 2001.
Page 64   Judith Kipper, personal interview, July 15, 2001.
Page 65   Jonathan Curiel, "Mideast News Network Has Fans Here: Al-Jazeera Coverage
           Uniquely Censored," *San Francisco Chronicle*, October 18, 2001.
Page 66   Nadia Semia, personal interview, July 30, 2001.
Page 66   Yasser Ahmed, personal interview, July 30, 2001.
Page 66   Davan Maharaj, "How Tiny Qatar Jars Arab Media," *Los Angeles Times*, May 7,
           2001.
Page 66   Ibid.
Page 67   Ned Parker, "Tiny Qatar Beams Big Signal to Arab World," *Christian Science
           Monitor*, August 4, 1999.
Page 67   Ibid.
Page 68   Ibid.
Page 68   Stephen Wu, "This Just In: Qatar's Satellite Channel," *Harvard International
           Review*, Fall 1999.
Page 68   Faisal Al-Kasim, personal interview, December 2, 2001.

CHAPTER 4

Page 73   Mary Anne Weaver, "Democracy by Decree," *New Yorker*, November 20, 2000.
Page 74   Ibid.
Page 77   "Qatar," 2000 *World Press Freedom Review*.
Page 77   Ibid.
Page 79   Mary Anne Weaver, "Democracy by Decree," *New Yorker*, November 20, 2000.

Page 80   Agence France Presse, February 29, 2000.
Page 82   *Al-Watan Online*, February 25, 2000.
Page 83   *Al-Watan*, December 5, 1997.
Page 84   Faisal Al-Kasim, personal interview, December 2, 2001.
Page 85   Qatari student, personal interview, November 19, 2001.
Page 85   Abdullah Al-Hajj, personal interview, November 10, 2001.
Page 86   Mohammed Arafa, personal interview, November 22, 2001.
Page 89   Ali Al-Hail, "Civil Society in the Arab World: The Role of Transnational Broadcasting," *Transnational Broadcasting Studies Journal*, Spring 2000.

CHAPTER 5

Page 93   Tony Karon, "The War for Muslim Hearts and Minds," *Time*, November 6, 2001.
Page 94   Zev Chafets, "Al-Jazeera Unmasked: An Arab Propaganda Machine in the Guise of Real Journalism," *New York Daily News*, October 14, 2001.
Page 94   Fouad Ajami, "What the Muslim World is Watching," *New York Times*, November 18, 2001.
Page 97   Faisal Al-Kasim, "Crossfire: The Arab Version," *Harvard International Journal of Press/Politics*, Summer 1999.
Page 104   Ibid.
Page 104   S. Abdallah Schleifer, "A Dialogue with Mohammed Jasim Al-Ali, Managing Director, Al-Jazeera," *Transnational Broadcasting Studies Journal*, Fall 2000.
Page 105   "Ala Hamesh Hewar Dr. Al-Kasim," *Al-Watan*, May 17, 1999.
Page 108   Yosri Fouda, "Al-Jazeera: Here We Stand; We Can Do No Otherwise," *Transnational Broadcasting Studies Journal*, Fall 2001.
Page 111   Stephen Wu, "This Just In: Qatar's Satellite Channel," *Harvard International Review*, Fall 1999.

CHAPTER 6

Page 114   Douglas A. Boyd, personal interview, December 22, 2001.
Page 115   Hafez Al-Mirazi, personal interview, July 20, 2001.
Page 115   Nail Al-Jubeir, personal interview, July 21, 2001.
Page 116   Al-Jazeera, March 14, 1998.
Page 116   Al-Jazeera, January 7, 1999.
Page 117   Al-Rai Al-Aam, February 3, 2000.
Page 117   Sheikh Hamad bin Jasim Al-Thani, "Interview with 'Inside Al-Jazeera,'" *60 Minutes II*, CBS, May 2001.
Page 118   Shaheen Sehbai, "Prince Abdullah Vents Fury at Al-Jazeera," *Al-Anwar*, January 17, 2002.
Page 119   David Hirst, "Al-Jazeera, the Arab TV Channel that Dares to Shock: Qatar Calling," *Le Monde*, August 15, 2000.
Page 120   "Barnamej Televesiouni Siasi Qatari Yotheer Ihtijajan Kuwaitiyyan," *Al-Watan*, July 15, 1999.
Page 120   Al-Siyassah, August 15, 1999.
Page 123   "Qatar," 1999 *World Press Freedom Review*.
Page 123   S. Abdallah Schleifer, "A Dialogue with Mohammed Jasim Al-Ali, Managing Director, Al-Jazeera," *Transnational Broadcasting Studies Journal*, Fall 2000.
Page 124   Qatar News Agency, May 2, 2000.
Page 125   "Controversial TV Channel Receives Protest Message from Baghdad," Agence France Presse, May 2, 2000.
Page 126   "Jordanian Government Halts Accreditation of Qatari Satellite Station," *Arabic News Online*, November 10, 1998.

Page 127   "Qatari Jazeera TV Office Closed in West Bank," *New York Times*, March 22, 2001.
Page 127   Ibid.
Page 130   Hazem Al-Abbadi, "Hamsat Etab," *Al-Raya*, March 16, 1998.
Page 130   Faisal Al-Kasim, personal interview, December 2, 2001.
Page 130   "Nikabat Al-Mouseekeyyen Taqta' Ta'molha Ma' Al-Jazeera," *Al-Akhbar*, November 2, 2000.
Page 132   Amira Ibrahim, "Qatari Broadcast Triggers Egyptian Anger," *Al-Ahram Weekly*, September 17, 1998.
Page 132   Ibid.
Page 133   Ibid.
Page 133   Amira Howeidy, "Too Hot to Handle," *Al-Ahram Weekly*, May 27, 1999.
Page 134   Paul Schemm, "Challenging Controversial Television. . . from Qatar?" *Middle East Times*, April 7, 1998.
Page 134   Paul Schemm, "Feisty Network Chooses Egypt," *Middle East Times*, April 21, 2000,
Page 135   S. Abdallah Schleifer, "A Dialogue with Mohammed Jasim Al-Ali, Managing Director, Al-Jazeera," *Transnational Broadcasting Studies Journal*, Spring 2000.
Page 135   Nadia Abul Magd, "A Stone's Throw Away," *Al-Ahram Weekly*, April 20, 2000.
Page 135   Ibid.
Page 136   Ibid.
Page 137   Mohammed Abdul Monem, Interview with *60 Minutes*, CBS, May 2001.
Page 137   Sharon Waxman, "Arab TV's Strong Signal: The Al-Jazeera Network Offers News the Mideast Never Had Before, and Views That Are All Too Common," *Washington Post*, December 4, 2001.
Page 137   Safwat Al-Sherif, Interview with *Good Morning Egypt*, Egyptian Television, October 26, 2000.
Page 138   Ezzat Al-Shami, "Hal Tarfa'a Misr Al-Jazeera Men Ala Al-Nile Sat?" *Rose Al-Youssef*, November 17, 2000.
Page 138   Hassan Al-Masry, "Al-Qana Al-Mashbouha Wal Irtibat Ma' Sahafat Israel," *Rose Al-Youssef*, April 21, 2000.
Page 138   Abdullah Kamal, "Mozei' Men Misr Ded Misr," *Rose Al-Youssef*, April 21, 2000,
Page 139   Tariq Hassan, "Qana Qatariyya Totheer Ghadab Al-Hokouma," *Al-Ahram*, October 27, 2000.
Page 139   Amir Kamal,"Egyptian Media Launch Attacks Against Al-Jazeera," *Al-Ahram Weekly*, October 28, 2000.
Page 140   Davan Maharaj, "How Tiny Qatar Jars Arab Media," *Los Angeles Times*, May 7, 2001.
Page 140   Paul Schemm, "Challenging Controversial Television. . . from Qatar?" *Middle East Times*, April 7, 1998.
Page 141   Amira Ibrahim, "Qatari Broadcast Triggers Egyptian Anger," *Al-Ahram Weekly*, September 17, 1998.

CHAPTER 7
Page 143   Deborah Bassett, personal interview, November 25, 2001.
Page 145   Tayseer Allouni, Interview with Al-Jazeera, November 22, 2001.
Page 145   Brian Whitaker, "Battle Station," *The Guardian*, October 9, 2001.
Page 145   Martin Bentham, "Pressure Mounts on TV Station over bin Laden," *London Sunday Telegraph*, October 14, 2001.
Page 147   Susan Sachs, "Bin Laden Finds His Audience: His Flowery Broadcast Wins over Some Muslims," *New York Times*, October 9, 2001.
Page 147   Sarah Schmidt, "Speech Translation Inaccurate, Experts Say," *National Post Online*, October 9, 2001.

Page 147   Ibid.
Page 147   Edmund Ghareeb, Interview with *NewsHour*, PBS, October 8, 2001.
Page 148   "Al-Jazeera Defends Airing of bin Laden Statements," The Associated Press, October 31, 2001.
Page 148   Warren Richey, "Arab TV Network Plays Key, Disputed Role in Afghan War," *Christian Science Monitor*, October 15, 2001.
Page 148   Martin Bentham, "Pressure Mounts on TV Station over bin Laden," *London Sunday Telegraph*, October 14, 2001.
Page 148   "Al-Jazeera Dealt with bin Laden," *Washington Times*, October 15, 2001.
Page 151   Bill Carter, "The News Media: Two Networks Get No Reply to Questions for bin Laden," *New York Times*, October 27, 2001.
Page 152   James Risen and Patrick Tyler, "Interview with bin Laden Makes the Rounds," *New York Times*, December 12, 2001.
Page 152   Tareq Al-Issawi, "Al-Jazeera: Interview was under Duress," The Associated Press, February 2, 2002.
Page 152   Elizabeth Jensen, "Bin Laden Interview Raises Questions," *Los Angeles Times*, October 18, 2001.
Page 153   "Arab TV Channel Says bin Laden's Last Speech 'Wasn't News,'" The Associated Press, November 6, 2001.
Page 154   Sarah Sullivan, "Interview with Mohammed Jasim Al-Ali," *Transnational Broadcasting Studies Journal*, October 2001.
Page 157   Shaden Shehab, "Fast and First," *Al-Ahram Weekly*, October 11, 2001.
Page 157   "Powell: Al-Jazeera Giving Too Much Air Time To Anti-U.S. Views," Agence France Presse, October 10, 2001.
Page 158   Sarahel Deeb, "Rumsfeld Defends U.S. Policy in Afghanistan to Arabs and Muslims," The Associated Press, October 17, 2001.
Page 159   Sarah Sullivan, "Interview with Mohammed Jasim Al-Ali," *Transnational Broadcasting Studies Journal*, October 2001.
Page 159   Ibid.
Page 160   Tayseer Allouni, Interview with Al-Jazeera, November 22, 2001.
Page 161   Eugene Wee, "Target Terrorism; Al-Jazeera's Strength, Its Newsmen," The Associated Press, October 13, 2001.
Page 162   Peter Jennings, Interview with *NewsHour*, PBS, October 8, 2001.
Page 163   Sarah Sullivan, "The Courting of Al-Jazeera," *Transnational Broadcasting Studies Journal*, October 2001.
Page 163   Ghida Fakhry, Interview with Foreign Policy Association, October 25, 2001.
Page 164   David Bauder, "CNN Backs Down from Exclusive Video Deal; Networks Cover Attack on Afghanistan," The Associated Press, October 2001.
Page 164   Ibid.
Page 165   Mark Jerkowitz, "Arab News Service's Exclusives Left U.S. Networks Wanting," *Boston Globe*, October 8, 2001.
Page 165   Ibid.
Page 166   Christian Miller, "Arab Satellite TV Station a Prime Battlefield in Information War," *New York Times*, October 12, 2001.
Page 166   Sarah Sullivan, "Interview with Mohammed Jasim Al-Ali," *Transnational Broadcasting Studies Journal*, October 2001.
Page 167   Peter Fueilhirade, "Qatar's Al-Jazeera Livens Up Arab TV Scene," *BBC News Online*, January 7, 1999.
Page 168   Tayseer Allouni, Interview with Al-Jazeera, November 22, 2001.
Page 169   Jim Rutenberg, "In October Interview, bin Laden Hinted at Role," *New York Times*, February 1, 2002.
Page 170   "Bin Laden: 'Freedom and Human Rights in America Are Doomed,'" *CNN Online*, January 31, 2002.

Page 170 "Al-Jazeera Statement and CNN Response on bin Laden Video," CNN Online, January 31, 2002.
Page 171 Ibid.
Page 171 Mohammed Jasim Al-Ali, personal interview, February 2, 2002.
Page 172 Tareq Al-Issawi, "Al-Jazeera: Interview was under Duress," The Associated Press, February 2, 2002.
Page 173 Fouad Ajami, "What the Muslim World Is Watching," *New York Times Magazine*, November 18, 2001.

CHAPTER 8

Page 175 U.S. State Department official, personal interview, July 15, 2001.
Page 176 Colin Powell, Interview with *Good Morning America*, ABC, October 9, 2000.
Page 176 Mohammed Jasim Al-Ali, personal interview, December 10, 2001.
Page 177 U.S. State Department official, personal interview, December 10, 2001.
Page 178 Jessica Hodgson, "Concern Grows over Media Censorship," *The Guardian*, October 15, 2001.
Page 178 Gerard Baker, "A Different Script," *London Times*, October 12, 2001.
Page 178 Howard Rosenberg, "To Air Is Human, Especially When It's Live," *Los Angeles Times*, October 15, 2001.
Page 178 Earl Lane, "Experts Doubt High-Tech Cues in Tapes," *Los Angeles Times*, October 11, 2001.
Page 179 Jessica Hodgson, "Concern Grows over Media Censorship," *The Guardian*, October 15, 2001.
Page 179 Zev Chafets, "Al-Jazeera Unmasked: An Arab Propaganda Machine in the Guise of Real Journalism," *New York Daily News*, October 14, 2001.
Page 179 "Al-Jazeera in the Balance," *New York Post*, October 15, 2001.
Page 179 "Al-Jazeera Dealt with bin Laden," *Washington Times*, October 15, 2001.
Page 180 Hatem Anwar, "New York Journalist Recommends Military Action Against Arab News Station, Al-Jazeera," *Middle East News Online*, October 15, 2001.
Page 180 Taieb Mahjoub, "Qatar's Al-Jazeera Stands Firm in Its Coverage Despite U.S. Displeasure," Agence France Presse, October 11, 2001.
Page 181 Susan Sachs, "U.S. Appears to be Losing Public Relations War So Far," *New York Times*, October 28, 2001.
Page 181 Frank Viviano, "Arab World Glued to TV Sets—Streets Appear Calm but Anger at U.S. Lies under Surface," *San Francisco Chronicle*, October 8, 2001.
Page 181 "Al-Jazeera Presents Arabic View of War?" The Associated Press, November 5, 2001.
Page 182 "For Some American Viewers, Al-Jazeera's News in Arabic Shapes Opposition to the War," The Associated Press, November 7, 2001.
Page 182 Ibid.
Page 182 "Matt Zoller Seitz on TV: Networks Not Strange Bedfellows," *Newark Star-Ledger*, October 11, 2001.
Page 183 Tayseer Allouni, Interview with Al-Jazeera, November 22, 2001.
Page 184 Mohammed Jasim Al-Ali, personal interview, December 10, 2001.
Page 184 "Spotlight Turns to Reporter for Arabic-Language Network," *Atlanta Journal-Constitution*, October 25, 2001.
Page 184 Faisal Al-Kasim, personal interview, December 10, 2001.
Page 185 Hafez Al-Mirazi, Interview with WNYC Radio, October 13, 2001.
Page 185 Ashraf Khalil, "White House Courts Arab TV Network: Al-Jazeera's Broadcasts Reach 35 Million," *San Francisco Chronicle*, October 20, 2001.
Page 185 "Arabic TV Runs Inflammatory Comments by U.S. Official," The Associated Press, October 16, 2001.

Page 186   "U.S. Finding It Tough to Reach Arabs," The Associated Press, October 19, 2001.
Page 189   Richard Sambrook, Interview with *CNN Online*, October 22, 2001.
Page 189   John Donnelly and Indira A.R. Lakshmanan, "Arab Station Finds New Access to U.S. Officials," *Boston Globe*, October 21, 2001.
Page 190   Nancy Benac, "U.S., Arab Misunderstandings Widespread," The Associated Press, October 18, 2001.
Page 190   John Donnelly and Indira A.R. Lakshmanan, "Arab Station Finds New Access to U.S. Officials," *Boston Globe*, October 21, 2001.
Page 191   "U.S. Considers Advertising on Al-Jazeera," *Daily Telegraph*, October 2, 2001.
Page 191   Peter Sinton, "War Must Be Waged with Words," *San Francisco Chronicle*, October 31, 2001.
Page 192   "U.S. Turn to Madison Avenue for PR War," *Chicago Tribune*, October 23, 2001.
Page 193   Al-Hayat, October 9, 2001.
Page 193   Gary Thatcher, personal interview, December 11, 2001.
Page 193   International Broadcasting Bureau is part of the Broadcasting Board of Governors.
Page 194   Douglas Boyd, personal interview, December 15, 2001.

EPILOGUE

Page 200   Sheikh Masha'al Al-Thani, personal interview, December 15, 2001.

Sources and References

Abu-Laban, Baha and Michael W. Suleiman 1989. *Arab Americans: Continuity and Change*: Association of Arab American University Graduates.

Abu-Lughod, Lila. 1989. Bedouins, cassettes and technologies of public culture. *Middle East Report* 159: 7–11, 47.

Abu-Lughod, Lila. 1993. Editorial comment: On screening politics in a world of nations. *Public Culture* 5(3): 465–467.

S. Abdallah Schleifer, "A Dialogue with Mohammed Jasim Al-Ali, Managing Director, Al-Jazeera," *Transnational Broadcasting Studies* Journal, Fall 2000.

Abul Magd, Nadia. "A Stone's Throw Away," *Al-Ahram Weekly*, 20 April 2000.

Afzal, Omar (1991, January). The American Media's Middle East War. *The Message International*: 19–20.

Agence France Presse, 29 February 2000.

Ahmad, Eqbal. 2001. *Terrorism: Theirs and Ours*. New York: Seven Stories Press.

Ahmed, Yasser. *Personal interview*, 30 July 2001.

Ajami, Fouad. "What the Muslim World is Watching," *New York Times*, 18 November 2001.

Al-Ali, Mohammed Jasim. *Personal Interview*, 2 February 2002.

Al-Ali, Mohammed Jasim. *Personal interview*, 10 December 2001.

Al-Hail, Ali. "Civil Society in the Arab World: The Role of Transnational Broadcasting," *Transnational Broadcasting Studies* Journal, Spring 2000.

Al-Hajj, Abdullah. *Personal interview*, 10 November, 2001.

Al-Issawi, Tareq. "Al-Jazeera: Interview was under Duress," *The Associated Press*, 2 February 2002.

"Al-Jazeera Dealt with bin Laden," *Washington Times*, 15 October 2001.

"Al-Jazeera Statement and CNN Response on bin Laden Video," *CNN Online*, 31 January 2002.

"Al-Jazeera in the Balance," *New York Post*, 15 October 2001.

"Al-Jazeera Dealt with bin Laden," *Washington Times*, 15 October 2001.

"Al-Jazeera Presents Arabic View of War?" *The Associated Press*, 5 November 2001.

Al-Jubeir, Nail. *Personal interview*, 21 July 2001.

Al-Kasim, Faisal. *Personal interview*, 2 December 2001.

Al-Kasim, Faisal. "Crossfire: The Arab Version," *The Harvard International Journal of Press/Politics*, summer 1999.

Al-Kasim, Faisal. *Personal interview*, 10 December 2001.

Al-Mirazi, Hafez. *Interview with WNYC Radio*, 13 October 2001.

Al-Mirazi, Hafez. *Personal interview*, 20 July 2001.

Al-Thani, Sheikh Masha'al. *Personal interview*, 15 December 2001.

Ali, M. 1984. Western Media and the Muslim World. *The Concept*, v. 4 (2): 13–19.

Allouni, Tayseer. *Interview with Al-Jazeera*, 22 November 2001.

Alterman, Jon B. 1998. *New Media, New Politics? From Satellite Television to the Internet in the Arab World* Washington, DC: Washington Institute For Near East Policy.

Anwar, Hatem. "New York Journalist Recommends Military Action Against Arab News Station, Al-Jazeera," *Middle East News Online*, 15 October 2001.

Arab American citizen in Baltimore, *Personal interview*, 30 July 2001.

"Arab TV Channel Says bin Laden's Last Speech 'Wasn't News,'" *The Associated Press*, 6 November 2001.

"Arabic TV Runs Inflammatory Comments by U.S. Official," *The Associated Press*, 16 October 2001.

Arafa, Mohammed. *Personal interview*, 22 November 2001.

Ayish, Muhammed I. "American-Style Journalism and Arab World Television: An Exploratory Study of News Selection at Six Arab World Satellite Television Channels," *Transnational Broadcasting Studies* Journal, Spring/Summer 2001.

Baker, Gerard. "A Different Script," *London times*, 12 October 2001.

Bauder, David. "CNN Backs Down from Exclusive Video Deal; Networks Cover Attack on Afghanistan," *The Associated Press*, 7 October 2001.

Benac, Nancy. "U.S., Arab Misunderstandings Widespread," *The Associated Press*, 18 October 2001.

Bentham, Martin. "Pressure Mounts on TV Station over bin Laden," *London Sunday Telegraph*, 14 October 2001.

"Bin Laden: 'Freedom and Human Rights in America are Doomed,'" *CNN Online*, 31 January 2002.

Boyd, Douglas A. *International Center Against Censorship Seminar*, Cairo, February 1999, page 30.

Boyd, Douglas A. 1999. *Broadcasting in the Arab World: A Survey of the Electronic Media in the Middle East*. Ames: Iowa State University Press.

Carey, Roane ed. 2001. *The New Intifada: Resisting Israel's Apartheid*. New York: Verso Books.

Carter, Bill. "The News Media: Two Networks Get No Reply to Questions for bin Laden," *New York Times*, 27 October 2001.

Chafets, Zev. "Al-Jazeera Unmasked: An Arab Propaganda Machine in the Guise of Real Journalism," *New York Daily News*, 14 October, 2001.

Cleveland, William L. 2000. *A History of the Modern Middle East*. Boulder: Westview Press.

"Controversial TV Channel Receives Protest Message from Baghdad," *Agence France Presse*, 2 May 2000.

Cook, Timothy E. 1998. *Governing With the News: The News Media As a Political Institution*. Chicago: University of Chicago Press.

Curiel, Jonathan. "Mideast News Network Has Fans Here: Al-Jazeera Coverage Uniquely Censored," *San Francisco Chronicle*, 18 October 2001.

Deeb, Sarahel. "Rumsfeld Defends U.S. Policy in Afghanistan to Arabs and Muslims," *The Associated Press*, 17 October 2001.

Donnelly, John and Indira A.R. Lakshmanan, "Arab Station Finds New Access to U.S. Officials," *Boston Globe*, 21 October 2001.

"Egyptian TV Fights Arab Rivals with Tepid Glasnost: A Plethora of Political Debates, Talk Shows and Social Comment is Now on Air After Years of Drab Propaganda," *Reuters*, 6 June 2001.

Eickelman, Dale F. and Jon W. Anderson ed. 1999. *New Media in the Muslim World: The Emerging Public Sphere* Bloomington: IU Press.

Esposito, John L. 1992. *The Islamic Threat: Myth or Reality?* New York: Oxford University Press.

Finkelstein, Norman G. 2001. *Image and Reality of the Israel-Palestine Conflict*. New York: Verso Books.

"For Some American Viewers, Al-Jazeera's News in Arabic Shapes Opposition to the War," *The Associated Press*, 7 November 2001.

Fouda, Yosri. "Al-Jazeera: Here We Stand; We Can Do No Otherwise," *Transnational Broadcasting Studies* Journal, Fall 2001.

Friedman, Thomas L. 1990. *From Beirut to Jerusalem*. New York: Anchor.

Friedman, Thomas L. 2000. *The Lexus and the Olive Tree*, New York, Random House, Inc.

Fueilhirade, Peter. "Qatar's Al-Jazeera Livens Up Arab TV Scene," *BBC News Online*, 7 January 1999.

Gerges, Fawaz A. 1999. *America and Political Islam: Clash of Cultures or Clash of Interests?* New York: Cambridge University Press.

Gerner, Deborah J., ed. 2000. *Understanding the Contemporary Middle East*. Boulder: Lynne Rienner Publishers.

Ghareeb, E. (1984). The Middle East in the U.S. Media. *The Middle East Annual Issues and Events*, v. 3: 185–210.

Hafez, Kai and David L. Paletz, eds. 2001. *Mass Media, Politics, and Society in the Middle East* Cresskill, NJ: Hampton Press.

Hafez, Kai. 2001. *Islam and the West in the Mass Media: Fragmented Images in a Globalizing World* Cresskill, NJ: Hampton Press.

Henry, Clement M. and Robert Springborg. 2001. *Globalization and the Politics of Development in the Middle East*. New York: Cambridge University Press.

Hess, Stephen. 1996. *International News and Foreign Correspondents*, Washington, D.C.: The Brookings Institution.

Hirst, David. "Al-Jazeera, the Arab TV Channel that Dares to Shock: Qatar Calling," *Le Monde*, 15 August 2000.

Hodgson, Jessica. "Concern Grows over Media Censorship," *The Guardian*, 15 October 2001.

Hourani, Albert. 1992. *A History of the Arab Peoples*. New York: Warner Books.

Howeidy, Amira. "Too Hot to Handle," *Al-Ahram Weekly*, 27 May 1999.

Huntington, Samuel P. 1998. *The Clash of Civilizations and the Remaking of World Order*. New York: Touchstone Books.

Ibrahim, Amira "Qatari Broadcast Triggers Egyptian Anger," *Al-Ahram Weekly*, 17 September 1998.

Iskandar, Adel and Mohammed el-Nawawy. Al-Jazeera and the Intifada. In Ethan Casey and Paul Hilder (Eds.). 2002. *Peace Fire: Fragments of the Israel-Palestine Story*. London: Free Association Books.

Jensen, Elizabeth. "Bin Laden Interview Raises Questions," *Los Angeles Times*, 18 October 2001.

Jerkowitz, Mark "Arab News Service's Exclusives Left U.S. Networks Wanting," *Boston Globe*, 8 October 2001.

"Jordanian Government Halts Accreditation of Qatari Satellite Station," *Arabic News Online*, 10 November 1998.

Kamal, Amir. "Egyptian Media Launch Attacks Against Al-Jazeera," *Al-Ahram Weekly*, 28 October 2000.

Kamalipour, Yahya R, ed. 1995. *The U.S. Media and the Middle East: Image and Perception*. Westport, Connecticut: Greenwood Press.

Kamalipour, Yahya R, ed. 1998. *Images of the U.S. Around the World: A Multicultural Perspective*. Albany, NY: State Univ. of New York Press.

Kamalipour, Yahya R. and Hamid Mowlana, eds. 1994. *Mass Media in the Middle East*. Westport, Conneticut: Greenwood Publishing Group.

Karon, Tony. "The War for Muslim Hearts and Minds," *Time*, 6 November 2001.

Kiefer, Francine and Ann Scott Tyson, "In War of Words, US Still Lags Behind," *The Christian Science Monitor*, October 17, 2001.

Khalidi, Rashid, Reeva S. Simon and Muhammad Y. Muslih, eds. 1993. *The Origins of Arab Nationalism*. New York: Columbia University Press.

Khalil, Ashraf. "White House Courts Arab TV Network: Al-Jazeera's Broadcasts Reach 35 Million," *San Francisco Chronicle*, 20 October 2001.

Kipper, Judith. *Personal interview*, 15 July 2001.

Kraidy, Marwan. "Transnational Television and Asymmetrical Interdependence in the Arab World: The Growing Influence of the Lebanese Satellite Broadcasters," *Transnational Broadcasting Studies* Journal, Fall/Winter 2000.

Lane, Earl. "Experts Doubt High-Tech Cues in Tapes," *Los Angeles Times*, 11 October 2001.

Lewis, Bernard. 2001. *What Went Wrong: Western Impact and Middle Eastern Response*. New York: Oxford University Press.

Liebes, Tamar. 1997. *Reporting the Arab Israeli Conflict: How Hegemony Works*. New York: Routledge.

Maharaj, Davan. "How Tiny Qatar Jars Arab Media," *Los Angeles Times*, 7 May 2001.

Mahjoub, Taieb. "Qatar's Al-Jazeera Stands Firm in its Coverage Despite U.S. Displeasure," *Agence France Presse*, 11 October 2001.

Mahroos, Tawfik. *Personal interview*, 15 November 2000.

"Matt Zoller Seitz on TV: Networks Not Strange Bedfellows," *Newark Star-Ledger*, 11 October 2001.

McAlister, Melani. 2001. *Epic Encounters: Culture, Media, and U.S. Interests in the Middle East, 1945–2000*. Berkeley, CA: University of California Press.

McChesney, Robert W. 2000. *Rich Media, Poor Democracy: Communication Politics in Dubious Times*. New York: The New Press.

Miller, Christian. "Arab Satellite TV Station a Prime Battlefield in Information War," *New York Times*, 12 October 2001.

Miller, Judith. 1997. *God Has Ninety-Nine Names: Reporting from a Militant Middle East*. New York: Touchstone Books.

Mousa, Issam S. 1984. *The Arab Images in the U.S. Press*. New York: Peter Lang.

Mowlana, Hamid, George Gerbner, and Herbert I. Schiller, eds. 1992. *Triumph of the Image: The Media's War in the Persian Gulf—A Global Perspective*. Boulder, CO: Westview Press

el-Nawawy, Mohammed. 2002. *The Israeli-Egyptian Peace Process in the Reporting of Western Journalists*. Westport, CT: Greenwood Publishing Group, Inc.

el-Nawawy, Mohammed, and Adel Iskandar. "The Minotaur of 'Contextual Objectivity': War Coverage and the Pursuit of Accuracy and Appeal." *Transnational Broadcasting Studies* Journal. Fall/Winter 2002.

Parker, Ned. "Tiny Qatar Beams Big Signal to Arab World," *The Christian Science Monitor*, 4 August 1999.

"Powell: Al-Jazeera Giving Too Much Air Time To Anti-U.S. Views," *Agence France Presse*, 10 October 2001.

Price, Monroe E. and Beata Rozumilowicz, eds. 2001. *Media Reform: Democratizing the Media, Democratizing the State*. New York: Routledge.

"Qatar," *2000 World Press Freedom Review*.

"Qatari Al-Jazeera TV Office Closed in West Bank," *New York Times*, 22 March 2001.

Qatari student, *Personal interview*, 19 November 2001.

Richey, Warren. "Arab TV Network Plays Key, Disputed Role in Afghan War," *The Christian Science Monitor*," 15 October 2001.

Risen, James and Patrick Tyler, "Interview with bin Laden Makes the Rounds," *New York Times*, 12 December 2001.

Rosenberg, Howard. "To Air is Human, Especially When It's Live," *Los Angeles Times*, 15 October 2001.

Rutenberg, Jim. "In October Interview, bin Laden Hinted at Role," *New York Times*, 1 February 2002.

Sacco, Joe. 1994. *Palestine: A Nation Occupied*. Seattle, WA: Fantagraphics Books.

Sachs, Susan. "Bin Laden Finds His Audience: His Flowery Broadcast Wins Over Some Muslims," *New York Times*, 9 October 2001.

Sachs, Susan. "U.S. Appears to be Losing Public Relations War So Far," *New York Times*, 28 October 2001.

Said, Edward, and Christopher Hitchens, ed. 1988. *Blaming the Victims: Spurious Scholarship and the Palestinian Question.* London, New York: Verso.

Said, Edward W. *The Politics of Dispossession: The Struggle for Palestinian Self Determination 1969–1994.* New York: Pantheon Books, 1994.

Said, Edward W. 1981. *Covering Islam: How the Media and the Experts Determine How We See Rest of the World.* New York: Pantheon Books.

Said, Edward W. 1978. *Orientalism.* New York: Pantheon Books.

Salhani, Claude, 1998, *Black September to Desert Storm: A Journalist in the Middle East,* Columbia: The University of Missouri Press.

Sambrook, Richard. *Interview with CNN Online,* 22 October 2001.

Schemm, Paul. "Challenging Controversial Television... from Qatar?" *The Middle East Times,* 7 April 1998.

Schemm, Paul. "Fiesty Network Chooses Egypt" *The Middle East Times,* 21 April 2000.

Schmidt, Sarah. "Speech Translation Inaccurate, Experts Say," *National Post Online,* 9 October 2001.

"Al-Jazeera Defends Airing of bin Laden Statements," *The Associated Press,* 31 October 2001.

Semia, Nadia. *Personal interview,* 30 July 2001.

Shaheen, Jack G. 1984. *The TV Arab.* Bowling Green: Bowling Green State University Popular Press.

Shehab, Shaden. "Fast and First," *Al-Ahram Weekly,* 11 October 2001.

"Shrine to legendary Egyptian diva," *BBC Online News,* December 28, 2001.

Sinton, Peter. "War Must be Waged with Words," *San Francisco Chronicle,* 31 October 2001.

Smith, Hedrick ed. 1992. *The Media and the Gulf War/the Press and Democracy in Wartime.* New York: Seven Locks Press.

"Spotlight Turns to Reporter for Arabic-Language Network," *The Atlanta Journal-Constitution,* 25 October 2001.

Straubhaar, Joseph. "Beyond Cultural Imperialism: Asymmetrical Interdependence and Cultural Proximity," *Critical Studies in Mass Communication,* 1991, 8 (1).

Sullivan, Sarah. "Interview with Mohammed Jasim Al-Ali," *Transnational Broadcasting Studies Journal,* October 2001.

Taylor, Philip M. 1998. *War and the Media : Propaganda and Persuasion in the Gulf War.* Manchester University Press.

Thatcher, Gary. *Personal interview,* 11 December 2001.

"U.S. Considers Advertising on Al-Jazeera," *Daily Telegraph,* 2 October 2001.

"U.S. Finding it Tough to Reach Arabs," The Associated Press, October 19 2001.

U.S. State Department official, *Personal interview,* 15 July 2001.

U.S. State Department official, *Personal interview,* 10 December 2001.

"U.S. Turn to Madison Avenue for PR War," *Chicago Tribune,* 23 October 2001.

Viviano, Frank. "Arab World Glued to TV Sets – Streets Appear Calm but Anger at U.S. Lies under Surface," *San Francisco Chronicle,* 8 October 2001.

Waxman, Sharon. "Arab TV's Strong Signal: The Al-Jazeera Network Offers News the Mideast Never Had Before, and Views That Are All Too Common," *The Washington Post,* 4 December, 2001.

Weaver, Mary Anne. "Democracy by Decree," *New Yorker,* 20 November 2000.

Wee, Eugene. "Target Terrorism; Al-Jazeera's Strength, Its Newsmen," *The Associated Press,* 13 October 2001.

Williams, Dan. "A Real Newsmaker," *The Jerusalem Post,* 2 September, 2001.

Whitaker, Brian. "Battle Station," *The Guardian,* 9 October 2001.

Wu, Stephen. "This Just In: Qatar's Satellite Channel," *Harvard International Review,* fall 1999.

INDEX

231

Pillar, Paul, 189–190
Political mobilization, 55–58, 161
Afghanistan and, 57–58
Palestinian Intifada and, 55–56, 64
Polygamy, 98
Powell, Colin, 157, 177
and Al-Jazeera allowing irresponsible
statements, 176
request to Al-Jazeera for censorship, 23
Prince of Egypt (motion picture), 14
Professionalism, 140
Programming, 11–12
and Algerian civil war, 49–50
backward, of Arabic television stations, 7
broadcasting of live events, 51–52
news, 45–46
normal compared with English-language
television, 50
and "Who is a Jordanian?," 50
See also "Opinion, the, and the other opinion";
Talk shows
Project Journalists, 184
"Protocol news," 39
Provocative and nontraditional views. *See*
Controversy
Public discourse, 68–69

Qaddafi, Muammar, 100, 124–125
Qandil, Hamdi, 158, 185
Qatar, 35–38
Central Municipal Council, 74–75, 87
civil society and, 89–90
coup attempt against Hamad and later trial,
80–81
democracy and, 73, 75, 82, 216
Egypt and, 131–132
freedom of association and, 76
free speech in, 37, 71–72, 200
government of, 35, 72–73, 87
human rights and, 80, 81, 89
Internet service in, 78–79
Iraq and, 36
Israel and, 36, 81–82
moderate course of action of, 36
more known since as Al-Jazeera more well-
known, 71
Morocco and, 123–124
oil economy of, 35–36
parliament establishment, 37, 82, 87
political weight increased with Al-Jazeera,
71
population of, 35
reform and change in, 73–74
religious practice in, 79–80
satellites in, 78
Saudi Arabia and, 81–82, 117–118
torture and, 77–78
and U.S. anger at Al-Jazeera, 180
women's rights and, 37–38, 74–75, 89

See also Freedom of media in Qatar; Hamad bin
Khalifa Al-Thani, Sheikh
Qatar and Al-Jazeera, 2, 23, 82–89
Al-Jazeera as hypocrite for not covering Qatar,
89–90
financial support, 88–89, 90
government dodging of criticisms of Al-Jazeera,
88
government launching of, 74
issues waiting to be covered, 86–87
lack of criticism of Qatar government, 83–85, 86
and Middle East economic summit in Doha and
Israel, 83
not covering local issues of Qatar, 49, 83–85, 86,
199–200
Qatar non-interference with affairs of, 141
separate foreign policies of, 140–141
Qatari News Agency (QNA), 124

Radio Egypt (radio show), 4
Radio Free Europe, 40
Radio Monte Carlo-Middle East, 17–18, 39, 40,
194
Radio Sawa, 213
Radio shows in Arabic, 4
Ragab family, 45
Reasons for watching
straightforward picture of what is going on,
66
survey regarding, 47–48
time of coverage of Middle Eastern issues, 12–13
as way of overcoming Jewish media conspiracy,
13–14
Reilly, Robert, 40
Reporters Sans Frontieres (Reporters Without
Borders), 179
Rice, Condoleezza, 24, 157–158
bin Laden videotapes and, 177–178
interview on Al-Jazeera and, 185–186
RMC-ME. *See* Radio Monte Carlo-Middle East
Rose Al-Youssef (magazine), 138–139
Rosenberg, Howard, 178
Ross, Christopher, 92–97, 154, 192, 196, 199
Rouleau, Eric, 108–109
Royal Military Academy, 34
Rugh, William, 182
Rumsfeld, Donald
and Al-Jazeera as "mouthpiece" for terrorists, 40
and Al-Jazeera coverage as inflammatory, 181
attempts at censorship of Voice of America, 40
interview on Al-Jazeera, 158
Rushdie, Salman, 99, 130

Al-Sabah, Sheikh Jaber Al-Ahmed, 39, 120
Sadat, Anwar, 131
Safi, Mohammed, 159
Salama, Ahmed Salama, 139
Saleh, Ali Abdulla, 125
Sambrook, Richard, 187